Best Practices for Human Rights and Humanitarian NGO Fact-Finding

Nijhoff Law Specials

VOLUME 78

The titles published in this series are listed at brill.nl/nlsp

Best Practices for Human Rights and Humanitarian NGO Fact-Finding

By

Gerald M. Steinberg
Anne Herzberg
and
Jordan Berman

MARTINUS
NIJHOFF
PUBLISHERS

LEIDEN • BOSTON
2012

Library of Congress Cataloging-in-Publication Data

Berman, Jordan.
Best practices for human rights and humanitarian NGO Fact-Finding / By Jordan Berman, Anne Herzberg, and Gerald Steinberg.
p. cm. -- (Nijhoff law specials ; v. 78)
Includes bibliographical references and index.
ISBN 978-90-04-21811-6 (pbk. : alk. paper) 1. Human rights--Evaluation. 2. Civil rights--Evaluation. 3. Non-governmental organizations. I. Herzberg, Anne. II. Steinberg, Gerald (Gerald M.) III. Title.
K3240.B465 2012
341.4'8--dc23

2011051926

ISSN 0924-4549
ISBN 978 90 04 21811 6 (paperback)
ISBN 978 90 04 21812 3 (e-book)

This book is printed on acid-free paper.

CONTENTS

ABOUT THE AUTHORS

Gerald M. Steinberg

Prof. Gerald Steinberg is president of NGO Monitor and professor of Political Studies at Bar Ilan University. His research interests include international relations, Middle East diplomacy and security, the politics of human rights and non-governmental organizations (NGOs), Israeli politics, and arms control. Steinberg works with a number of international organizations (NATO, UN University, OSCE, SIPRI); participates in track-two workshops and in the Inter-parliamentary Coalition for Combating Antisemitism (ICCA); and is the founder of the Program on Conflict Management and Negotiation at Bar Ilan University. His op-ed columns have been published in the *Wall Street Journal*, *Financial Times*, *Ha'aretz*, *International Herald Tribune*, *Jerusalem Post*, and other publications. Recent academic publications include "The Politics of NGOs, Human Rights and the Arab-Israeli Conflict" (*Israel Studies*); "Realism, Politics and Culture in Middle East Arms Control Negotiations" (*International Negotiation*); and "The UN, the ICJ and the Separation Barrier: War by Other Means" (*Israel Law Review*).

Anne Herzberg

Anne Herzberg is the Legal Advisor of NGO Monitor. Her areas of expertise include international human rights and humanitarian law, NGOs and the UN system, universal jurisdiction, and international criminal law. She is a graduate of Oberlin College and Columbia University Law School, where she was named a James Kent Scholar and a Harlan Fiske Stone Scholar. She also served as the Managing Editor for the *Columbia Journal of Transnational Law*. Prior to joining NGO Monitor, Anne worked as a litigation associate in New York. As part of her pro bono work as an associate, she assisted asylum seekers and performed work for the International Criminal Tribunal for Rwanda. Her publications have appeared in major news outlets including the *Wall Street Journal* (Europe), *Ha'aretz*, *Jerusalem Post*, *YNet*, and *Jewish Ideas Daily*. She is the author of *NGO 'Lawfare': Exploitation of Courts in the Arab-Israeli Conflict*, co-editor of *The Goldstone Report "Reconsidered": A Critical Analysis*, and has also published on the

International Criminal Tribunal for the former Yugoslavia ("Rule 61: The Voice of the Victims Screams Out for Justice") in the *Columbia Journal of Transnational Law*.

Jordan Berman

Jordan Berman received a J.D. from UCLA School of Law in 2008 and a B.A. from Brandeis University in 2003. He is a licensed attorney in the state of Illinois, where he worked for two years as a Staff Law Clerk for the U.S. Court of Appeals for the Seventh Circuit. During law school, he served as Managing Editor of the *UCLA Law Review*, which published his 2007 article, "The Presumption of Sanity and Clark's Categorization of Mens Rea Evidence." He also worked as the Legal Research Assistant to the Chancellor of UCLA, as a Law Clerk for the California Attorney General's Office, and as a Prosecution Extern for the International Criminal Tribunal for the former Yugoslavia in The Hague. In 2010–11, Jordan served as the Legal Research Fellow for NGO Monitor's "Best Practices" project.

ABOUT NGO MONITOR

NGO Monitor's mission is to provide information and analysis, promote accountability, and support discussion on the reports and activities of NGOs claiming to advance human rights and humanitarian agendas in the framework of the Arab-Israeli conflict. NGO Monitor is a project of the Amutah for NGO Responsibility (R.A. 580465508).

ACKNOWLEDGEMENTS

The authors wish to thank Peter Simpson for his generous support in making this project a reality. The authors would also like to thank the Wechsler Family Foundation for its longstanding support of and commitment to the work of NGO Monitor. Finally, we wish to thank Paula Kweskin and Naftali Balanson for their research and editorial assistance with this publication.

CHAPTER ONE

INTRODUCTION

The importance of human rights non-governmental organizations (NGOs) in the implementation and monitoring of international human rights and humanitarian law is widely acknowledged. In her book *Diplomacy of Conscience,* Ann Marie Clark notes that Amnesty International and other NGOs were among the creators of many of the human rights norms in existence today.[1] Clark, citing statements from UN treaty bodies, committee chairs, and the General Assembly, argues that the major contribution of NGOs in particular is their basic fact-finding role.[2] NGO fact-finding reports help draw public attention to human rights violations, prioritize human rights issues in the global agenda, and monitor state compliance with various human rights covenants.[3] These reports are often considered more independent and reliable than those from overtly politicized organs of states or inter-governmental organizations (IGOs).[4] The United Nations' *Manual on Human Rights Reporting* encourages governments to consult NGOs when preparing human rights reports in order to have access to different sources of information and perspectives.[5]

In light of this crucial fact-finding role, NGO reports require "accuracy, independence, and impartiality" in order to achieve legitimacy and efficacy in the international context.[6] These qualities are especially important because, as Clark notes, NGOs do not simply transmit factual information, but rather "must verify accuracy, supply

---

[1] Clark, Ann Marie, Diplomacy of Conscience: Amnesty International and Changing Human Rights Norms 5 (2001).

[2] Id. at 16.

[3] Ajibade, Idowu Mopelola, *A Synopsis: Rights, Responsibilities and Roles of Human Rights NGOs under International Law* 18 (2008), available at http://papers.ssrn.com/sol3/papers.cfm?abstract_id=1300103.

[4] Id. at 19.

[5] United Nations Office of the High Commissioner for Human Rights, *Manual on Human Rights Reporting* 50 (1997), available at http://www.ohchr.org/Documents/Publications/manualhrren.pdf.

[6] Clark, *supra* note 1, at 33.

context, and strategize about how best to use the facts to attain principled goals."[7]

When these qualities are absent, an NGO's reputation and credibility suffer, as does its ability to affect change and to promote universal human rights principles.[8] Despite the centrality of the need for accuracy in NGO reporting, few mechanisms regulate reporting methods. Most strikingly, the NGO community has not fixed any methodological standards for fact-finding.[9] Without guidelines or standards for NGO fact-finding output, the international community risks relying on reports that have no clear measure of reliability, and may in fact be detrimental to the pursuit of human rights.

This work outlines available resources and proposed standards for international NGO fact-finding missions:

- Chapter One presents an introduction to the issue of NGO fact-finding.
- Chapter Two discusses the problems caused by the lack of any generally-accepted guidelines for NGO fact-finding, in contrast with contexts where NGOs have achieved consensus.
- Chapter Three surveys proposed guidelines for human rights and humanitarian NGOs. In addition, this section examines United Nations fact-finding standards, as well as examples of internal fact-finding standards for major NGOs.
- Chapter Four analyzes the fact-finding standards used in five specific cases: the International Crisis Group (Kosovo, 1999), the Independent International Fact-Finding Mission on the Conflict in Georgia (2008), United Nations Office of the High Commissioner for Human Rights Mapping Exercise on the Democratic Republic of Congo (1993–2003), Conflict Analysis Resource Center/University London study on Amnesty International and Human Rights Watch (Colombia, 1988–2004), and Human Rights Watch (Lebanon, 2006).
- Chapter Five offers conclusions and recommendations.

---

[7] Id. at 130. See also Steiner, Henry J., Diverse Partners: Non-Governmental Organizations in the Human Rights Movement – The Report of a Retreat of Human Rights Activists 34 (1991). ("INGOs do work in advocating sanctions and educating the public. The principal INGOs are more than the statisticians of violence that some participants seemed to suggest.")

[8] Clark, *supra* note 1, at 132.

[9] Fitzpatrick, Joan, "Human rights fact-finding," in The UN Human Rights Treaty System in the 21st Century 65 (Anne F. Bayefsky ed., 2000).

CHAPTER TWO

THE NEED FOR STANDARDIZED FACT-FINDING METHODOLOGY

The Importance of NGO Fact-Finding

Credible factual claims concerning the behavior and intentions of states and conflict parties are essential for efforts to reduce the adverse humanitarian and human rights impacts of armed conflicts. Only by ascertaining the facts can decision-makers, advisors, and critics design better policies. Parties to an armed conflict, for example, may obtain information to assess their military successes and failures, but the results are usually limited to strategic requirements. Officials are often reluctant to make the details public. When they release this information, individuals lacking relevant military knowledge cannot readily understand it or filter out the political influences. At the same time, in the context of intense violence, the gathering of information by journalists, governments, and United Nations officials is *ad hoc*, impressionistic, and occasionally inaccurate.

As a result of the need for additional fact-finding sources, publications from the major non-governmental international human rights organizations—such as the UK-based Amnesty International (AI) and the US-based Human Rights Watch (HRW)—are highly influential. AI began as a campaign on behalf of "prisoners of conscience" and the abolition of torture, mainly in Eastern Europe and Africa.[1] Similarly, HRW grew out of "Helsinki Watch," founded in the 1970s as a research-oriented alternative to AI. AI's and HRW's influence begins with the press: reports generate prominent headlines in influential media outlets throughout the world. The headlines are then quoted by governments and the UN, where ECOSOC (the UN Economic and Social Council) accredits NGOs and grants them special privileges. NGOs are also often cited as authoritative sources in scholarly works on

[1] Amnesty International, *Amnesty International - Who are We*, available at http://www.amnesty.org/en/who-we-are/history (last visited Apr. 3, 2011).

human rights, international law, and the humanitarian impact of conflict. AI's reputation was both reflected and enhanced by its receipt of the 1977 Nobel Peace Prize.

After the end of the Cold War, NGOs such as HRW and AI sought to maintain and increase their influence by claiming to be experts in asymmetric warfare and advanced military technology, as well as arbiters of international law, military necessity, proportionality, and human rights.[2] This transformation allowed NGOs to increase their influence in the media and in the diplomatic sphere, and in some cases move the organizations "ahead of international law."[3] London School of Economics Professor Mary Kaldor refers to the emergence of a "global civil society" resulting from "a growing consciousness of a set of duties towards mankind, which developed as a consequence of the wars of the twentieth century."[4] The increased role of NGOs in conflict regions was justified by moral concepts such as the 'duty to interfere' (*Devoir d'Ingerence*) in the context of humanitarian disasters. Similarly Volker Heins notes that NGOs "often attempt to shame national governments into accepting standards or provisions promulgated by international organizations, something these organizations cannot do themselves."[5]

The increased influence of NGOs on international political processes, particularly following the end of the Cold War, is accompanied by a growth of academic publications, including laudatory comments and, more recently, some independent critical analysis. For example, Shamima Ahmed and David Potter trace the impact of environmental NGOs "in helping create international regimes to protect animal species and to reduce the harmful effects of industrial and other forms of pollution."[6] Organizational theorist William Powell refers to

---

[2] Clark, Roger, Amnesty International Canada Section (English Speaking), *The Evolution of the Mandate* (Oct. 28, 1996), http://www.amnesty.org/aboutai/eom.htm; *see* Anderson, Kenneth, Questions re: Human Rights Watch's Credibility in Lebanon Reporting, Kenneth Anderson Laws of War Blog, Aug. 23, 2006, http://kennethandersonlawofwar.blogspot.com/2006/08/questions-re-human-rights-watchs.html.

[3] See Ben-Ari, Har'el, *The Normative Position of International Non-Governmental Organizations (INGOs) Under International Law* (2010)(unpublished Ph.D. dissertation, Bar-Ilan University)(on file with the author).

[4] Kaldor, Mary, Global Civil Society: An Answer to War 129 (2003).

[5] Heins, Volker, Nongovernmental Organizations in International Society 58 (2008).

[6] Ahmed, Shamima and David Potter, NGOs in International Politics 11 (2006).

non-hierarchical NGOs as "lighter on their feet" in comparison to formal diplomatic structures,[7] and William Fisher characterizes the perception of NGOs as "everything that governments are not."[8] David Chandler labels the moral claims of NGOs as "oriented around universal beliefs and motivations."[9] Margaret Keck and Kathryn Sikkink argue that "governments are the primary guarantors of rights, they are also their primary violators," leaving individuals or minorities with "no recourse within domestic political or judicial arenas."[10] Therefore they commend NGOs that extend their power as they "bypass their state and directly search out international allies to bring pressure on their states from the outside."[11]

Common Problems - Questionable Reliability, Lack of Training

Although the influence and reputations of human rights NGOs has increased significantly, the lack of a consistent and appropriate fact-finding methodology has resulted in major inconsistencies across many dimensions. Without methodological standardization, fact-finders face a wide range of challenges. Robert Charles Blitt notes that "the rejection of generally accepted procedures necessarily detracts from each [human rights organization's] ability to authoritatively ascertain truth or falsity with any degree of legitimacy, and moreover, from the industry as a whole."[12] For example, Eric Meldrum writes that investigators for the International Criminal Tribunal for the former Yugoslavia noticed severe deficiencies in clarity and neutrality in NGO fact-finding reports and were unable to ascertain which statements were literal transcriptions from witnesses and which were added by the

---

[7] Powell, William W., *Neither Market nor Hierarchy: Network Forms of Organization*, 12 Research in Org. Behav. 295–96, 303–04 (1990).

[8] Fisher, William F., *Doing Good? The Politics and Antipolitics of NGO practices*, 26 Ann. Rev. of Anthropology 444 (1997), available at http://www.jstor.org/stable/2952530.

[9] Chandler, David, Constructing Civil Society: Morality and Power in International Relations 1 (2004).

[10] Keck, Margaret E. and Kathryn Sikkink, Activists beyond Borders, Advocacy Networks in International Politics 12 (1998).

[11] Id. at 12.

[12] Blitt, Robert Charles, *Who will watch the watchdogs? Human rights Non-governmental Organizations and the case for regulation*, 10 Buff. Hum. Rts. L. Rev. 261, 339 (2004), available at http://www.ngo-monitor.org/data/images/File/SSRN-id753487.pdf.

interviewer.[13] In addition, the lack of sufficient procedural safeguards has led NGOs to mishandle and damage potential forensic evidence.[14] Critics also note that NGO missions often lack terms of reference, a clear agenda, selection procedures for team members, detailed descriptions of on-site methodology, distinction between direct evidence and inferences from indirect evidence, explanation of legal standards used, and a separate section for conclusions and recommendations.[15] That last item is especially troubling, as it prevents readers from clearly separating fact from opinion, and also risks erasing differences in opinion that may have occurred in the group.[16]

Some analysts have noted the NGO 'accountability deficit': David Chandler views NGOs as an unregulated and nebulous sector, "fuzzy at the edges,"[17] and Blitt describes a number of examples of how NGO reporting on human rights issues is "easily subject to manipulation."[18] Sovereign democratic governments are generally held accountable through political processes. Analysts such as Volker Heins and Hugo Slim note,[19] in contrast, that NGO officials are accountable only to their donors or – in the case of mass membership organizations such as AI – to their members, usually through an opaque and amorphous process.[20] Similarly, Anne Marie Slaughter highlights the limitations of "supranational governance" leading to the lack of NGO accountability and transparency.[21] In *The Journal of Global Ethics*, Louis Logister observes that while NGOs "have taken roles that traditionally have been the sole province of states or intergovernmental institutions,"

---

[13] Meldrum, Eric, *Time for a Change?: The Traditional Human Right NGO Fact Finding Methodology in relation to National and International Prosecutions of Gross Human Right Violations* 40 (2009), available at http://www.brookes.ac.uk/schools/be/oisd/architecture/cendep/dissertations/EricMeldrum.pdf.

[14] Id. at 43.

[15] Blitt, *supra* note 12, at 335–39. *See also* Conflict Research Consortium, University of Colorado, *International Online Training Program On Intractable Conflict* (1998), available at http://www.colorado.edu/conflict/peace/problem/factfinding.htm.

[16] Thoolen, Hans and Berth Verstappen, Human Rights Missions: A Study of the Fact-finding Practice of Non-governmental Organizations 135 (1986).

[17] Chandler, *supra* note 9, at 1.

[18] Blitt, *supra* note 12, at 263.

[19] Slim, Hugo, International Council on Human Rights Policy, By What Authority? The Legitimacy and Accountability of Non-Governmental Organisations (2002).

[20] Heins, *supra* note 5, at 34.

[21] Slaughter, Anne-Marie, A New World Order (2004); see also Mitchell A. Orenstein, and Hans Peter Schmitz, *Review: The New Transnationalism and Comparative Politics*, 38 Comp. Pol. 470–500 (2006).

their officials "are not bound to act in the public interest. Neither are their actions justified by formal democratic procedures, as is the case with states."[22]

The accountability deficits of NGOs are exacerbated by the 'halo effect,' by which groups perceived to promote 'good' principles are insulated from scrutiny by a cloak of morality. This 'halo effect' compensates not only for the lack of accountability but also for the lack of expertise in the military and diplomatic spheres with which many NGOs concern themselves. According to Peter Willets, "There is a widespread attitude that NGOs consist of altruistic people campaigning in the general public interest, while governments consist of self-serving politicians… such an attitude should not be adopted as an unchallenged assumption…"[23] David Chandler cites assertions by NGO officials and advocates that they promote "political emancipation," the empowerment of individuals, and the extension of democracy.[24] Volker Heins argues that NGOs create "symbolical" victims and then portray themselves as altruistic rescuers.[25]

In addition, some scholars find a consistent ideological bias in many NGO publications. Kenneth Anderson notes that NGO reports "focus to near exclusion on what the attackers do, especially in asymmetrical conflicts where the attackers are Western armies," and the reports tend "to present to the public and press what are essentially lawyers' briefs that shape the facts and law toward conclusions that [they] favor… without really presenting the full range of factual and legal objections to [their] position."[26] And as Blitt notes, NGOs "identify their primary goals as monitoring and reporting of government behavior on human rights … building pressure and creating

---

[22] Logister, Louis, *Global Governance and Civil Society: Some Reflections on NGO Legitimacy*, 3 J. Global Ethics 165–79 (2007).

[23] Willetts, Louis, *Introduction*, *in* The Conscience of the World': The Influence of Non-Governmental Organisations in the UN System (Peter Willets, ed., 1996); see also Louis Willets, *The Impact of Promotional Pressure Groups in Global Politics*, *in* Pressure Groups in the Global System: The Transnational Relations of Issue-Oriented Non-Governmental Organizations (Peter Willets, ed., 1982).

[24] Chandler, *supra* note 9, at 1.

[25] Heins, *supra* note 5, at 24.

[26] Anderson, Kenneth, Questions re: Human Rights Watch's Credibility in Lebanon Reporting, Kenneth Anderson Laws of War Blog, Aug. 23, 2006, available at http://kennethandersonlawofwar.blogspot.com/2006/08/questions-re-human-rights-watchs.html.

international machinery to end the violations and to hold governments accountable."[27]

NGOs function like lobbies and interest groups, in a manner that Kaldor refers to as the "domestication of the international" political process.[28] Their influence is based on the application of soft power: "the ability to get what you want through attraction rather than coercion or payments."[29] Nye notes that "NGOs and network organizations have soft power resources and do not hesitate to use them."[30] Among those resources, the perception of expertise and commitments to a universal morality untainted by partisan politics or economic objectives are crucial for human rights NGOs. The moral leverage claimed by NGOs that promote human rights, international law, environmental causes, and similar goals increases their soft power impact.

Using strategies based on naming and shaming, NGOs often seek to "modify behavior not with logic, but by isolating or embarrassing the target."[31] Human Rights Watch in particular promotes this strategy as a means to encourage democratic reforms from abusive regimes.[32] NGO officials assert that "even questionable, unverified allegations ought to be sanctioned as a basis for shaming in urgent situations."[33] And as Heins notes, in such NGO reports, it is "not the event, but the event's telling that counts," and "the process of establishing the facts of victimhood plays itself out through language (including pictures), which

---

[27] Blitt, *supra* note 12, at 288, citing F. Gaer, Reality Check, in NGOs, The UN, and Global Governance 56 (T.G. Weiss & L. Gordenker, eds., 1996).

[28] Kaldor, *supra* note 4, at 78.

[29] Nye, Joseph S., Jr., Soft Power: The Means to Success in World Politics x (2004).

[30] Id. at 94.

[31] Blitt, *supra* note 12, at 290, citing T. Risse & K. Sikkink, *The Socialization of International Human Rights Norms into Domestic Practices: Introduction in* The Power of Human Rights: International Norms and Domestic Change (Thomas Risse, Stephen C. Ropp, & Kathryn Sikkink, eds., 1999). For more on the use of "naming and shaming," see Robert F. Drinan, The Mobilization of Shame (2002).

[32] Human Rights Watch, *Our History*, available at http://www.hrw.org/en/node/75134 (last visited Apr. 11, 2011); see also Hafner-Burton, Emilie M., *Sticks and Stones: Naming and Shaming the Human Rights Enforcement Problem*, 62 Int'l Org. 689, 693 (2008), available at http://ilar.ucsd.edu/assets/001/11945.pdf. ("The NGO Human Rights Watch considers the strategy to be 'one of the most effective human rights tools' to oblige governments, at a minimum, to protect some civil and political rights.")

[33] Blitt, *supra* note 12, at 290, citing H. Hannum, *Implementing Human Rights: An Overview of NGO Strategies and Procedures*, Guide to International Human Rights Practice 36 (Hurst Hannum, ed., 2d ed. 1992).

implies that it is inherently contestable."[34] In a study in *International Organization*, Emilie Hafner-Burton concludes that naming and shaming leads to mixed results: "Governments put in the global spotlight for violations often adopt better protections for political rights afterward, but they rarely stop or appear to lessen acts of terror. Worse, terror sometimes increases after publicity."[35] Hafner-Burton posits that leaders often have more capacity to address political legislation than to curb terror, or that leaders view political legislation as a simpler way to appease the world community (while continued acts of terror prevent a real effect to any political reform).[36]

The lack of standardization for NGO fact-finding methodology means, perhaps most critically, that no standard training exists for investigators. Due to the unique complexities in international NGO missions, the need for reliable investigators is paramount. In her book *Fact-Finding Without Facts*, Nancy Combes outlines some of the challenges that face international investigators (in the context of international tribunals).[37] She divides these challenges into three categories: 1) education, literacy, and life experience; 2) interpretation errors; and 3) cultural divergences.[38] First, witnesses often invoke their lack of education when unable to answer a question, for example where or when an incident occurred. Witnesses in certain countries may have no concept of how to read a map or of standard units of time.[39] Next, Combes notes that inaccuracies in interpretation are prolific in international cases, and even subtle errors can be "distortive."[40] And in many instances, the errors are less than subtle, such as a case in which a court provided Spanish interpreters for someone who was in fact Mixtec.[41] Finally, Combes notes that Western fact-finders easily misinterpret cultural norms. Different cultures associate different meanings with the same gestures. For example, avoiding eye contact is a sign of respect in some countries and a sign of disingenuousness in others.[42] NGOs risk skewing information when they are unaware of cultural

[34] Heins, *supra* note 5, at 24.
[35] Hafner-Burton, *supra* note 32, at 707.
[36] Id. at 707–10.
[37] Combes, Nancy Armoury, Fact-Finding Without Facts: The Uncertain Evidentiary Foundations of International Criminal Convictions (2010).
[38] Id. at 63.
[39] Id. at 65–66.
[40] Id. at 67.
[41] Id.
[42] Id. at 80.

norms, especially in less-visited Third World countries. Other sources are equally concerned about "adopting homogenizing approaches to human rights that draw little from non-Western realities."[43] NGOs themselves acknowledge that their managing boards include few people from the Third World, even while most of their work concerns those countries.[44]

Proper training for investigators is one of the most important requirements for a fact-finding mission. Combes notes that many of the deficiencies in international investigations come from investigators failing to ask the right questions initially.[45] In addition, interviewers must include in their report what questions they posed. Otherwise interviewees can later deny that the question ever occurred, and readers of the report, including policy makers, journalists, and members of UN investigatory commissions, are unable to place responses in context.

Another aspect of training is making sure to include team members with the necessary expertise. Michael Schmitt notes the importance of an investigator with military experience for investigations of violations of international law in armed conflict:

> An investigator who does not understand, for example, weapons options, fuzing, guidance systems, angle of attack, optimal release altitudes, command and control relationships, communications capabilities, tactical options, available intelligence options, enemy practices, pattern of life analysis, collateral damage estimate methodology, human factors in a combat environment, and so forth, will struggle to effectively scrutinize an air strike.[46]

Without a trained investigator to navigate potential stumbling-blocks or to provide the relevant expertise, critics will continue to call into question the reliability of witness statements.

---

[43] Ibhawoh, Bonny, *Human Rights INGOs and the North-South Gap: The Challenge of Normative and Empirical Learning*, in Daniel A. Bell and Jean-Marc Coicaud, Ethics in Action: The Ethical Challenges of International Human Rights Nongovernmental Organizations 80 (2007).

[44] Steiner, Henry J., Diverse Partners: Non-Governmental Organizations in the Human Rights Movement – The Report of a Retreat of Human Rights Activists 34 (1991).

[45] Combes, *supra* note 37, at 279–80. For that reason it is critical that investigators' reports don't contain mere summaries but rather transcripts of the interviews.

[46] Schmitt, Michael N., *Investigating Violations of International Law in Armed Conflict*, 2 Harv. Nat'l Sec. J. 31, 84 (2011).

Robert Blitt sums up the problem of having no standardized training procedures: "In short, no prerequisite or certification is required for pursuing classic [human rights organization] activities, and none is in place to distinguish or legitimize [human rights organizations] from any other third party."[47] In other words, there is no clear distinction between the reliability of a report from an established NGO and that from any individual reporting from the ground. Investigators for the International Criminal Tribunal for the former Yugoslavia (ICTY) found a clear difference between professional police/prosecutorial standards and those used by NGOs and other third parties.[48] The *ICTY Manual on Developed Practices* warns that taking witness statements is a "professional process that is best left to … trained investigators" rather than to the humanitarian agencies in the area.[49] Human Rights First also notes that if an NGO investigator conducts interviews or collects evidence without proper training, those actions could "have a serious negative impact on any subsequent criminal investigation and … NGOs could harm a prosecution, or a defense case."[50]

The academic literature suggests several explanations for why NGOs do not align their standards with those of the police or prosecutorial investigators. One reason is that NGOs have different mandates than government or international investigative agencies. For example, NGOs assert that they have an "early warning" function that allows them to repeat claims of questionable reliability for the limited purpose of sounding "an alarm bell within the international community."[51] Others note that NGOs are not mechanisms of criminal justice, but rather are concerned with, for example, "establishing and publishing the occurrence of human rights abuses in order to pressurise the offending state or party to stop committing them."[52] Another explanation is simply that human rights NGOs are "so devoid of expertise, time and resources, that they lack the ability to develop any regular

[47] Blitt, *supra* note 12, at 288.

[48] Meldrum, *supra* note 13, at 40.

[49] United Nations Interregional Crime and Justice Research Institute and the International Criminal Tribunal for the former Yugoslavia, *ICTY Manual on Developed Practices* 16 (2008).

[50] Human Rights First, *The Role of Human Rights NGOs in Relation to ICC Investigations* (2004), available at http://www.amicc.org/docs/Human%20Rights%20First%20NGO_Role_Discussion_Paper.pdf.

[51] Blitt, *supra* note 12, at 343; Steiner, *supra* note 7, at 35.

[52] Meldrum, *supra* note 13, at 36; see also Human Rights First, *supra* note 50, at 5.

procedures. Instead they live from press release to hastily drawn report, without time for methodology."[53] NGOs also assert that they need flexibility in order to adapt their fact-finding efforts to countries and situations across the globe, or that a uniform standard would endanger their individual employees, allowing governments to attack domestic human rights professionals for failure to adhere to those standards.[54] To a certain extent, NGOs see regulation as contrary to their very nature, especially if efforts to regulate them come from those "who have been obliged to change their policies and practices as a result of NGO campaigning."[55] In short, critics attribute the lack of generally applicable guidelines to a concern among NGOs about ceding some of their independence.[56]

One element not addressed by these writers, however, is a comparison to fact-finding standards utilized by law enforcement in criminal investigations. Although NGOs may have different mandates than criminal investigators, both are "primarily concerned with establishing the veracity of accounts and in investigating the same situations."[57] Given that methodologies utilized by police and prosecutors are designed to obtain the most accurate information in a variety of contexts, perhaps similar standards could be employed in NGO fact-finding.[58]

The NGO role as an "early warning" system is similarly confusing, particularly in light of the fact that the vast majority of human rights reporting is not an "early warning" situation. Even in such circumstances, an early warning role is only effective and contributory if the information is accurate. The case of Operation Defensive Shield, where Israeli forces entered the town of Jenin on April 3, 2002 to combat Palestinian terrorist groups, is instructive.[59] After a week of fighting in

---

[53] Weissbrodt, David and James McCarthy, *Fact-Finding by Nongovernmental Organizations*, in International Law and Fact-Finding in the Field of Human Rights 186, 189 (B.G. Ramcharan, ed., 1982); see also Blitt, *supra* note 12, at 341.

[54] Orentlicher, Diane F., *Bearing Witness: The Art and Science of Human Rights Fact Finding*, 3 Harv. Hum. Rts. J. 83, 105–06 (1990); see also Steiner, Henry J., Philip Alston and Ryan Goodman, International Human Rights in Context: Law Politics and Morals 748 (3d ed. 2008).

[55] Steiner, *International Human Rights in Context*, *supra* note 44, at 1423.

[56] Blitt, *supra* note 12, at 339; Steiner, *Diverse Partners*, *supra* note 44, at 67.

[57] Meldrum, *supra* note 13, at 41.

[58] Id.

[59] United Nations, *Report of the Secretary-General prepared pursuant to General Assembly resolution ES-10/10* (June 7, 2002), http://www.un.org/peace/jenin/index.html.

the streets of Jenin, NGOs were quick to allege that Israeli soldiers massacred 200 or more Palestinian civilians and even used bulldozers to bury people alive.[60] The UN Security Council sent a mission to examine the massacre claims, and reported back that

> [t]he number of Palestinian fatalities, on the basis of bodies recovered to date, in Jenin and the refugee camp in this military operation can be estimated at around 55. Of those, a number were civilians, four were women and two children. There were 23 Israeli fatalities in the fighting operations in Jenin.[61]

Even after claims of a massacre and summary executions were widely dismissed, the myth continued to circulate even years later.[62]

In another incident in 1990, Amnesty International released a report accusing Iraqi soldiers of murdering Kuwaiti babies by removing them from hospital incubators after the invasion of Kuwait.[63] The story was in fact a fabrication of an American public relations firm hired by the Kuwaitis to influence world opinion about the Gulf crisis.[64] Amnesty was criticized for publishing the report without obtaining corroborating evidence of the allegations, while at the same time the report quickly gained traction in the push for action against Iraq.[65] Even years after Amnesty disavowed the report, President George H.W. Bush continued to cite the murders as justification for the invasion.[66]

More recently, when the Israeli army bombed targets in the southern Lebanon village of Qana in July 2006, NGOs such as HRW issued reports estimating there were 54 to 63 civilian casualties, mostly

---

[60] See, e.g., Dr. Eyad El-Sarraj, *Don't Take Part in War Crimes: Boycott Israel Now*, http://www.gcmhp.net/File_files/PressApr222k2.html (last visited November 17, 2010).; see also Amnesty International, *Israel/Occupied Territories: The cycle of abuse must stop* (April 8, 2002), http://www.amnesty.org/en/library/asset/MDE15/044/2002/en/66894365-d85e-11dd-9df8-936c90684588/mde150442002en.html. ("Reports suggest that 200 people may have been killed in Jenin.")

[61] *United Nations, Report of the Secretary-General prepared pursuant to General Assembly resolution ES-10/10* (June 7, 2002), http://www.un.org/peace/jenin/.

[62] Bennet, James, *Death on the Campus: Jenin; U.N. Report Rejects Claims Of a Massacre Of Refugees*, N.Y. Times, Aug. 2, 2002, available at http://query.nytimes.com/gst/fullpage.html?res=9D04E6DD1E3BF931A3575BC0A9649C8B63&scp=2&sq=jenin&st=cse.

[63] Blitt, *supra* note 12, at 350.

[64] Id.

[65] Clark, *supra* note 2, at 132.

[66] Id.

women and children.[67] HRW published these allegations even though they were aware that the Lebanese Red Cross reported that there were only 28 bodies in the rubble.[68] Lucy Mair, a researcher for Human Rights Watch, told the *L.A. Times*, "The original 54 number actually came from the fact that one of the survivors was saying, 'We were 63 people from two families camped out in the basement.' They identified only nine living people, and immediately people started doing the subtraction."[69] Human Rights Watch later admitted that only 28 bodies were confirmed, but most sources continued to report the higher estimate.[70] Coverage of the 2006 Lebanon War is examined in further detail in the case studies in Chapter Four.

Despite the need to maintain independence and flexibility, the effectiveness of NGO reporting is diminished if it is conveying false information. Moreover, inaccurate reporting can place human rights professionals and vulnerable populations at risk of retaliation either by governments or non-state forces. There is also a concern that the promotion of false claims may lead to the blocking of future access. As a result, it is critical that NGOs must implement at least a basic "meaningful evidentiary baseline."[71]

Another troubling issue is the use of NGO reports in contexts where the report itself does not follow the standards of the body relying on it.[72] For example, the International Bar Association learned that its country reports, which were not created as legal documents, nor intended to be used as such, were relied upon in New Zealand courts and other national courts as proof of country conditions.[73] This application is not necessarily promoted by NGOs, unless they themselves submit papers to judicial bodies, but the problem is significant. It is important, therefore, to have a set of guidelines, so at a minimum, a

---

[67] Kalb, Marvin, and Carol Saivetz, Harvard University Kennedy School of Government, *The Israeli-Hezbollah War of 2006: The Media as a Weapon in Asymmetrical Conflict* 8–9 (2006).

[68] Murphy, Kim, *Officials Say 28 Died in Qana, Not 54*, L.A. TIMES, Aug. 4, 2006, available at http://articles.latimes.com/2006/aug/04/world/fg-qana4.

[69] Id.

[70] Kalb, Marvin, and Carol Saivetz, Harvard University Kennedy School of Government, *The Israeli-Hezbollah War of 2006: The Media as a Weapon in Asymmetrical Conflict* 8–9 (2006).

[71] Blitt, *supra* note 12, at 351.

[72] E-mail from Prof. Abraham Bell, Bar Ilan University, Feb. 13, 2011.

[73] Interview with Alan Stephens, Director of Research, Clemens Nathan Research Centre, Feb. 16, 2011.

court or fact-finding body can point to some international metric when deciding whether or not to accept NGO findings.[74]

Political Considerations

Without clear methodological standards, it becomes exceedingly difficult for a reader to filter out fact-finding from advocacy in human rights reports. A distorted interpretation of facts may be of even greater impact than their collection.[75] Critics note that NGOs structure their interpretation so as to assert moral authority and rally public opinion in order to influence a particular government.[76] Consequently there is "a great deal of incentive for the parties to manipulate the fact-finding process in ways which strengthen their position."[77]

Some critics suggest that NGOs use fact-finding data—especially when collected through a single visit and without systematic monitoring - in order to emphasize issues that are "designed more to promote their own image and fundraising efforts than to advance the public interest."[78] This impression is strengthened in instances where, for example, the fact-finding report is presented only in the NGO's base city and not in the language of the visited country. In such instances, the reports appear to be geared more towards "home-generated considerations" than to the needs of the human rights situation.[79]

Similarly, critics also accuse NGOs of not sending missions to areas where the most severe human rights violations are taking place, but rather basing their decisions on criteria such as "media engagement, international donor strategy and whether the country being investigated is 'powerful.'"[80] These critics compare NGO missions to UN *ad*

---

[74] Id.

[75] Clark, *supra* note 2, at 33.

[76] Blitt, *supra* note 12, at 290.

[77] Conflict Research Consortium, University of Colorado, *International Online Training Program On Intractable Conflict* (1998), available at http://www.colorado.edu/conflict/peace/problem/cinterest.htm.

[78] Simmons, P.J., *Learning to live with NGOs*, 112 Foreign Pol'y 82, 83 (1998); see also Bukovská, Barbora, *Perpetrating Good: Unintended Consequences of International Human Rights Advocacy*, 9 Sur Int'l J. on Hum. Rts. 6, 11 (2008).

[79] Thoolen, *supra* note 16, at 139.

[80] Mallinder, Louis, *Law, Politics and Fact-Finding: Assessing the Impact of Human Rights Reports*, 2 J. Hum. Rts. Prac. 166, 168 (2010), citing James Ron, Howard Ramos & Kathleen Rodgers, *Transnational Information Politics: NGO Human Rights Reporting, 1986–2000*, *in* International Studies Quarterly 49:557–587 (2005).

hoc investigative committees, which are seen as responding to the political objectives of the relevant UN body "without really judging the veracity of the information and therefore the value of the information."[81] In short, as in the Jenin case, "the opportunity for political gain is too great and the cost too cheap for many NGOs to turn down" an opportunity for political expediency and sensationalism.[82] Some NGO staffers have reportedly acknowledged concern that their organizations are becoming too focused on media impact, creating a "Faustian bargain" that pressures them to focus on high-profile countries to the detriment of less-visible nations.[83]

The important question is balancing priorities – whether the underlying human rights or legal violations deserved attention themselves or whether the mission was undertaken with a specific political end (other than the promotion of human rights).[84] NGO reports must in some way be designed to affect change. For example, timing reports to coincide with relevant legislative debates or the visit of a particular head of state is a frequent and widely accepted NGO practice.[85] But this means that there is no simple solution for filtering out the political considerations or media impact calculus. For that reason, it is all the more important that NGOs devise guidelines to ensure that their fact-finding missions are actually reporting facts, while advocacy is relegated to a separate section.

Accountability in Other Contexts – Financial Accountability, Efficacy

Although NGOs have yet to come together on commonly-accepted fact-finding guidelines, these same organizations have succeeded

[81] Ermacora, F., *The Competence and Functions of Fact-Finding Bodies*, in International Law and Fact-Finding in the Field of Human Rights 90 (1982); see also Blitt, *supra* note 12, at 338.

[82] Blitt, *supra* note 12, at 347.

[83] Ron James, Howard Ramos and Kathleen Rodgers, *What Shapes the West's Human Rights Focus?, in* The Social Movements Reader: Cases and Concepts 345, 351–52 (2d. ed. 2009). The authors discuss the tension caused by the NGOs' need to engage Western media and the temptation to cater coverage to suit Western media tastes. For example, the authors note that during the 1990s AI issued almost 70 press releases about Kosovo and only 2 about Congo-Brazzaville, despite similar levels of violence, presumably because the Western media was more interested in the Balkan conflict. Id. at 351.

[84] Id. at 38.

[85] Hannum, Hurst, *Implementing Human Rights: An Overview of NGO Strategies and Available Procedures*, in Guide to International Human Rights Practice 37 (4th ed. 2004).

in creating standardization and accountability in other contexts. One major example is the 2005 "International Non-Governmental Organisations Accountability Charter," a document signed by major international organizations including AI and Greenpeace.[86] The charter focuses on financial accountability and proper governance. For example, the charter requires "[w]ritten procedures covering the appointment, responsibilities and terms of members of the governing body, and preventing and managing conflicts of interest," as well as "a regular general meeting with authority to appoint and replace members of the governing body."[87] The charter is voluntary and not exclusive, and outlines a framework for greater transparency, stakeholder communication, and ethical fundraising. The charter, however, does not contain much information on liability and enforcement, such as setting up reporting mechanisms.[88]

The Accountability Charter is not the only attempt to create a consensus on proper financial governance for NGOs. The charter follows efforts such as One World Trust, an NGO that publishes an annual accountability index that rates prominent international NGOs in terms of their accountability to both internal and external stakeholders.[89] The idea behind organizations like One World Trust is that it would be hypocritical of NGOs to demand accountability of others and not themselves.[90]

The charter follows after several instances of concern in the academic literature about the lack of transparency and internal democracy in certain NGO operations.[91] Such concerns resonate with those now voiced about transparency in fact-finding. In regard to financial transparency, one author wrote that "the rapid growth in the number

---

[86] International Advocacy Non-Governmental Organizations (IANGO) Workshop, *International Non Governmental Organization Accountability Charter* (2005), available at http://www.ingoaccountabilitycharter.org.

[87] Id. at 6.

[88] Anheier, Helmut K. and Amber Hawkes, *Accountability in a Globalising World: International Non-Governmental Organisations and Foundations, in* LEADERSHIP IN SOZIALEN ORGANISATIONEN (J. Eurich and A. Brink, eds., 2009).

[89] Steiner, *International Human Rights in Context*, *supra* note 44, at 1431.

[90] Id. at 1423–24.

[91] Wouters, Jan and Ingrid Rossi, Institute for International Law, University of Leuven, HUMAN RIGHTS NGOS: ROLE, STRUCTURE AND LEGAL STATUS 11–12 (2001); see also Kerstin Martens, *Examining the (Non-) Status of NGOs in International Law*, 10 IND. J. GLOBAL LEGAL STUD. 2–3 (2003), available at http://www.sfb597.uni-bremen.de/homepages/martens/download/MARTENS_GLS2003.pdf. ("Most importantly, in the light of the increasing participation of NGOs in international political processes, the lack of regulation raises questions about NGO representativity and legitimacy.")

of NGOs across the globe and the needs to distinguish credible groups from 'self-seeking bandits,' is a real challenge, one that underscores the need for clearly stipulated legal guidelines for international operations of NGOs."[92] And Jan Wouters and Ingrid Rossi wrote, "NGO accountability depends entirely on public opinion and self-regulation either through the own structure of the NGO or through a network of NGOs to which the particular NGO is affiliated."[93] The authors concluded that NGOs must have a code of conduct that holds them accountable, and that the NGOs should themselves be involved in writing the code so as to prevent NGO-hostile states from using the code to restrict the organizations' activities.[94]

Several NGOs also adhere to the Sphere Project's Humanitarian Charter and Minimum Standards in Disaster Response, a code of conduct on responses to humanitarian crises.[95] This charter was created in 1990s, primarily as a code of obligations to provide assistance in natural disaster situations. It applies to humanitarian work in armed conflicts as well. The charter follows and elaborates on a ten-point code of conduct prepared by the International Federation of Red Cross and Red Crescent Societies and the International Committee of the Red Cross.[96] A core group of international NGOs created the charter by

---

[92] Ajibade, Idowu Mopelola, *A Synopsis: Rights, Responsibilities and Roles of Human Rights NGOs under International Law* 18 (2008), available at http://papers.ssrn.com/sol3/papers.cfm?abstract_id=1300103.

[93] Wouters and Rossi, *supra* note 91, at 12.

[94] Id. at 13.

[95] Slim, Hugo, *Claiming a Humanitarian Imperative: NGOs and the Cultivation of Humanitarian Duty, in* HUMAN RIGHTS AND CONFLICT: EXPLORING THE LINKS BETWEEN RIGHTS, LAW, AND PEACEBUILDING 159, 161 (Julie Mertus and Jeffrey W. Helsing, eds., 2006).

[96] The Sphere Project, *Humanitarian Charter and Minimum Standards in Humanitarian Response* 370–72 (3rd ed. 2011), available at http://www.sphereproject.org/. ("The Code of Conduct: Principles of Conduct for The International Red Cross and Red Crescent Movement and NGOs in Disaster Response Programmes: 1) The humanitarian imperative comes first; 2) Aid is given regardless of the race, creed or nationality of the recipients and without adverse distinction of any kind. Aid priorities are calculated on the basis of need alone; 3) Aid will not be used to further a particular political or religious standpoint; 4) We shall endeavour not to act as instruments of government foreign policy; 5) We shall respect culture and custom; 6) We shall attempt to build disaster response on local capacities; 7) Ways shall be found to involve programme beneficiaries in the management of relief aid; 8) Relief aid must strive to reduce future vulnerabilities to disaster as well as meeting basic needs; 9) We hold ourselves accountable to both those we seek to assist and those from whom we accept resources; 10) In our information, publicity and advertising activities, we shall recognise disaster victims as dignified humans, not hopeless objects." Available at http://www.ifrc.org/Docs/idrl/I259EN.pdf.)

canvassing other NGOs and academic personnel to "produce precise and quantifiable standards for describing what their humanitarian duty would look like in practice."[97] While the charter is praised as an "extraordinary attempt" to outline rights and responsibilities of humanitarian organizations, some critics accuse the charter of failing to factor in the complexities of various possible operations.[98]

If NGOs can come together in these contexts, then a common code of conduct for fact-finding methodology is not out of reach. NGOs have demonstrated a willingness to cede some authority in the interests of transparency and legitimacy. In spite of criticisms, these ventures provide organizations with a certain baseline of reliability and guidance. Without a baseline in the fact-finding context, the accuracy of NGO reports continues to vary.

---

97 Slim, *supra* note 19, at 162–63.
98 Id. at 163, 166.

CHAPTER THREE

GUIDELINES FOR NGOs

Guideline Proposals

Thomas M. Franck and H. Scott Fairley's 1980 article, "Procedural Due Process in Human Rights Fact-Finding by International Tribunals" in the *American Journal of International Law,* lays much of the groundwork for framing subsequent discussions of NGO methodology.[1] Although the output of NGOs has changed dramatically in recent decades—including the level of technical complexity and public scrutiny—many of the most in-depth articles on fact-finding methodology were written 20 to 30 years ago. Franck and Fairley note that a basis to test validity is critical to assessing fact-finding reports and securing cooperation of the investigated state.[2]

In their article, they list five indicators of impartiality for fact-finding missions: "(1) choice of subject, (2) choice of fact finders, (3) terms of reference, (4) procedures for investigation, and (5) utilization of product."[3] The authors explain why each category is integral to the credibility of a mission, and they list practice suggestions from the United Nations Economic and Social Council (ECOSOC) and the International Labour Organisation (ILO) on procedures such as election of mission members, decision-making through majority vote, drafting of the agenda, place of meeting, and whether sessions are open or *in camera*.[4] But the authors also note that the ECOSOC rules miss many key questions, such as who sets the mission's agenda, whether the mission has the right to meet with imprisoned witnesses, the extent to which an accused can confront an accuser, and the role of hearsay evidence.[5] Franck and Fairley do not propose any model set of rules, preferring to instead point out concepts that a model should address.

---

1 Franck, Thomas M. and H. Scott Fairley, *Procedural Due Process in Human Rights Fact-Finding by International Tribunals*, 74 AM. J. INT'L L. 308 (1980).

2 Id. at 312.

3 Id. at 311.

4 Id. at 320.

5 Id. at 321.

In Belgrade, in August 1980, the delegates of the 59th Conference of the International Law Association approved the "Belgrade Minimal Rules of Procedure for International Human Rights Fact-finding Missions" (Belgrade Rules), based in part on Franck and Fairley's work. The Rules are a "set of minimal procedures to protect the integrity of human rights fact-finding by nongovernmental organizations."[6] The effort was designed to address departures from due process by fact-finding missions, to encourage states to cooperate with investigations, and to bolster the credibility of findings. The International Law Association, itself an NGO, designed the guidelines with the idea that its broad membership base would encourage other organizations to adopt their findings.[7] The guidelines provide basic standards for creating terms of reference, selecting fact-finders, collecting evidence, on-site investigating, and writing up findings after the mission.[8]

Many of the rules stem from a "Memorandum of Understanding with the Government of Chile" negotiated in advance of a 1978 visit by an *ad hoc* working group of the UN Commission on Human Rights, not by an NGO.[9] The group investigated allegations that the government of Augusto Pinochet committed "constant and flagrant violations of human rights and fundamental freedoms," in particular by use of "torture, disappearance of persons for political reasons and the refusal to adequately account for about one thousand missing detainees, limitations on freedom of expression, the suspension of political activity, the systematic campaign against suspected opponents of the régime," as well as "infringement of the right to a nationality and the right to return to one's country, arbitrary arrest, detention and exile."[10]

Most NGOs did not adopt the Belgrade Rules, and some scholars criticized the rules for their lack of detail and, simultaneously, for being inflexible.[11] For example, the rules strictly do not allow the addition or

---

[6] Franck, Thomas M., ed., *The Belgrade Minimum Rules of Procedure for International Fact-Finding Missions*, 75 AM. J. INT'L L. 163, 163 (1981).

[7] Id.

[8] Id.

[9] Steiner, Henry J., Philip Alston, and Ryan Goodman, INTERNATIONAL HUMAN RIGHTS IN CONTEXT: LAW POLITICS AND MORALS 748 (3d ed. 2008).

[10] UN Commission on Human Rights, *Study of reported violations of human rights in Chile, with particular reference to torture and other cruel, inhuman or degrading treatment or punishment* E/CN.4/RES/12 (1978), available at http://www.unhcr.org/refworld/publisher,UNCHR,,CHL,3b00f0b22c,0.html.

[11] Raoul Wallenberg Institute of Human Rights and Humanitarian Law, International Bar Association, and British Institute of International and Comparative

the removal of any member of a fact-finding team (with an exception for gross misbehavior), which some organizations found too rigid.[12] The rules state that the mission "should make its own determination as to whether it needs to conduct an on-site inspection," but they provide no guidance about factors to consider.[13] Several academics opined that the rules were based on the experiences of IGOs (like the working group in Chile) rather than NGOs and are therefore unworkable.[14] The requirement that all mission members serve "in their personal capacities,"[15] for example, is out of place for NGOs, who often send members of their organizations.[16] Despite these concerns, the Belgrade Rules contain a number of important standards—such as the requirement that a mission's report should include views of any dissenting members—and provide a framework for future efforts.[17]

At around the same time, David Weissbrodt and James McCarthy recommended in the *Virginia Journal of International Law* against creating a uniform standard for NGO methodology. In a 1981 article, they are highly critical of the Belgrade Rules and Franck and Fairley's work as too narrow and adversarial.[18] They conclude that while NGOs may benefit from adopting certain rules from the IGO community, NGOs must be able to choose which procedures they wish to follow in order to retain their flexibility. They later suggest that concerns about NGO fact-finding procedure can be alleviated by disclosing the investigative methods in the final report.[19] In their view, NGO reports should include the names of the mission members, government statements in

---

Law, *Human Rights Fact-Finding Missions: Seminar Report* 8 (June 1–2, 2009), available at http://www.biicl.org/files/4462_fact_finding_report_updated_2.pdf [hereinafter Lund-London Guidelines].

[12] Franck, *Belgrade Rules*, *supra* note 6, at 163–64.

[13] Id. at 164.

[14] Id. See also Blitt, Robert Charles, *Who will watch the watchdogs? Human rights Nongovernmental Organizations and the case for regulation*, 10 BUFF. HUM. RTS. L. REV. 261, 348 (2004), *available at* http://www.ngo-monitor.org/data/images/File/SSRN-id753487.pdf.; Hans Thoolen and and Berth Verstappen, HUMAN RIGHTS MISSIONS: A STUDY OF THE FACT-FINDING PRACTICE OF NON-GOVERNMENTAL ORGANIZATIONS 135–36 (1986).

[15] Franck, *Belgrade Rules*, *supra* note 113, at 164.

[16] See, e.g. Weissbrodt, David and James McCarthy, *Fact-Finding by International Nongovernmental Human Rights Organizations*, 22 VA. J. INT'L L. 1 (1981).

[17] Id. at 16.

[18] Weissbrodt, *supra* note 16, at 15–17 (1981).

[19] Weissbrodt, David and James McCarthy, *Fact-Finding by Nongovernmental Organizations*, in INTERNATIONAL LAW AND FACT-FINDING IN THE FIELD OF HUMAN RIGHTS 215 (B.G. Ramcharan, ed., 1982).

response to the report (where possible), accounts of information the team rejected as inaccurate, and the legal norms cited.[20] They note that, with the adoption of fact-finding rules, more governments may cooperate and accept NGO findings. But they reflect concern that standardization would impede the NGOs from reporting when they "know" a violation is occurring but are unable to reveal sources or prove it.[21]

Despite the flexibility of Weissbrodt and McCarthy's approach, the informality creates troubling concerns about reliability. Weissbrodt and McCarthy do not set any baseline standards for measuring fact-finding techniques or any way to strengthen "the confidence of the international community" in a particular report.[22] When information is quickly cited and disseminated throughout the world, it is problematic to assume that anyone taking advantage of the report will thoroughly review and cite the description of investigative methods before spreading the information. In addition, in the nearly three decades since Weissbrodt and McCarthy's article, the NGO community has not widely adopted even their basic suggestions about disclosure.[23]

At a seminar in 1989, representatives from 25 NGOs tried to grapple with some of these issues, including the difficulties for international NGOs to grasp the complex political phenomena in each particular country.[24] The meeting did not attempt to create guidelines but debated ideas for improving accuracy.[25] One suggestion was to avoid the practice of selecting public figures to head fact-finding missions and instead selecting investigators with the requisite expert knowledge (and leaving the public figures to instead publicize the mission findings).[26]

Similar to Weissbordt and McCarthy, Diane Orentlicher, a fellow at Yale Law School, concluded in 1990 in the *Harvard Human Rights Journal* that—in light of the considerable variations between investigations in different countries—it is impossible to create a single standard for human rights workers everywhere.[27] Orentlicher's article examines

---

[20] Id. at 217.
[21] Id. at 216.
[22] Thoolen, *supra* note 14, at 19.
[23] Blitt, *supra* note 14, at 349.
[24] Steiner, *supra* note 9, at 64.
[25] Id.
[26] Id.
[27] Orentlicher, Diane F., *Bearing Witness: The Art and Science of Human Rights Fact Finding*, 3 Harv. Hum. Rts. J. 83, 106 (1990); see also Steiner, Henry J., Philip Alston and Ryan Goodman, International Human Rights in Context: Law Politics and Morals 748 (3d ed. 2008).

the evolving role of NGOs in light of the Reagan administration's focus on human rights compliance in its foreign policy.[28] The administration certified to Congress that El Salvador met its human rights obligations and was thus eligible to receive federal aid in the early 1980s.[29] According to Orentlicher, the administration worked to discredit any NGO that portrayed El Salvador—or the contra insurgents in Nicaragua—as violators of human rights. She concludes that this battle between NGOs and the US government led to increased public scrutiny on human rights reports and to improvements in human rights reporting on both sides.[30]

In her article, Orentlicher makes a detailed summary of preferred NGO methodologies, including avoiding politically-biased sources where possible, interviewing witnesses outside of the presence of third persons, asking relentless follow-up questions to witnesses (to work through cultural divides and test credibility), and working with domestic human rights groups.[31] She also points out the advantage of having well-trained investigators with encyclopedic knowledge of a particular country, so that they more easily evaluate and test witness accounts.[32]

Rather than attempting to standardize methodology, Orentlicher suggests other avenues to improve credibility. For example, she suggests that NGOs must be internally consistent in different countries and be able to explain any variation in approach "by reference to variations in factual conditions."[33] She also argues that NGOs need only make a "prima facie" case by developing probative—even if inconclusive—evidence of human rights abuses, and, if persuasive, the government in question will be pressured to respond.[34] Orentlicher's proposal conveys a somewhat idealized view of the interaction between NGOs and governments, similar to the Wilsonian idealist notion that all international diplomacy must be conducted "in the public view."[35] Her article does not acknowledge the potential for abuses by NGOs under her model, which risks allowing NGOs to issue specious reports with

---

[28] Id. at 89.
[29] Id. at 90–91.
[30] Id. at 91–92.
[31] Id. at 109, 113, 117, 125–34.
[32] Id. at 119.
[33] Id. at 104.
[34] Id. at 107–08.
[35] Wilson, Woodrow, *Transcript of President Woodrow Wilson's 14 Points* (1918), available at http://www.ourdocuments.gov/doc.php?doc=62&page=transcript.

the expectation that governments would bear the burden to refute the allegations.

In 2000, the Asian Human Rights Commission released a guide to "Human Rights Monitoring and Fact-Finding," which focuses on ensuring thorough analysis and socio-cultural understanding of the facts.[36] The guide provides tips for monitoring government human rights practices, including seeking technical and legal assistance where necessary.[37] The guide also lays out numerous principles:

1. All inquiries must be thorough and many-sided. No conscious or unconscious deletion of any information that may be considered adverse.
2. Accuracy is guaranteed by the use of diverse sources of information.
3. Impartiality; willingness to abandon any hypothesis, if there are reasons to do so.
4. Fair hearing to every party - particularly to the suspected party.
5. Application of International standards.
6. Following inquiries till it is brought to a logical ending.
7. All inquiries are likely to come under many obstacles. The inquirers must be resourceful to deal with such obstacles.[38]

The guide offers very basic advice in very basic language, emphasizing the need for investigative training while remaining vague as to what the training should include. The focus on accuracy and impartiality is noteworthy, but the notion that a diversity of sources guarantees accuracy is an oversimplification.

The Human Rights Centre at the University of Essex produced two manuals to "define specific rights, outline the legal protections against their violation, and provide ways in which testimony and evidence from victims can be collected."[39] The "Torture Reporting Handbook" in 2000 and the "Reporting Killings as Human Rights Violations Handbook" in 2002 are designed to assist NGO fieldworkers (and any other individual engaged in human rights reporting) in documenting

---

[36] Asian Human Rights Commission (ARDC), *Human Rights Monitoring and Fact-Finding* (2000), available at http://www.hrschool.org/modules/6.pdf.

[37] Id. at 5.

[38] Id. at 6.

[39] Landman, Todd, STUDYING HUMAN RIGHTS 81 (2006).

allegations and reporting them to international bodies.[40] The projects were funded in part by the United Kingdom Foreign Office's Human Rights Fund.[41] The handbooks emphasize maximizing the accuracy and reliability of the collected information.[42]

In order to ensure quality and accuracy, the handbooks provide a number of practical suggestions. The Torture Reporting Handbook encourages fact-finders to examine, for example, the sources of their information, the level of detail provided, the number of contradictions within an account, and the presence of corroborating evidence.[43] The handbook also provides an outline of the optimal information to seek during an interview, including any official response to the incident and the forms of the holding conditions.[44] These models are primarily useful to the specific type of violation (torture, killing) in question, and both handbooks are not standards of conduct so much as practice suggestions.[45] In a few cases, however, the handbooks provide bright-line rules for practitioners. The handbooks insist that qualified medical professionals must conduct any physical or psychological examination for evidence of torture, in case the reports are later used in court.[46] For the most part, the handbooks note that many of the practice suggestions are not amenable to a systemic approach but rather dependent on the particulars of the situation.[47]

In 2003, The Human Rights Information System (HURIDOCS), a global network of over 100 human rights organizations, provided a series of manuals that include "What is Monitoring" and "What is Documentation."[48] The organization itself does not engage in fact-finding

---

[40] Giffard, Camille and Kate Thompson, Human Rights Centre, University of Essex, *Reporting Killings as Human Rights Violations Handbook* 3 (2002), available at http://www.essex.ac.uk/reportingkillingshandbook/; Camille Giffard, Human Rights Centre, University of Essex, *Torture Reporting Handbook* 4 (2000), available at http://www.essex.ac.uk/torturehandbook/handbook(english).pdf.

[41] Cook, Robin, *Statement at the Launch of the Torture Reporting Handbook* (2000), available at http://www.essex.ac.uk/torturehandbook/news.htm.

[42] Giffard, *Torture Reporting Handbook, supra* note 40, at 30. ("As you will see below, the degree of quality, accuracy and reliability necessary may vary according to the course of action selected, but you should always aim to reach the highest standard possible in the circumstances.")

[43] Id. at 30–31.

[44] Id. at 38.

[45] See, e.g., Giffard, *Reporting Killings Handbook, supra* note 42, at 47–48.

[46] Id. at 48.

[47] Id. at 7.

[48] Guzman, Manuel and Bert Verstappen. HURIDOCS, *What is Documentation* (2003), available at http://www.huridocs.org/wp-content/uploads/2010/08/

but rather works to improve methodologies for documenting and accessing public information on human rights.[49] The "Monitoring" handbook focuses on long-term monitoring practices rather than fact-finding missions, and lays out general concepts for monitoring rather than specific practice standards.[50] For example, the handbook emphasizes the importance of using consistent standards or norms in order to objectively assess the situation in a particular country.[51] The "Documentation" handbook goes into slightly more depth about common forms of on-site fact-finding methodology (including interviewing, process observation, and video/audio recording).[52] The handbook includes tips such as using photographs and video recordings. But it refers to other resources (including the UN sources discussed above) for any detailed discussion of fact-finding technique.[53]

Julie Mertus, a professor at American University's Program in Ethics, Peace, and Global Affairs, laid out her suggested guidelines in the early 2000s in the article "Considerations for Human Rights Fact Finding by NGOs."[54] She sets out criteria for selecting a team, collecting evidence, conducting on-site interviews and inspections, and writing the report.[55] Many of her rules draw from older sources including Weissbrodt and McCarthy and Orentlicher, as well as from her experiences in the field.[56] She emphasizes the objectivity and training of investigators, and she highlights proper training as a higher consideration than local language skills.[57] She also emphasizes creating clear terms of reference for the mission, as well as establishing direct and corroborating evidence.[58] She notes that witnesses should be interviewed separately

---

whatisdocumentation-eng.pdf; Guzman, Manuel and Bert Verstappen. HURIDOCS, *What is Monitoring* (2003), available at http://www.huridocs.org/wp-content/uploads/2010/08/whatismonitoring-eng.pdf.

[49] Dueck, Judith, "HURIDOCS Standard Formats as a Tool In the Documentation of Human Rights," *in* HUMAN RIGHTS AND STATISTICS: GETTING THE RECORD STRAIGHT 127, 127–28 (Richard P. Claude and Thomas B. Jabine, eds., 1992) ; see also Landman, *supra* note 39, at 81.

[50] Guzman, HURIDOCS, *What is Monitoring*, *supra* note 48, at 7, 27–31.

[51] Id. at 7.

[52] Guzman, HURIDOCS, *What is Documentation*, *supra* note 48, at 20–21.

[53] Id. at 21, 40.

[54] Mertus, Julie, *Considerations for Human Rights Fact Finding by NGO's*, http://academic3.american.edu/~mertus/HR%20fact-finding.htm (last visited Mar. 3, 2011).

[55] Id.

[56] Id. at n.1.

[57] Id.

[58] Id.

and should not be informed of what other witnesses have stated. She also states that final reports should provide the goals and methodology of the mission, as well as the methods for checking information.[59] Some of the guidelines are vague, perhaps so as to retain a degree of flexibility. For example, Mertus suggests that the mission teams draw up their own guidelines for collection of evidence and mission goals. In addition, she recommends that the team prepare members with any specialized training or background information that may be needed, but she does not specify what that training may include.[60]

Tarisai Mutangi of Makere University in Uganda, in a 2005 analysis of the Franck and Fairley article, discusses how to make findings as impartial as possible. For example, he suggests keeping political considerations outside of the terms of reference.[61] Mutangi's analysis was primarily in response to a controversy between the government of Zimbabwe and the African Commission on Human and People's Rights (ACHPR). In 2004, the government asserted that it did not have a chance to respond to the allegations in the ACHPR's annual report.[62] The African Union suspended publication of the report in order to include an appendix of comments from concerned states parties. In its submission to the appendix, the government of Zimbabwe said that the ACPHR's fact-finding mission did not spend enough time in the country and did not interview people who were fairly representative of the population.[63] The government subsequently instituted harsher disclosure requirements for local NGOs, who were upset that the ACPHR revealed their participation.[64] Mutangi uses this incident as an opportunity to gauge the ACHPR's practices.

Mutangi suggests that reports should only be utilized by political organs like the UN and not the fact-finders themselves; rather, the fact-finders should focus on information gathering and balancing the interests of both parties. He concludes that basic rules are necessary but must also be flexible enough for use by any organ.[65] Mutangi drafts a

---

[59] Id.

[60] Id.

[61] Mutangi, Tarisai, Human Rights and Peace Centre, Makere University, Uganda, *Fact-Finding Missions or Omissions: A Critical Analysis of the African Commission on Human and Peoples' Rights and Lessons to be Learnt from the Inter-American Commission on Human Rights* 21 (2005).

[62] Id. at 1.

[63] Id. at 2.

[64] Id.

[65] Id. at 22.

model set of rules to govern fact-finding missions for the ACHPR, an IGO. His model uses rules from UN *ad hoc* bodies, ECOSOC, ILO, and The Inter-American Commission on Human Rights. With the focus on IGOs, his proposal is very similar to the Belgrade Rules.[66]

The Lund-London Guidelines

In 2009, the International Bar Association's (IBA) Human Rights Institute and the Raoul Wallenberg Institute released the "Guidelines on International Human Rights Fact-Finding Visits and Reports" (Lund-London Guidelines) at a conference at the British Institute of International and Comparative Law in London.[67] The guidelines aim to set an agreed international standard of good practice "in the conduct of fact-finding visits and in the compilation of reports."[68] The guidelines emphasize objectivity, transparency, and proper sourcing, to ensure that a report prepared in adherence to the guidelines "can be reasonably relied upon, thus enhancing the efficacy and credibility of the report."[69] The guidelines focus specifically on NGOs rather than IGOs, and grew out of detailed analysis of NGO reports and interviews with their authors.[70]

According to Har'el Ben-Ari, the guidelines were prepared in response to a concern that media and international tribunals were relying on NGO reports without looking for any indication of reliability.[71] For example, Ben-Ari notes that the drafters found it problematic that some tribunals—such as the British House of Lords and the South African Constitutional Court—insist on high standards of objectivity for their own proceedings, but are willing to accept NGO reports without any safeguards.[72] The project proposal explained the situation: "It is paradoxical that tribunals which in their own proceedings insist

---

[66] Id. at 51.

[67] Office of the United Nations High Commissioner for Refugees, *Refworld: The Leader in Refugee Decision Support*, available at http://www.unhcr.org/cgi-bin/texis/vtx/refworld/rwmain (last visited September 13, 2011).

[68] *The Lund-London Guidelines, supra* note 1.

[69] Id. See also American Society of International Law, *International Law in Brief* (June 12, 2009), available at http://www.asil.org/ilib090612.cfm#r3.

[70] *The Lund-London Guidelines, supra* note 11.

[71] Ben-Ari, Har'el, *The Normative Position of International Non-Governmental Organizations (INGOs) Under International Law* 345 (2010)(unpublished Ph.D. dissertation, Bar-Ilan University)(on file with the author).

[72] Id; *The Lund-London Guidelines, supra* note 11.

on principles of objectivity, impartiality, and due process, are sometimes prepared to accept the findings of fact-finding commissions at their face value...."[73] In fact, the guidelines were initially inspired by an incident in which a Dutch court accepted the veracity of a report without question solely because—in the eyes of the court—it was from a "reputable NGO."[74] Another concern of the guideline drafters, as noted by Geoffrey Robertson, was that errors in fact-finding reports could potentially open an NGO to liability for libel.[75]

At a 2004 conference in Lund, the IBA working group discussed how it researched the guidelines.[76] First, it selected over 100 fact-finding reports (based on geographic, racial, and religious differences), then it analyzed each report in detail and where necessary called the organizations to discuss their findings.[77] During this research phase, the working group paid particular attention to the UN system, AI, HRW, the Commonwealth Human Rights Initiative, International Helsinki Federation, "and various religion-based NGOs."[78] The group discovered several patterns in the NGO reports. For example, the group noted that no NGO report had any information about investigative training or selection process of fact-finders.[79] In addition, most of the examined reports did not expressly state mandates for the teams or goals for the mission, nor did they contain much information on the circumstances of the interviews or whether interviewees were informed of the mandate.[80] The working group outlined its main concerns—including transparency and accuracy—and gave the results to a team to draft informal guidelines for fact-finding.[81]

The Lund-London Guidelines balance the principles of independence and self-sufficiency of NGOs with concerns about credibility and

[73] Document provided by Alan Stephens, Director of Research, Clemens Nathans Research Centre, Feb. 16, 2011. Alan Stephens initiated the Lund-London Guidelines project [hereinafter Alan Stephens document].

[74] Interview with Alan Stephens, Director of Research, Clemens Nathan Research Centre, Feb. 16, 2011 [hereinafter interview with Alan Stephens].

[75] Robertson, Geoffrey, *Human Rights Fact Finding: Some Legal and Ethical Dilemmas*, HUM. RTS. INST., INT'L BAR ASS'N, THEMATIC PAPERS 4, 20 (May 2010).

[76] Mugambe, Lydia, *Lund Workshop on fact finding held from 30 November 2004 – 2 December 2004* at 1, document provided by Alan Stephens, Clemens Nathans Research Centre, Feb. 16, 2011.

[77] Id.

[78] Alan Stephens document, *supra* note 73.

[79] Id. at Table of Contents, #12 at 3.

[80] Id. at 5.

[81] Id. at 2.

legitimacy. Although the guidelines have yet to be officially adopted, they already provide a contrast to the standards used in current NGO fact-finding reports. The mission of the guidelines is to "encapsulate accepted standards of fairness, serve as a check-list for all organizations setting up fact-finding missions, lead to uniformity of practice in the conduct of enquiries and serve as criteria for judging the reliability of reports, and their admissibility as evidence."[82] The guidelines include several provisions to filter bias: ensuring that the terms of reference do not reflect any predetermined conclusion (while allowing flexibility to extend the terms of reference); that interpreters are independent and professional; and that all team members receive training on "any relevant cultural, economic, political, historical and legal information."[83]

Alan Stephens, Director of Research at the Clemens Nathan Research Centre, initiated the Lund-London Guidelines project. He states that the two most important provisions were those concerning the nature of the mission and the wording of the mandate, and those concerning selection of personnel.[84] Both sections place emphasis on the impartiality of the mission. Stephens says that of similar importance are the training and competence of the fact-finders, as well as the nature of the writing—namely, using sober, neutral language rather than emotionally charged rhetoric.[85] In addition, Stephens notes that NGOs must have standards for any forensic analysis—or at least have a policy as to whether they will conduct analysis.[86]

The drafters intended for the guidelines to be the first step in a series of reforms to improve the professionalism of fact-finding missions.[87] According to Alan Stephens, the next step should have been an institute for training fact-finders.[88] But the momentum of the project collapsed, around the time that the international community became more focused on debating the methodology of the 2009 United Nations Fact-Finding Mission on the Gaza Conflict (Goldstone Mission).[89]

---

[82] Id.
[83] *The Lund-London Guidelines*, *supra* note 11, at ¶20.
[84] Interview with Alan Stephens, *supra* note 74.
[85] Id; see also *The Lund-London Guidelines*, *supra* note 68, at ¶59 (2009).
[86] Interview with Alan Stephens, *supra* note 74.
[87] Id.
[88] Id.
[89] United Nations Human Rights Council, *United Nations Fact-Finding Mission on the Gaza Conflict* (Sept. 25, 2009), available at http://www2.ohchr.org/english/bodies/hrcouncil/specialsession/9/factfindingmission.htm.

Richard Goldstone, leader of the Mission, and Christine Chinkin, a member of the Mission, both initially agreed to be keynote speakers for the launch of the Lund-London Guidelines.[90] Their willingness to participate indicates endorsement, so the Goldstone Mission's subsequent decision not to adopt or adhere to the guidelines is unexplained. Although the Goldstone Mission was not an NGO, the guidelines provide standards applicable to any fact-finding mission. If the Goldstone Mission had adhered to the guideline to "fairly reflect all the information gathered,"[91] Goldstone may not have needed to write a 2011 article reconsidering his mission's findings. In that article, published in the *Washington Post*, he writes, "[i]f I had known then what I know now, the Goldstone Report would have been a different document."[92] But the original report failed to account for information presented to the Mission at that time, including "official papers issued by Israel's Foreign Ministry, legal opinions, facts and media cuttings regarding the Hamas rocket barrages, violations, ambulance hijackings and the like."[93]

Goldstone is the Chair of the IBA's Task Force on International Terrorism, and the IBA has taken no further steps to advance the guidelines after the release of the Goldstone Mission's report. Seven organizations, including Center for Human Rights and Rehabilitation and British Irish Rights Watch, endorsed the guidelines almost immediately, but the IBA has not updated the endorsement list or any other part of the guidelines website since 2009.[94]

---

90 Interview with Alan Stephens, Director of Research, Clemens Nathan Research Centre, Apr. 12, 2011.

91 *The Lund-London Guidelines*, *supra* note 68, at ¶59.

92 Goldstone, Richard, *Reconsidering the Goldstone Report on Israel and war crimes*, WASH. POST, Apr. 1, 2011, available at http://www.washingtonpost.com/opinions/reconsidering-the-goldstone-report-on-israel-and-war-crimes/2011/04/01/AFg111JC_story.html.

93 Baker, Alan, *Just what did Goldstone expect?* JERUSALEM POST, Oct. 18, 2009, available at http://www.jpost.com/Opinion/Article.aspx?id=157889. The Mission also included large sections of NGO information, particularly on points that Goldstone later reconsidered, and the report indicated only that it tried to "ascertain the methodologies used" and not that it sought independent verification of the evidence as required by the guidelines. United Nations Human Rights Council, *United Nations Fact-Finding Mission on the Gaza Conflict* ¶170 (Sept. 25, 2009), available at http://www2.ohchr.org/english/bodies/hrcouncil/specialsession/9/factfindingmission.htm. See also The Goldstone Report *Reconsidered*: A Critical Analysis (G. Steinberg & A. Herzberg, eds., 2011).

94 *The Lund-London Guidelines*, *supra* note 11.

Post-Lund London

In 2008, Diakonia, a Swedish government-funded framework that supports many NGOs, initiated and then dropped a project to establish guidelines on "Good Monitoring Practices" because it could not find common ground among partner organizations on principles for monitoring.[95] Instead of a conference on monitoring, Diakonia held a conference with the groups B'Tselem and Al Haq to strategize on bringing cases against Israeli officials in third-party countries under universal jurisdiction statutes, a topic not at all related to best practices.[96] As a result, Diakonia was not able to measure whether the quality of human rights reporting by its partner agencies had increased.[97]

In a 2009 article, Eric Meldrum interviewed sources who worked with or for the International Criminal Tribunal for the former Yugoslavia (ICTY) and the national war crimes court in Uganda to see which issues an NGO must address upfront when it works in cooperation with a war crimes tribunal.[98] The list includes the following issues: how to record details of anyone who travels with the team (interpreters, drivers, etc.), if and how sensitive information is passed along to tribunals, and whether staff should handle physical evidence or give evidence in court. After establishing its position on these issues, the NGO could then follow up with appropriate training.

Human Rights First similarly provides questions for NGO investigators who are cooperating with the International Criminal Court: "When conducting interviews, what should an interviewer tell people about what will happen to the information they give? What sorts of reassurances can be given, if any, concerning their protection? How can confidentiality be safeguarded if a person wishes to speak in confidence?"[99] Human Rights First concludes that victims and witnesses

---

[95] Sthlm Policy Group, *Evaluation of the Diakonia IHL program: Occupied Palestinian territory (oPt) and Israel* 39 (2009), available at http://www.diakonia.se/Documents/public/RESULTS_AND_HIGHLIGHTS/Evaluation_IHL_Programme_2009.pdf.

[96] Id.

[97] Id. at 53.

[98] Meldrum, Eric, TIME FOR A CHANGE?: THE TRADITIONAL HUMAN RIGHT NGO FACT FINDING METHODOLOGY IN RELATION TO NATIONAL AND INTERNATIONAL PROSECUTIONS OF GROSS HUMAN RIGHT VIOLATIONS 49 (2009), available at http://www.brookes.ac.uk/schools/be/oisd/architecture/cendep/dissertations/EricMeldrum.pdf.

[99] Human Rights First, *The Role of Human Rights NGOs in Relation to ICC Investigations* (2004), available at http://www.amicc.org/docs/Human%20Rights%20

must be informed of the purpose of the interview and how the information will be used. In addition, the NGO should ascertain if the witness would cooperate in a potential future prosecution.[100]

In his 2010 article in *Transitional Law and Contemporary Problems*, Tyler Musselman recommends practices to improve the impartiality of fact-finding organs, mostly in the context of IGOs.[101] In particular, he examines the methods of the Independent International Fact-Finding Mission on the Conflict in Georgia—discussed at greater length in Chapter Four—and other responses to the 2008 Russia-Georgia conflict.

First, Musselman suggests that those overseeing fact-finding should not be representatives of any country involved in or neighboring the conflict. He recommends that a fact-finding mission avoid developing legal conclusions and instead leave legal questions to the international community and courts.[102] Also, he emphasizes timely collection of evidence. He notes that staff should have experience with armed conflicts and fact-finding techniques, gather information from neutral sources or at least from both sides, and attempt to substantiate all information.[103]

Other organizations make tangential references to best practices, but an actual list of guidelines is difficult to identify. The Centre for Civil and Political Rights released 2010 guidelines specifically for NGO reports submitted to the UN Human Rights Committee.[104] The guidelines address the structure and content of the report, but they make only passing references to the importance of objective fact-finding methodology.[105] The guidelines note that each legal point must be supported by specific information, including dates of cases or violations. In addition, the report must be updated to include the latest judicial

First%20NGO_Role_Discussion_Paper.pdf http://www.humanrightsfirst.org/international_justice/pdf/NGO_Role_Discussion_Paper.pdf at 8.

[100] Id.

[101] Musselman, Tyler B., *Skirmishing for Information: The Flaws of the International Legal System as Evidenced by the Russian-Georgian Conflict of 2008*, 19 TRANSNAT'L L. & CONTEMP. PROBS. 317, 348 (2010), available at http://fog.its.uiowa.edu/~tlcp/TLCP%20Articles/19-1/musselman.finalfinal.mlb.022710.pdf.

[102] Id.

[103] Id.

[104] Brett, Peggy, and Murzenberg, Patrick, Centre for Civil and Political Rights, *UN Human Rights Committee, Participation in the Reporting Process: Guidelines for Non-Governmental Organisations (NGOs)* (2nd ed. 2010), available at http://www.ccprcentre.org/doc/CCPR/Handbook/CCPR_Guidelines%20for%20NGOs_en.pdf.

[105] Id. at 24.

processes and current sources.[106] In 2006, the Swedish International Development Cooperation Agency (Sida) released a "Manual for Conflict Analysis," which does not directly address human rights fact-finding but provides questions to consider when observing a country for conflict analysis.[107]

United Nations Standards for NGOs

The UN has never clearly explicated its standards for accepting NGO material, even though NGOs have long been an integral part of United Nations fact-finding. In fact, the term "non-governmental organization" only came into popular use with the establishment of the UN in 1945, and the UN Charter itself gives a consultative role to NGOs.[108] The UN's 1997 *Manual on Human Rights Reporting*—a training manual for government officials tasked with drafting reports in compliance with human rights treaties—lists the ways that several states seek information from non-governmental sources. The *Manual* discusses Norway's Advisory Committee on Human Rights and Italy's Interministerial Committee on Human Rights, as well as the International Labour Organization's Committee of Experts, which all have mechanisms for screening NGO information.[109] Norway's committee has the ability to comment on draft human rights reports, and allows governmental and NGO sources to coordinate and exchange views.[110] In Italy, the committee must study and examine reports in order to approve their submission to international treaty bodies.[111]

[106] Id.

[107] Sida, Division for Peace and Security Through Development Cooperation, *Manual for Conflict Analysis* 5 (2006), available at http://www.conflictsensitivity.org/sites/default/files/Manual_for_Conflict_Analysis.pdf. ("What is/are the main mechanism(s) driving the conflict: for example, structural instability, struggles for power and influence, security dilemmas, or a combination of the above?")

[108] Ajibade, Idowu Mopelola, University of McGill, *A Synopsis: Rights, Responsibilities and Roles of Human Rights NGOs under International Law* 18 (2008), available at http://papers.ssrn.com/sol3/papers.cfm?abstract_id=1300103.

[109] United Nations Office of the High Commissioner for Human Rights, *Manual on Human Rights Reporting* 34 (1997), available at http://www.ohchr.org/Documents/Publications/manualhrren.pdf. See also International Labour Organization, Civil Society, available at http://www.ilo.org/public/english/bureau/pardev/civil/index.htm (last visited Jan. 2, 2010).

[110] Id.

[111] Id.

In a 2001 article, Jan Wouters and Ingrid Rossi assert that UN bodies value NGO fact-finders as "more independent from political forces than States or IGOs and thus are more able to identify and criticize human rights violations."[112] Wouters and Rossi go on to note that, while NGOs play a prominent role in providing fact-finding information to UN human rights bodies, the accuracy of the information varies widely between organizations.[113] In 2005, Frans Viljoen similarly noted that the United Nations Human Rights Committee should look to NGOs for information but should not rely exclusively on NGO fact-finding, "as their information may suffer from bias or inaccuracy."[114]

Standards for United Nations Staff and Member States

There is no standardized fact-finding procedure or format that applies to all UN human rights officers.[115] Instead the various organs emphasize a few common principles, such as the principle of hearing from both sides.[116] The delegates at the 1968 International Conference on Human Rights held in Tehran, marking the 20th anniversary of the Universal Declaration of Human Rights, recommended that the Commission on Human Rights create model rules of procedure for bodies dealing with violations of human rights.[117] Nonetheless, provisions remain largely on an *ad hoc* basis. Issues such as who sets the mission's itinerary or the right of a group to interview witnesses of its choosing were not addressed.

The UN General Assembly issued a "Declaration on Fact-finding by the United Nations in the Field of the Maintenance of International Peace and Security" in 1991.[118] The declaration establishes basic principles for UN fact-finding missions, including a commitment to

---

[112] Wouters, Jan and Ingrid Rossi, Institute for International Law, University of Leuven, HUMAN RIGHTS NGOs: ROLE, STRUCTURE AND LEGAL STATUS 5 (2001).

[113] Id. at 12. ("While certain NGOs provide valuable and reliable information and expertise, other NGOs have sometimes simplistic and poorly researched positions.")

[114] Viljoen, Frans, *Fact-Finding by UN Human Rights Complaints Bodies – Analysis and Suggested Reforms*, MAX PLANCK Y.B. OF UNITED NATIONS L. 49, 76 (2005), available at http://www.mpil.de/shared/data/pdf/pdfmpunyb/viljoen_8.pdf.

[115] Id.

[116] Id. at 55.

[117] United Nations, *Final Act of the International Conference on Human Rights: Tehran, 22 April to 13 May 1968* A/CONF. 32/41 (1968).

[118] United Nations, *Declaration on Fact-finding by the United Nations in the Field of the Maintenance of International Peace and Security* A/RES/46/59 (1991).

"comprehensive, objective, impartial and timely" fact-finding and to receiving consent from the concerned state.[119] The declaration also requires a clear mandate and notes that "[t]he report should be limited to a presentation of findings of a factual nature."[120] The idea of using fact-finding in the context of conflict prevention is discussed in greater depth in an article by the Organization for Economic Co-operation and Development, "Guidance for Evaluating Conflict Prevention and Peacebuilding Activities."[121] The publication includes sample terms of reference, as well as a list of questions to evaluate the perception of bias of team members. For example, "Might certain individual characteristics—based on (perceived) religion, skin colour, gender, nationality and language, for instance—expose the team to additional risks or accusations of bias in this particular conflict context?"[122]

The 1991 "Minnesota Protocol" outlines procedures for independent commissions of inquiry into allegations of extra-legal, arbitrary, and summary executions.[123] The protocol was a follow up to the Economic and Social Council's "Principles on the effective prevention and investigation of extra-legal, arbitrary and summary executions" in 1989.[124] An international group of lawyers, human rights workers, forensic scientists, and other experts wrote the protocol, and the Minnesota Lawyers International Human Rights Committee facilitated their efforts. The protocol outlines the targeted information a commission must collect, a list of potential types of interviewees, and ways to protect the identity of the witness (such as through *in camera* proceedings).[125] Much of the protocol advice assumes that the commission will take part in examining the decedent and processing the crime scene, a role that generally does not apply to NGOs. The protocol also contains several principles more applicable to NGOs, such as

---

[119] Id.

[120] Id.

[121] Development Assistance Committee, Organization for Economic Co-operation and Development, *Guidance on Evaluating Conflict Prevention and Peacebuilding Activities: Working draft for application period* 33 (2008), available at http://www.oecd.org/secure/pdfDocument/0,2834,en_21571361_34047972_39774574_1_1_1_1,00.pdf.

[122] Id. at 34.

[123] United Nations, *Manual for the Prevention of Extra-Legal, Arbitrary and Summary Executions* (1991), available at http://www1.umn.edu/humanrts/instree/executioninvestigation-91.html.

[124] Id.

[125] Id.

an emphasis on appointing commissioners who are impartial (have no connections with government entities or victims), competent (with expertise in law, medicine, or other specialized fields, if possible), and independent.[126]

In 1995, the Legal Counsel of the United Nations prepared a set of guidelines and procedures for the conduct of UN inquiries into allegations of massacres.[127] The Legal Counsel was responding most directly to the massacre in June 1993 of nearly 600 Liberians, most of them women, children, and elderly persons.[128] The Secretary General appointed a three-member panel of inquiry chaired by Mr. Amos Wako, Attorney General of Kenya, to research the facts. The panel concluded that the massacre was planned and executed by the Armed Forces of Liberia. The panel also recommended the creation of systematic procedures to collect and preserve evidence for future investigations.[129]

The Legal Counsel's guidelines include proposed terms of reference, guidelines for collection of physical evidence, a list of items to include in the report (including final recommendations, if applicable to the mandate), as well as a list of assurances of access that a commission requires from relevant authorities (freedom of movement, access to prisoners, and protected status of all recording equipment and documentation).[130] In addition, the guidelines contain recommendations about how to conduct an interview. They recommend that interviewers have a specialized background (as lawyers or trained military/police investigators), that at least two people conduct the interview, and that a background interview take place to "identify any bias, motive, or inconsistencies in the interviewee's statement."[131] Like other guidelines, this list emphasizes impartiality, competence, and independence of commission members.[132]

The UN Office of the High Commissioner for Human Rights produced a 1997 *Manual for Human Rights Reporting* to provide a few

---

[126] Id.

[127] United Nations, *Guidelines for the Conduct of United Nations Inquiries into Allegations of Massacres* (1995), available at http://www.icrc.org/themissi.nsf/b5a5eed1a93ca649c12569dd00505aca/ee82c7e78d0175d3c1256b02002984df!OpenDocument.

[128] Id.

[129] Id.

[130] Id.

[131] Id.

[132] Id.

simple guidelines for government officials who wish to engage in human rights fact-finding. Those guidelines place a strong emphasis on training, on forming questions and a realistic mission time frame *before* gathering information, and on making the purpose of the interview clear to any potential interviewee.[133]

The UN Office of the High Commissioner for Human Rights also has a 2001 training manual that details its own information gathering process.[134] The manual begins with a note that previous human rights field operations—in Bosnia-Herzegovina, Burundi, Cambodia, El Salvador, Guatemala, Haiti, Rwanda, and other locales—largely developed their own fact-finding practices and methodology. The manual provides a basic practice framework so that each operation need not face delays by developing its own practices while setting up the mission.[135] The manual contains a general list of steps for identifying violations, including "pursuing an inquiry meant to verify information concerning the violation, as well as the response of the authorities, including the military, police, and the legal system as relevant."[136] In addition, the manual requires that officers assess and compensate for the bias of any contact persons and verify all information by, among other tactics, locating any family or friends who can corroborate the information, interviewing all witnesses individually and promptly, and promising (but not guaranteeing) to endeavor to protect the witnesses.[137] In a commitment to "relevance, veracity, reliability, and probity," the manual insists that all information must be examined in context with other independent sources, with its own internal consistence and coherence, as well as with physical/psychological symptoms of the interviewee.[138] The manual provides great detail about how to conduct an interview, touching on everything from the number of interviewers (two is optimal), how to vet interpreters (to ensure they are not part of the government or opposition groups, among other concerns), and interview locations (avoid hotels and other easily

[133] United Nations Office of the High Commissioner for Human Rights, *Manual on Human Rights Reporting* 49–50 (1997), available at http://www.ohchr.org/Documents/Publications/manualhrren.pdf.

[134] United Nations Office of the High Commissioner for Human Rights, *Training Manual on Human Rights Monitoring* 100 (2001), available at http://www.ohchr.org/EN/PublicationsResources/Pages/TrainingEducation.aspx.

[135] Id. at 3.

[136] Id. at 100.

[137] Id. at 101–04.

[138] Id. at 104–06.

monitored locations).[139] It contains a sample list of questions for interviewers to use to verify details about a statement,[140] and it states that it "may assist other intergovernmental or non-governmental organizations engaged in human rights work to develop their own methodologies and train their staff."[141]

The 2004 "Istanbul Protocol" is a manual for states to effectively investigate and document torture and other cruel, inhuman, or degrading treatment or punishment.[142] More than 40 organizations and 75 experts in law, health, and human rights helped draft the protocol, which is based in part on the "Minnesota Protocol." The Human Rights Foundation of Turkey and Physicians for Human Rights (USA) initiated the project, which was originally inspired by efforts to investigate the death of Turkish prisoner Baki Erdogan.[143] Erdogan died in a state hospital in Turkey after eleven days in custody. The official medical report concluded that he died of acute pulmonary edema as the result of a ten-day hunger strike.[144] In an independent investigation, the Turkish Medical Association discovered mistakes in the autopsy, and the Protocol was conceived during the subsequent outcry for accountability.

The "Istanbul Protocol" emphasizes impartiality, and instructs state commissions to create clear terms of reference that are neutrally framed and do not "suggest a predetermined outcome."[145] The Protocol also recommends appointing counsel from outside of state's ministry of justice, conducting public hearings (except when safety concerns necessitate otherwise), and evaluating evidence in light of "the demeanour and overall credibility of the witness."[146] The Protocol notes that a commission must be sensitive to social, cultural, and gender issues,

---

139 Id. at 112–15.

140 Id. at 118.

141 Id. at 6.

142 United Nations Office of the High Commissioner for Human Rights, *Istanbul Protocol: Manual on the Effective Investigation and Documentation of Torture and Other Cruel, Inhuman or Degrading Treatment or Punishment* (2004), available at http://www.ohchr.org/Documents/Publications/training8Rev1en.pdf [hereinafter Istanbul Protocol].

143 International Rehabilitation Council for Torture Victims, *The Istanbul Protocol*, available at http://www.irct.org/investigation—documentation/the-istanbul-protocol.aspx (last visited Mar. 7, 2011).

144 Istanbul Protocol, *supra* note 142.

145 Id. at 22.

146 Id. at 24.

and must corroborate evidence from several sources where possible. Also if a commission is not unanimous in its findings, the Protocol requires that the final report include the dissenting opinion from the minority commissioners.[147]

Mandate-holders of the UN Human Rights Council must abide by a 2007 code of conduct, which directs them to "seek to establish the facts, based on objective, reliable information emanating from relevant credible sources, that they have duly cross-checked to the best extent possible."[148] The code emphasizes that mandate-holders strictly observe their mandate and that their recommendations not exceed the mandate.[149] The mandate-holders must gather information while adhering to "principles of discretion, transparency, impartiality, and even-handedness," preserving the confidentiality of sources, and giving representatives of the concerned state the opportunity to respond.[150] The code also requires filtering out one's personal political opinions and recognizing the independent nature of the mandate.[151] These procedures are also described in the reports of the Special Rapporteurs, such as the Special Rapporteur on torture or the Special Rapporteur on extrajudicial, summary, or arbitrary executions.[152]

Throughout the UN documents, several common themes recur. For instance, the words "impartiality, competence, and independence" appear in the majority of guidelines. The guidelines also often address concerns about confidentiality and protection of witnesses, how to conduct an effective interview, and strict adherence to a mandate. All of these concerns are important, but a number of other concerns, such as selection of team members, are rarely or tangentially addressed. In addition, in the majority of circumstances, the state being investigated must approve of any fact-finding mission, which is one of the

---

147 Id.

148 United Nations, *Code of Conduct for Special Procedures Mandate-Holders of the Human Rights Council* (2007), available at http://www1.umn.edu/humanrts/codeofconduct.html.

149 Id.

150 Id.

151 Id.

152 United Nations Human Right Council, *Methods of Work of the Special Rapporteur on torture*, available at http://www2.ohchr.org/english/issues/torture/rapporteur/docs/methodswork.doc; United Nations Human Rights Council, *Report of the Special Rapporteur on extrajudicial, summary or arbitrary executions* (2010), available at http://daccess-dds-ny.un.org/doc/UNDOC/GEN/G10/135/03/PDF/G1013503.pdf?OpenElement.

major limitations on UN fact-finding efforts and the International Humanitarian Fact-Finding Commission.

The International Humanitarian Fact-Finding Commission

The International Humanitarian Fact-Finding Commission (IHFFC), a fact-finding body in the area of humanitarian law, is a decentralized procedure that cedes most of the control to the states related to the investigation.[153] In 1991, the IHFFC was created under Article 90 of the First Additional Protocol to the Geneva Conventions of 1949 as "a permanent international body whose main purpose is to investigate allegations of grave breaches and serious violations of international humanitarian law."[154] The norms and challenges of investigating violations of humanitarian law are frequently different and more complex than in human rights law, as the investigations often occur during armed conflict.[155] The Commission consists of 15 members elected by the 71 member states. Each inquiry is conducted by five members who are not nationals of any party to the conflict and two *ad hoc* commissioners (also not nationals), one to be appointed by each side.[156]

The scope of the Commission's fact-finding powers is limited and deferential to the concerned states. The IHFFC will only investigate with the consent of both parties, and even then relies largely on presentations from the parties and not on independent investigation.[157] In addition, the Commission must fully disclose all information to both parties and may not report its findings publicly, unless all the parties to the conflict agree.[158]

Although 71 states have recognized the IHFFC, no state has ever called upon the Commission to conduct an investigation.[159] At an

---

[153] Bothe, Michael, *Fact-Finding as a means of ensuring respect for international humanitarian law*, in INTERNATIONAL HUMANITARIAN LAW FACING NEW CHALLENGES 249, 266–67 (Volker Epping and Wolff Heintschel von Heinegg, eds., 2007).

[154] International Humanitarian Fact-Finding Commission, *About Us*, available at http://www.ihffc.org/en/aboutus.html (last visited Jan. 5, 2011).

[155] Schmitt, Michael N., *Investigating Violations of International Law in Armed Conflict*, 2 HARV. NAT'L SEC. J. 31, 84 (2011).

[156] Geneva Convention Relative to the Treatment of Prisoners of War, art. 90, Aug. 12, 1949, 6 U.S.T. 3316, 75 U.N.T.S. 135.

[157] Musselman, *supra* note 101, at 346.

[158] International Humanitarian Fact-Finding Commission, *Rules of the International Humanitarian Fact-Finding Commission* (1992), http://www.ihffc.org/.

[159] International Humanitarian Fact-Finding Commission, *About Us*, http://www.ihffc.org/index.asp?Language=EN&page=aboutus_general (last visited Jan. 5, 2011).

International Bar Association seminar, Professor Charles Garraway of the British Red Cross gave three possible reasons for this lack of use: 1) states do not know about the Commission; 2) states have no use for reports that are generally kept confidential; or 3) unlike most human rights organs, the Commission does not offer conclusions.[160] Others consider that states might be concerned that the Commission will be too diplomatic and too neutral to examine state violations.[161]

Regardless of whether the Commission is ever utilized, its procedures embody important principles for fact-finding organizations. The IHFFC commissioners are neutral third-party individuals who are not connected to either party in a conflict. In addition, the Commission emphasizes seeking experts such as lawyers, doctors, or high-ranking military personnel.[162] And as a permanent commission, the IHFFC can issue reports in a timelier fashion than could an *ad hoc* body. Until a state calls upon the IHFFC, these points remain theoretical. The IHFFC has the potential to play an important role in the field of humanitarian law, especially in cases where states prefer to retain control and are concerned that the Security Council or ICC prosecutor may usurp it.[163]

Internal NGO Guidelines

Amnesty International

According to Clark, Amnesty International "forged many of the techniques that are now the common stock" of NGO fact-finders, so its methodology has particular significance for the international NGO community.[164] In a 2002 handbook, AI acknowledges that its reports deal with "allegations rather than undisputed facts" and serve primarily as a call for investigation.[165] The handbook briefly defines the organization's fact-finding practices:

---

[160] Raoul Wallenberg Institute of Human Rights and Humanitarian Law, International Bar Association And British Institute of International and Comparative Law, *Human Rights Fact Finding Missions: Seminar Report* (2009).

[161] Interview with Alan Stephens, *supra* note 74.

[162] Musselman, *supra* note 101, at 346.

[163] Bothe, Michael, *supra* note 153, at 265.

[164] Clark, Ann Marie, DIPLOMACY OF CONSCIENCE: AMNESTY INTERNATIONAL AND CHANGING HUMAN RIGHTS NORMS 8 (2001).

[165] Amnesty International, *Amnesty International Handbook* (2002), available at http://www.amnesty.org/en/library/asset/ORG20/001/2002/en/76e976ef-d8a8-11dd-ad8c-f3d4445c118e/org200012002en.html.

> AI sends fact-finding missions—openly and after informing the authorities of their intention to visit—to assess situations on the spot. The delegates might interview prisoners, relatives, lawyers, witnesses to human rights violations and local human rights activists. They may also observe trials and meet government officials. Where AI is denied access to a country, research teams may have to rely on sources of information outside the country, including news media reports, refugees and diplomatic representatives abroad.

This broad outline of what AI "may" do is not a definitive template for fact-finding but provides a window into how AI approaches the task. The handbook notes several potential sources of information - from local community workers to religious bodies to media outlets.[166] The handbook also notes that the text of any report must be approved by the AI's International Secretariat "to ensure it is accurate, politically impartial and falls within AI's mandate."[167]

On its website, AI makes only tangential reference to methodology. Its mandate includes commitments to principles of accuracy and impartiality, and the FAQ section includes an assurance that "[b]efore any statement, publication or report is issued, its text is subject to close review to ensure it is factually accurate, politically impartial and consistent with Amnesty International's mission."[168]

AI does not publish any overall best-practices guidelines, only regional guidelines. The most detailed descriptions of AI's methodology and standards come from their published manuals for fact-finders, including a series of publications for the Special Programme on Africa (SPA).[169] Amnesty International created the SPA in June 1994 in order to "find a more effective response to the human rights crisis in Africa."[170] One publication explains AI's methodology in particular detail: "UKWELI: Monitoring and Documenting Human Rights Violations

---

[166] Id.

[167] Id. Review by the Secretariat, however, raises its own concerns that the home office may try to suppress or edit local fact-finding reports if the conclusions reached do not match the goals or political ideology of the central organization.

[168] Amnesty International, *Amnesty International: Frequently Asked Questions*, available at http://www.amnesty.org/en/who-we-are/faq (last visited Jan. 9, 2011); Amnesty International, *Statute of Amnesty International, available at* http://www.amnesty.org/en/who-we-are/accountability/statute-of-amnesty-international (last visited Jan. 9, 2011).

[169] Amnesty International Nederland, *Special Programme on Africa - Publications*, available at http://www.amnesty.nl/special-programme-africa-publication (last visited Apr. 4, 2011).

[170] Amnesty International Nederland, *Programme on Africa*, http://www.amnesty.nl/special-programme-africa (last visited Apr. 4, 2011).

in Africa," a joint publication by AI and the Council for the Development of Social Science Research in Africa (CODESRIA).[171] A staff member of AI drafted the text, and an editorial advisory committee of human rights monitors from across Africa reviewed and approved the draft.[172] The text was based on discussions from AI-led conferences of African human rights activists in 1997 and 1998, conferences that discussed the progress of human rights monitoring in the years following African governments' adoption of the African Charter on Human and People's Rights in October 1986.[173]

The UKWELI manual (UKWELI is Swahili for "truth") is a best-practices guide for NGOs and individual activists who engage in human rights fact-finding and documentation. The manual outlines preparations prior to a fact-finding visit, including researching domestic law, listing objectives for the mission, preparing an interview checklist, and consulting with forensic pathologists, lawyers, and other relevant experts.[174]

The manual makes several suggestions for the composition of the delegation: excluding members who "may be perceived as partial" based on their political affiliations or other reasons, making sure the team is gender and ethnically balanced, and including experts from any necessary field.[175] In addition to a section on interview tactics, the manual also has a section emphasizing principles such as accuracy and impartiality.[176] To ensure accuracy, fact-finders must assess the political agenda or record of the original source of information, compare allegations with patterns in other countries, and cross-check all information.[177] To ensure impartiality, fact-finders must document violations by all sides (including those perpetrated by opposition groups), develop a code of conduct, and screen staff for "possible conflicts of interest and accusations of bias."[178] Another handbook by

---

[171] Amnesty International and CODESRIA, *UKWELI: Monitoring and Documenting Human Rights Violations in Africa* viii–ix (2000), http://www.hrea.org/erc/Library/Ukweli/ukweli-en.pdf.

[172] Id. at xi.

[173] Id. at vii.

[174] Id. at 12.

[175] Id. at 12–13.

[176] Id. at 32–46.

[177] Id. at 33–34.

[178] Id. at 40–41.

AI, "Monitoring and Reporting Human Rights Violations in Africa: A Handbook for Community Activists," covers the same points.[179]

These handbooks list important tenets of fact-finding, but AI has not clarified if these standards apply throughout the organization or only in Africa. Several critics over the years have accused AI of failing to live up to standards such as those in the handbooks. For example, Robert Charles Blitt notes that, as early as 1977, AI violated its self-imposed policy of impartiality when it dispatched two members of its West German section to investigate their own country (in a visit to Red Army Faction prisoners and prison officials in West Germany).[180] A former AI observer similarly discussed an early AI mission to Rhodesia that was discredited when it was revealed that the government of Britain—one of the concerned parties—funded the inquiry.[181] Even after this early episode, AI continues to receive significant funds from the UK and other governments.[182]

Criticism of AI methodology goes beyond accusations of bias. Another critique is a lack of even-handedness in its focus. The same former observer mentioned that AI views its role as investigating the state and not the conduct of those opposed to the state.[183] Thus, for example, he contends that AI did not denounce the actions of ANC guerillas, while it condemned the apartheid policies of the South African Government.[184] In such cases AI is criticized for evaluating the legitimacy of state counter-insurgency policies in a vacuum, without reference to how reasonable they are in light of the conduct of

---

[179] Amnesty International, *Monitoring and Reporting Human Rights Violations in Africa: A Handbook for Community Activists* (2002), available at http://www.amnesty.nl/documenten/spa/handbook_community_eng.pdf.

[180] Blitt, *supra* note 14, at 322.

[181] Robertson, Geoffrey, *Human Rights Fact Finding: Some Legal and Ethical Dilemmas*, HUM. RTS. INST., INT'L BAR ASS'N, THEMATIC PAPERS 4, 20 (May 2010); see also Raoul Wallenberg Institute of Human Rights and Humanitarian Law, International Bar Association, and British Institute of International and Comparative Law, *Human Rights Fact-Finding Missions: Seminar Report* 2 (June 1–2, 2009), available at http://www.biicl.org/files/4462_fact_finding_report_updated_2.pdf.

[182] Amnesty International Charity Limited, *Report and financial statements for the year ended 31 March 2010* 20, available at http://www.amnesty.org/en/library/asset/FIN40/013/2010/en/1efe033e-9922-4495-b4f7-36198a545a0f/fin400132010en.pdf; Amnesty International Limited and Amnesty International Charity Limited, *Report and financial statements for the year ended 31 March 2007* 16, available at http://www.amnesty.org/sites/impact.amnesty.org/files/PUBLIC/documents/AI-Ltd-and-AI-Charity-Ltd-Report-and-Financial-Statements.pdf.

[183] Robertson, *supra* note 181, at 8.

[184] Id.

insurgents.[185] In the UKWELI manual, AI notes that in order to ensure impartiality, fact-finders must "[d]ocument violations whether they are perpetrated by the government, political opponents or armed opposition groups."[186]

In a review of AI's interview techniques, Weissbrodt and McCarthy note that a 1975 AI mission to Israel and Syria to investigate allegations of torture and mistreatment of prisoners of war refused to thoroughly question the veracity of the prisoners' accounts. AI asserted that, in light of the fragile state of the prisoners, "it would not have been very reasonable … to conduct the kind of cross-examination in which the truthfulness of statements was seriously challenged."[187] Weissbrodt and McCarthy approve adjusting the approach of the interview in these circumstances, while Blitt concludes that NGOs run the risk of appearing to "await—or worse, even encourage—tales of horror and abuse" when they deviate from established interview techniques.[188] In addition, these instances may conflict with AI's own suggested guidelines demanding following up with more "direct and directive" questions when answers seem inconsistent.[189] The tenor of an interview has to be moderated in order to obtain the maximum amount of information without traumatizing an interviewee. But any interview runs the risk of awakening some level of post-traumatic stress, and an interviewer must be willing to go through some level of discomfort in order to maintain a commitment to accuracy.[190]

Some critics assert that AI (as well as HRW) lends its name to reports prepared by local NGOs, reports that they have "no control over whatsoever."[191] Additional criticisms of AI will be addressed more specifically in the case study in Chapter Four about the organization's work in Kosovo and Colombia.

---

[185] Id.

[186] Amnesty International and CODESRIA, *UKWELI: Monitoring and Documenting Human Rights Violations in Africa* 41 (2000), available at http://www.amnesty.nl/documenten/ukw_eng.pdf.

[187] Weissbrodt, *supra* note 19, at 205–06 (1982); see also Blitt, *supra* note 14, at 336.

[188] Blitt, *supra* note 14, at 336.

[189] *Amnesty International and CODESRIA, UKWELI: Monitoring and Documenting Human Rights Violations in Africa 68–69 (2000),* http://www.hrea.org/erc/Library/Ukweli/ukweli-en.pdf.

[190] Id. at 65.

[191] Alan Stephens document, *supra* note 73.

Human Rights Watch

Human Rights Watch (HRW), a major force in the international NGO community, devotes a prominent section of its website to explaining its "research methodology."[192] The text includes many important dimensions used in fact-finding guidelines: conducting thorough background research in order to understand the context of a situation, committing to obtain interviews from both sides, and consulting with legal and medical experts when relevant.[193] HRW does not have a uniform interview methodology and instead lists its commonly employed techniques: conducting interviews in private, asking multiple witnesses about the same incident, focusing on details, and asking witnesses to repeat or clarify information.[194]

Several aspects of HRW's methodology raise concern, however, particularly the failure to clearly separate fact-finding functions from advocacy. According to HRW:

> Researching the problem goes hand-in-hand with researching the advocacy approach: our research is not just about victims and perpetrators, but about determining who can and should take responsibility for stopping rights violations and providing redress, the detailed and specific steps they need to take, and who else can bring influence and leverage to bear.[195]

In addition, HRW recruits researchers with "a powerful commitment to human rights and an existing expertise," but the organization does not mention any measures to screen for potential bias or the need to temper enthusiasm with careful reporting. When interpreters are necessary, HRW suggests recruiting "local human rights activists working with the researcher."[196] HRW states that using local activists will ensure impartial interpretation, but local human rights activists are often far from impartial. In fact, the *UN Training Manual on Human Rights Monitoring* discourages using interpreters from the visited country, especially if they are connected to groups that oppose

[192] Human Rights Watch, *HRW – Our Research Methodology*, available at http://www.hrw.org/en/node/75141 (last visited Jan. 10, 2011).

[193] Id.

[194] Id.

[195] Id.

[196] Id.

the government.[197] As will be discussed in the case studies, these dimensions of HRW's approach to fact-finding create credibility problems in the organization's reports.

Extensive research conducted by NGO Monitor regarding the methodological practices of HRW was presented in the monograph "Experts or Ideologues."[198] Criticisms include accusations that HRW hired researchers with an advocacy background heavily weighted to one side in a conflict.[199] The monograph demonstrated HRW's failure to abide by several standards highlighted by the Lund-London Guidelines, including failing to verify all alleged facts where possible with "an independent third party," to write transparently and without bias, and to identify the standards "against which the delegation members weigh the information obtained."[200] In particular, and as discussed in Chapter Four, NGO Monitor found that HRW credited questionable witnesses and unverifiable reports from one side of the conflict (while rejecting statements from the other side), relied on local NGOs with questionable credibility, distorted international legal standards, issued conclusory allegations, failed to explain which reports were written and interviews conducted under the watch of officials from a closed regime, artificially narrowed the focus of reports to strip away "the wider context" of violence and self-defense leading up to a particular conflict or incident, and used inconsistent definitions for legal terms like "human shields" and "collective punishment."[201] One example highlighting these methodological issues involved Israel's defense against rocket attacks from Gaza. NGO Monitor found that this situation was the only one in which HRW alleged that a partial blockade in response to

---

[197] *United Nations Office of the High Commissioner for Human Rights, Training Manual on Human Rights Monitoring* 113 (2001), available at http://www.ohchr.org/EN/PublicationsResources/Pages/TrainingEducation.aspx.

[198] Mandel, Sarah, NGO Monitor, *Experts or Ideologues? A Systematic Analysis of Human Rights Watch's Focus on Israel* (2009).

[199] Id.

[200] *The Lund-London Guidelines*, *supra* note 11, at ¶59.

[201] Mandel, *supra* note 198, at 22–34. One example is the 2006 Gaza Beach incident, in which HRW's "military expert" relied on unverified and contradictory eyewitness accounts to accuse Israel of killing eight Palestinian civilians in an artillery strike. After the Israeli military cited evidence that the shrapnel was not from an Israeli shell, HRW reversed its position several times and eventually admitted that the blast was most likely from unexploded ordnance. Id. at 22–25. For similar criticisms of HRW from HRW's founder, see Robert L. Bernstein, *Rights Watchdog, Lost in the Mideast*, N.Y. Times, Oct. 19, 2009, available at http://www.nytimes.com/2009/10/20/opinion/20bernstein.html.

deliberate attacks on the civilian population constituted "collective punishment."[202] Cases that are somewhat parallel to that of Israel and Gaza, but were not labeled by HRW as "collective punishment," include blockades of Chechnya, Nagorno-Karabakh, and Armenia.[203] Similarly, in an April 2009 report on Sri Lanka, HRW condemned the LTTE (Tamil Tigers) for "deploy[ing] their forces close to civilians, thus using them as 'human shields.' "[204] In contrast, HRW's statements on the Arab-Israeli conflict apply a much more narrow definition of "human shielding" that would appear to absolve Hamas and Hezbollah of culpability for operating in densely populated urban areas.[205]

Criticisms of HRW's methodology in Gaza were particularly acute after Judge Richard Goldstone, head of the UN Human Rights Council's fact-finding mission to investigate the 2009 Gaza conflict, recanted his support for his report, which was based in part on HRW's findings.[206] In his 2011 op-ed in the *Washington Post*, "Reconsidering the Goldstone Report on Israel and war crimes," Goldstone acknowledged that his "fact-finding mission had no evidence" for many of the allegations, particularly the claim that Israel intentionally targeted civilians "as a matter of policy."[207] Goldstone, previously a member of HRW's board, referenced unsubstantiated HRW publications more than 30 times in his 2009 report; these references included HRW's conclusion that "human shielding" did not take place.[208] In response to Goldstone's op-ed, HRW Director Kenneth Roth claimed that HRW had never accused Israel of targeting civilians as a matter of policy.[209] Later in the same statement, however, Roth accuses Israel of "massive and

---

[202] Id. at 37–38.

[203] Id.

[204] Human Rights Watch, *Sri Lanka: Urgently Evacuate Civilians* (Mar. 4, 2009), available at http://www.hrw.org/en/news/2009/03/04/sri-lanka-urgently-evacuate-civilians.

[205] Human Rights Watch, *Rockets from Gaza: Harm to Civilians from Palestinian Armed Groups' Rocket Attacks* (Aug. 6, 2009), available at http://www.hrw.org/en/reports/2009/08/06/rockets-gaza-0. *See also* Mandel, *supra* note 198 at 38–40, appendix 4.

[206] Goldstone, *supra* note 92.

[207] Id.

[208] United Nations Human Rights Council, *United Nations Fact-Finding Mission on the Gaza Conflict* (Sept. 25, 2009), available at http://www2.ohchr.org/english/bodies/hrcouncil/specialsession/9/factfindingmission.htm.

[209] Roth, Kenneth, *Gaza: the stain remains on Israel's war record*, GUARDIAN (UK), Apr. 5, 2011, at A28, available at http://www.guardian.co.uk/commentisfree/2011/apr/05/gaza-stain-remains-israel-war-record.

deliberate destruction of civilian buildings and infrastructure without a lawful military reason. This misconduct was so widespread and systematic that it clearly reflected Israeli policy."[210] Roth did not offer an explanation for this apparent contradiction, nor regarding the several other HRW publications that also implied that Israel carried out a deliberate policy of targeting civilians.[211] For other specific methodological criticisms of HRW, see the Colombia and Lebanon analyses in Chapter Four.

---

[210] Id.

[211] See Bernstein, David, Human Rights Watch (and Amnesty International) on Goldstone Retraction, The Volokh Conspiracy, Apr. 6, 2011, available at http://volokh.com/2011/04/06/human-rights-watch-lies-re-goldstone-retraction/.

CHAPTER FOUR

FACT-FINDING CASE STUDIES

The following five case studies—fact-finding missions in Kosovo, Georgia, the Democratic Republic of Congo, Colombia, and Lebanon – highlight issues in fact-finding methodology. With the current lack of universally accepted methodological standards, missions are left to create their own guidelines. Some missions developed workable guidelines, while others did not establish guidelines at all. These cases show the range of practices that exist in the absence of standardization.

Case Study 1: Documenting Violations of International Humanitarian Law in Kosovo (1999) – The International Crisis Group

In 1999, the International Crisis Group (ICG) conducted seven months of field research in Kosovo and Albania as part of its Humanitarian Law Documentation Project.[1] The research was primarily focused on the conflict in Kosovo in early 1999 between the Federal Republic of Yugoslavia / Serbian forces and the Kovoso Liberation Army.[2] Serbian forces were readying for a ground invasion of Kosovo while at the same time, attempting to shield themselves from a NATO bombing campaign by laying anti-personnel and anti-tank mines against NATO forces. The Kosovars accused the Serbian army of systematically terrorizing them in order to forcibly expel them from the province.[3]

The ICG project aimed to support the International Criminal Tribunal for the former Yugoslavia (ICTY) in investigating violations of international humanitarian law in Kosovo. The European Commission Humanitarian Office funded the project with the aim to 1) gather

---

[1] International Crisis Group, *Reality Demands: Documenting Violations of International Humanitarian Law in Kosovo 1999* 1 (2000), available at http://www.crisisgroup.org/~/media/Files/europe/Kosovo%2021.ashx. ("The purpose of the Project was to support the efforts of the International Criminal Tribunal for the former Yugoslavia ... to investigate serious violations of international humanitarian law committed in Kosovo and bring to justice persons responsible for such crimes.")

[2] Id. at 67–68.

[3] Id. at 68.

information from victims and witnesses; 2) standardize all information in a central uniform database; and 3) provide informational assistance where possible to local NGOs and individuals.[4] The mission had no official or representative relationship with the ICTY. The staff gathered over 4,700 statements from victims and witnesses, and presented them to the ICTY Prosecutor's office.[5]

The ICG mission is impressive because it started with a clear and limited mandate, which it did not exceed. The ICG only reported on violations within the subject matter jurisdiction of the ICTY and did not endorse the political claims of any party to the conflict (and in fact, noted evidence of crimes against Kosovo Serbs as well).[6] The ICG consulted with the Prosecutor's office as to how to compile information in the format most useful to the Tribunal.[7] Local staff received specialized training by international staff on familiarization with the database system, legal issues, interview techniques, and the importance of accuracy.[8] Interviewers made clear to witnesses that their statements would be shared with the ICTY and asked witnesses about any previous statements that they provided to other organizations.[9]

The ICG's efforts were widely praised for setting a new standard in cooperation with an international tribunal. Human Rights First noted the impressive usefulness of the ICG's systematized documentation procedures.[10] The Crimes of War Project also praised the methodology of the ICG as setting "a new precedent for war crime documentation work."[11] The Project noted the ICG's efforts to mark newly discovered casualties with Global Positioning Satellites, record crime scenes with digital cameras, and generally preserve evidence for the Tribunal.[12] The ICG also facilitated the delivery of humanitarian items to

---

[4] Id. at 1–2, 7.

[5] Id. at 1.

[6] Id. at 4–6.

[7] Id. at 9.

[8] Id. at 9–13.

[9] Id. at 15.

[10] Human Rights First, *The Role of Human Rights NGOs in Relation to ICC Investigations* 7 (2004), available at http://www.amicc.org/docs/Human%20Rights%20First%20NGO_Role_Discussion_Paper.pdf.

[11] Griffiths, Hugh, Crimes of War Magazine: The Tribunals, *Evidence Gathering: The Role of NGOs* (2001), available at http://www.crimesofwar.org/tribun-mag/relate_ngo_print.html.

[12] Id. When NGOs attempt to preserve material, they risk breaking the chain of custody, contaminating, or otherwise ruining evidence. These organizations should be very selective about when they choose to take such actions.

communities not yet served by other international humanitarian relief agencies. The ICG offered teams of psychologists and social workers to assist victims. These efforts were possible in large part due to close cooperation with local human rights NGOs.[13]

The work of the ICG is an effective contrast to the work of other human rights organizations in the same area. Amnesty International, in its work in the former Yugoslavia, did not employ a specific format for interviews and left the questions up to the discretion of the statement-taker.[14] And while most of the national NGOs in the former Yugoslavia discussed with witnesses the possibility of involvement in future criminal proceeding and requested authorization to pass on information to prosecutors, AI did not.[15] AI had an organizational policy not to hand over material to the ICTY.[16] If requested, AI would go back to the witnesses and ask permission to pass on their details.[17] These policies led to confusion among witnesses as to whether interviewers were from human rights NGOs or the ICTY.[18] When the roles of each organization were not clearly explained by NGO staff, some witnesses believed they already made a statement to prosecutors. This confusion caused "unnecessary delays as investigative teams had to work out who had already spoken to the witness."[19]

These reported AI practices run counter to the UN's *Training Manual on Human Rights Monitoring*, which notes that human rights organizations in the area should promptly inform investigators of any information that might fall under their purview.[20] The manual also notes that humanitarian organizations should only collect basic information, while leaving comprehensive interviewing to trained investigators.[21] This model is endorsed in the ICTY practice manual, which

---

[13] Id.

[14] Meldrum, Eric, Time for a Change?: The Traditional Human Right NGO Fact Finding Methodology in relation to National and International Prosecutions of Gross Human Right Violations 39 (2009), available at http://www.brookes.ac.uk/schools/be/oisd/architecture/cendep/dissertations/EricMeldrum.pdf.

[15] Id. at 41.

[16] Id. at 45.

[17] Id. at 26.

[18] Id. at 42.

[19] Id. at 32.

[20] United Nations Office of the High Commissioner for Human Rights, *Training Manual on Human Rights Monitoring* 107 (2001), available at http://www.ohchr.org/EN/PublicationsResources/Pages/TrainingEducation.aspx.

[21] Id.

states that interviews by human rights organizations should be a tool for UN professionals and not a final source of information:

> [NGO interview information] requires careful verification, and should not be unquestioningly relied on to select cases for prosecution. Instead, institutions and agencies should be encouraged to record the details of potential witnesses, including and especially their future contact information, but should be encouraged not to attempt to take comprehensive witness statements. Rather, they should simply record in a general way the statements of potential witnesses based on their own direct experiences, and they should understand that the taking of statements is a professional process that is best left to the criminal justice system and to trained investigators. It is good practice to issue guidelines to outside agencies regarding proper practices.[22]

The ICG project documented basic information in a clear and searchable format for the ICTY. As one author noted, with the creation of the International Criminal Court, this model can be part of a growing trend of NGOs collecting and storing testimony that fits the requirements sought by an international tribunal.[23] More importantly, the reason that the ICG project is an example of a successful NGO mission is not due to its close collaboration with a tribunal, but rather due to its adherence to a specific, clearly-defined mandate. The witnesses were briefed on exactly how their statements would be used, the NGO kept in close cooperation with local groups, and the NGO vetted all of its information several times for accuracy.

---

[22] United Nations Interregional Crime and Justice Research Institute and the International Criminal Tribunal for the former Yugoslavia, *ICTY Manual on Developed Practices* 16 (2008).

[23] Griffiths, *supra* note 11.

Case Study 2: The Independent International Fact-Finding Mission on the Conflict in Georgia (2008)

In December 2008, the Council of the European Union formed the Independent International Fact-Finding Mission on the Conflict in Georgia (IIFFMCG - CEIIG), headed by the Swiss diplomat, Ambassador Heidi Tagliavini, who previously spent years monitoring conflicts in Georgia and Chechnya.[24] The mission was not an NGO, as it fell under the auspices of the European Union, but it serves as a useful example of the benefits and limits of *ad hoc* methodology. The mission was set up to investigate the large-scale conflict between Georgia and Russia that began in August 2008. On the night of August 7, Georgian forces attacked the town of Tskhinvali in South Ossetia, a disputed territory within the former Georgian Soviet Socialist Republic.[25] In response, Russian forces pushed back deep into Georgia, almost as far as Tbilisi, Georgia's capital city. At the same time, Georgia continued to fight armed groups of South Ossetians and Abkhaz fighters. Georgia and Russia negotiated a ceasefire agreement after five days of fighting.[26]

The mandate of the Tagliavini Mission went beyond mere fact collection, requiring a legal analysis and an allocation of fault. Its aim was to "investigate the origins and the course of the conflict in Georgia, including with regard to international law (including the Helsinki Final Act), humanitarian law and human rights, and the accusations made in that context (including allegations of war crimes)."[27]

The composition of the mission, as well as its procedures and working methods, were left to Ambassador Tagliavini.[28] According to the mandate, the team members were recognized experts in the fields of law, history, military, or human rights.[29] In addition, a Senior Advisory

---

[24] *Independent International Fact-Finding Mission on the Conflict in Georgia* (2009), available at http://www.ceiig.ch/Index.html [hereinafter Independent Fact-Finding Mission]; Barry, Ellen, *E.U. Report to Place Blame on Both Sides in Georgia War*, N.Y. TIMES, Sept. 29, 2009, available at http://www.nytimes.com/2009/09/29/world/europe/29georgia.html.

[25] Id.

[26] Id. at 10–11.

[27] Id. at 5.

[28] Id. at 6.

[29] Council of the European Union, *Mandate of the Independent International Fact-Finding Mission on the Conflict in Georgia* (2008), available at http://eur-lex.europa.eu/Notice.do?mode=dbl&lang=en&ihmlang=en&lng1=en,fr&lng2=bg,cs,da,de,el,en,es,et,fi,fr,hu,it,lt,lv,mt,nl,pl,pt,ro,sk,sl,sv,&val=484042:cs&page.

Board, composed of international relations and conflict management experts, reviewed the mission's work and provided guidance.[30] The mission stayed independent from either state party by setting up its main office in the Geneva Center for Security Policy (while also setting up offices in Belgium and Tbilisi).[31]

The mission directly requested comprehensive evaluations of the conflict from each side, as well as answers to questionnaires on the military, legal, humanitarian, and political aspects of the events in Georgia.[32] In addition, the mission reviewed and repeatedly checked information from available books, articles, studies, videos, and photographs, though the mission report does not explain how they gathered these sources or how they analyzed and corroborated the information.[33] Mission members repeatedly travelled to both Georgia and Russia to examine sites and interview witnesses, government officials, military leaders, academics, and other independent experts in the region.[34] The mission also invited other countries and IGOs to contribute any material in their possession.[35]

On September 30, 2009, the mission formally presented the results of its investigation in a report to the Council of the European Union, the Organization for Security and Co-operation in Europe (OSCE), and the UN, as well as to the parties of the conflict.[36] Russia embraced the Mission's finding that the conflict started with an unjustified shelling of Tskhinvali by Georgian armed forces. Meanwhile, Georgia embraced the finding that Russia was preparing for war for months and that, even if Russia's initial response to the shelling was justified, its later push into Georgia proper was not in self-defense and constituted a violation international law.[37]

---

[30] *Report of the Independent International Fact-Finding Mission on the Conflict in Georgia* 6 (2009), available at http://www.ceiig.ch/index.html [hereinafter Report of Independent Fact-finding Mission].

[31] Id.

[32] Id.

[33] Id. at 7.

[34] Id.

[35] Id.

[36] Independent Fact Finding Mission, *supra* note 24.

[37] *Georgia 'started unjustified war,'* BBC News, Sept. 30, 2009, available at http://news.bbc.co.uk/2/hi/8281990.stm; *Uncomfortable conclusions for Georgia*, BBC News, Sept. 30, 2009, available at http://news.bbc.co.uk/2/hi/europe/8284046.stm; *EU: Russia, Georgia share responsibility for 2008 conflict*, CNN World, Sept. 30, 2009, available at http://articles.cnn.com/2009-09-30/world/russia.georgia.eu_1_south-ossetia-russia-and-georgia-georgian-territory?_s=PM:WORLD.

Even while both sides welcomed certain aspects of the report, they stated objections to the mission's methodology. Temuri Yakobashvili, Georgia's minister for reintegration, publicly accused two mission researchers of pro-Russian bias, saying they worked for organizations that received money from the Russian gas company, Gazprom.[38] The Georgian government also accused European investigators of ignoring evidence that Russian soldiers and volunteers were already in South Ossetia prior to August 2008, and that Georgia therefore had attacked in self-defense.[39] At the same time, the Russian Foreign Ministry issued a statement that the report included "a number of diffuse and ambiguous formulations that, as we understand them, reflect the previous politicized approach of many of the European Union to the events of August 2008."[40]

The mission adhered to several methodological principles, but its work also contained many flaws. One positive step was the mission's commitment not only to use legal experts, but also military experts.[41] In addition, the mission did not include personnel from either party to the conflict and had the backing and influence of a large international body.[42] The commitment to remain neutral while also commanding the respect of the parties was a major advantage. On the other hand, as an *ad hoc* venture, the mission was not formed until months after the conflict ended and did not release a report until the following year.[43] Thus, the international community could not rely on the report's findings to provide an immediate response to the conflict. In addition, the mission had an inconsistent conception of its mandate—at some points, it emphasized that it was not a judicial tribunal and was "strictly limited" to establishing facts, while at other points, it offered legal conclusions about the course of the conflict.[44]

---

[38] Barry, Ellen, *E.U. Report to Place Blame on Both Sides in Georgia War*, N.Y. Times, Sept. 29, 2009, available at http://www.nytimes.com/2009/09/29/world/europe/29georgia.html?pagewanted=allhttp://www.nytimes.com/2009/09/29/world/europe/29Georgia.html.

[39] Barry, Ellen, *Georgia Challenges Report That Says It Fired First Shot*, N.Y. Times, Sept. 30, 2008, available at http://www.nytimes.com/2009/10/01/world/europe/01russia.html.

[40] Id.

[41] Musselman, Tyler B., *Skirmishing for Information: The Flaws of the International Legal System as Evidenced by the Russian-Georgian Conflict of 2008*, 19 Transnat'l L. & Contemp. Probs. 317, 348 (2010), available at http://fog.its.uiowa.edu/~tlcp/TLCP%20Articles/19-1/musselman.finalfinal.mlb.022710.pdf.

[42] Id.

[43] Id. at 347.

[44] Report of Independent Fact-finding Mission, *supra* note 30; Independent Fact-finding Mission, *supra* note 24.

Another major concern was that, as most of the mission's evidence collection occurred well after the conflict, it had to rely on second-hand reports from other organizations.[45] As a result, the Mission based many of its findings on information collected by regional and international organizations such as AI, HRW, ICG and others, all of whom employ varying methodological standards, if any.[46] Despite the fact that the mission thoroughly reviewed all the submitted information, the report's accuracy suffers in comparison to that of a first-hand investigation that can directly access primary sources.

45 Independent Fact-finding Mission, *supra* note 24.
46 Id. at 8.

Case Study 3: Democratic Republic of Congo Mapping Exercise (1993–2003) – UN Office of the High Commissioner for Human Rights

In 2008, the UN Secretary General established a fact-finding mission for the Democratic Republic of Congo (DRC) to conduct a mapping exercise of violations of human rights and international humanitarian law occurring in the country between 1993 and 2003. The methodology applied by the mapping team was highly detailed and transparent, which sets it apart from the other case studies analyzed. Again, although this investigation was also carried out under the auspices of an international organization rather than an NGO, many aspects of the mapping exercise can serve as best practices to be adopted by NGOs in future fact-finding missions.

Background

The mapping exercise was prompted by the 2005 discovery of three mass graves in Eastern Congo. The conflict in the DRC, one of the worst since World War II, began in the early 1990s as a result of opposition to the oppressive regime of Mobutu Sese Seko, but intensified significantly in the wake of the 1994 Rwandan genocide. In Rwanda, the Tutsi-led Rwandan Patriotic Front (RPF) battled against the Hutu-dominated government, ending the genocide of 800,000 Tutsis and taking control of the country. As a result, more than a million Hutu refugees, ex-government and army officials (ex-FAR), and thousands of genocidaires (Interwahame) fled to the DRC (then known as Zaire). Once inside the DRC, the ex-FAR and Interwahame launched attacks on Rwanda, often from within refugee camps, prompting counterattacks from the RPF. This fighting was coupled with ethnic violence and incitement fueled by longstanding discrimination against Congolese Tutsis, as well as organized efforts by neighboring governments, militias, and revolutionary forces to overthrow the Mobutu regime.

By 1996, Rwandan, Congolese, and Ugandan armies and militias were locked in hostilities over control of the DRC. The conflict erupted into a regional war enveloping Burundi, Angola, Zimbabwe, and other countries. Peace accords were signed in 2003, though fighting and ethnic skirmishes have continued. Civilians were brutally targeted by all parties during the conflict and were the victims of horrific murders, cannibalism, forced expulsions, and systematic rape. More than five million, including hundreds of thousands of women and children, were estimated killed.[47]

The discovery of the mass graves in 2005 was a reminder of these gross human rights violations and prompted discussions within the UN Secretariat to reactivate a 1997–1998 UN investigation about those abuses. Rather than reopen the old investigation, Secretary General Ban Ki-Moon decided to launch a new inquiry with a broader mandate. In June 2006, he notified the UN Security Council of his intention to "dispatch a human rights team to the Democratic Republic of the Congo to conduct a mapping of the serious violations committed between 1993 and 2003." The Terms of Reference for the "mapping exercise" were drafted and then approved by the Secretary General in May 2007, encompassing three specific objectives:

- Conduct a mapping exercise of the most serious violations of human rights and international humanitarian law committed within the territory of the DRC between March 1993 and June 2003.
- Assess the existing capacities within the national justice system to deal appropriately with such human rights violations that may be uncovered.
- Formulate a series of options aimed at assisting the Government of the DRC in identifying appropriate transitional justice mechanisms to deal with the legacy of these violations, in terms of truth, justice, reparation and reform, taking into account ongoing efforts by the DRC authorities, as well as the support of the international community.[48]

The investigation was carried out jointly under the auspices of the UN Organization Mission in the DRC (MONUC) and the UN Office of the High Commissioner for Human Rights (OHCHR). Headed by Montreal jurist Luc Cote,[49] the final report of the mapping exercise describes more than 600 violent incidents and summarizes what steps

---

[47] For an excellent overview of the conflict, see Jason Stearns, Dancing in the Glory of Monsters (2011).

[48] "Terms of Reference," *U.N. Office of the High Commissioner for Human Rights, "Report of the Mapping Exercise documenting the most serious violations of human rights, and international humanitarian law committed within the territory of the Democratic Republic of the Congo between March 1993 and June 2003"* (August 2010), at Annex 3. [hereinafter *Mapping Report]*, available at http://www.ohchr.org/Documents/Countries/ZR/DRC_MAPPING_REPORT_FINAL_EN.pdf.

[49] Cote was also the head of the legal office for the International Criminal Tribunal for Rwanda from 1995–1999.

have been taken to hold perpetrators judicially accountable. A seminar on the mapping exercise sponsored by the Great Lakes Policy Forum and Johns Hopkins University characterized the report as "very significant for the DRC," because while the "findings are not new, the report brings them together in a comprehensive way, and with an authority that previous accounts have not been able to establish."[50]

What is Mapping?

Mapping is a fact-finding methodology increasingly applied to the human rights context. It can take the form of cartographical and graphical "concept" maps or, as in the case of the DRC report, involve "conflict mapping."[51] As noted by Betts and Gisvold, conflict mapping originated as "a methodology for studying conflict through separating the constituent parts of a conflict, such as the historical background, parties, issues involved, and context within which the conflict is occurring so as to better devise means of resolving it."[52] It "involves data collection and reporting on a larger and different scale from more common forms of human rights reporting," which "usually involves portraying a situation through a few particular instances of grievous human rights violations."[53] A major premise of conflict mapping is that it "does not seek to gather evidence that would be admissible in court." Rather, it "provides the basis for the formulation of initial hypotheses of investigation by giving a sense of the scale of violations, detecting patterns and identifying potential leads or sources of evidence." This information can then be "used to better and devise global investigation and prosecution strategies."[54] Mapping exercises have been conducted in several conflict zones including India, Afghanistan, and Sierra Leone.[55]

---

[50] Great Lakes Policy Forum, *Congo: The UN Mapping Report and the Responsibility to Justice*, December 2, 2010, available at http://www.sfcg.org/programmes/forums/pdf/GLPF%2012-02-10%20Summary.pdf.

[51] See, e.g., Amnesty International, "Mapping for Human Rights," available at http://www.amnesty.nl/documenten/spa/mapping%20for%20human%20rights.pdf.

[52] Wendy S. Betts and Gregory Gisvold, *Conflict Mapping: Innovation in International Responses in Post-Conflict Societies*, 10 No. 3 HUM. RTS. BRIEF 24 (2003).

[53] Id.

[54] *See* Mapping report, *supra* note 48, at para. 94.

[55] Usha Ramanathan, *Human Rights in India: A Mapping*, Environmental Law Research Center, available at http://www.ielrc.org/content/w0103.pdf; Betts & Grisvold, *supra* note 52. For other examples of mapping studies, see Report of the Special Representative of the Secretary-General (SRSG) on the issue of human rights and

Methodology of the DRC Mapping Exercise

As mentioned, the DRC report mandate was focused on three concrete objectives: mapping the most serious human rights abuses, assessing the capabilities of the Congolese justice system, and formulating options for transitional justice. What distinguishes this document from other fact-finding reports, however, are the clear terms of reference and the detailed and transparent methodology provided by the report's authors. Prior to conducting any work, a five-page terms of reference was drafted detailing the objectives for the mission, the professional requirements for the investigators,[56] and the division of labor among involved UN bodies. It also mandated that procedures be established to ensure confidentiality and the preservation of evidence.[57] The methodology section of the mapping report itself comprises more than 20 pages of the 538-page document.[58] It addresses the timeframe and scope of the investigation, working methods for the mapping team, how evidence was verified, and the standard of proof applied for the investigation. The mapping team was also candid in qualifying its methodology and conclusions when warranted.

Unlike other fact-finding inquiries with an ambitious mandate, but a limited timeframe, the DRC mapping team was clear and realistic about what it could accomplish. The team was very conscious that the allotted six-month schedule to investigate ten years of violations throughout the country would pose serious challenges. The DRC is roughly the size of Western Europe with fewer than 300 miles of paved roads, making travel extremely difficult, if not impossible.[59] In addition to the great temporal and geographic scope of the task, the violations had occurred between five and fifteen years prior, making

transnational corporations and other business enterprises, "Business and Human Rights: Mapping International Standards of Responsibility and Accountability for Corporate Acts," February 9, 2007, UN Doc. A/HRC/4/035; NGOs and Humanitarian Reform Project; "NGOs and Humanitarian Reform Mapping Study Democratic Republic of Congo Report," December 2008, available at http://www.icva.ch/doc00003652.pdf; International Human Rights Funders Group, "Mapping Human Rights Funding," available at http://www.ihrfg.org/policy-research/mapping-human-rights-funding.

[56] See *supra* note 54, at sections 2.1, 2.2 of the Terms of Reference, Mapping Report at Annex III.

[57] Id. at sections 3.2, 4.3, 4.4.

[58] See, e.g., *Mapping Report, supra* note 48, at 1–7, 33–47, 510–45.

[59] Elena Baylis, *Tribunal-Hopping with the Post-Conflict Justice Junkies*, 10 Oregon Rev. Int'l L. 361, 386 (2008).

identification of witnesses and collection of evidence complicated, if they were available at all.

As a result of these obstacles, the mapping team chose to forgo "in-depth investigations or gathering of admissible evidence for judicial proceedings," but instead, formulated "initial hypotheses of investigation by giving a sense of the scale of violations, detecting patterns and identifying potential leads or sources of evidence."[60] The mapping team also applied a "gravity threshold" in order to limit inclusion in the report to only the most serious incidents.[61]

According to the report, the mapping team conducted its work in three phases. The first phase began in July 2008, establishing the team members and collecting documents and other evidence for analysis. Surprisingly, while the report is careful in detailing its method of work, the names of team members are not included and were not publicly released by the UN. This was a departure from the otherwise transparent methods of work. The second phase, beginning in October 2008, involved deployment of three team members to each of five field offices. Interviews were conducted at the offices, and information gathered in phase one was verified and corroborated. The third phase involved the closing of field offices in May 2009, consulting with civil society representatives on transitional justice, and drafting the final report, which was submitted to the OHCHR for review and comments on June 15, 2009.[62]

The mapping team analyzed more than 1,500 documents (which are listed in an annex to the report) and conducted 1,280 witness interviews.[63] The mapping team also consulted more than 200 NGOs, members of the Congolese government, and UN agencies. A list of several of these meetings is provided in the report, though it is not comprehensive. The team did not appear to consult with officials from neighboring countries involved in the conflict, most notably, Rwanda—a fact that would prove problematic when the report was issued.

---

[60] *Mapping Report, supra* note 48, at para. 5.

[61] Four criteria were applied to determine whether an incident was of sufficient gravity: "1) nature of the crimes and violations linked to a given incident, 2) scale (number) of crimes and violations linked to an incident, and number of victims, 3) how the crimes and violations were committed and 4) impact of crimes and violations on communities, regions or the course of events." *Mapping Report* at para. 6. Paragraph 100 provides a detailed description of how these standards were applied.

[62] *Mapping Report, supra* note 48, at para. 14

[63] Id. at para. 10.

The mapping team explained that evidence was evaluated according to a two-step review method known as the "admiralty scale." The team first evaluated the reliability and credibility of its sources by looking at

> the nature, objectivity and professionalism of the organisation providing the information, the methodology used and the quality of prior information obtained from the same source.[64]

Only after the source was credited did the team then analyze the "validity and the veracity of the information itself ... by comparing it to other available data relating to the same incidents to ensure that it tallies with already verified elements and circumstances."[65] The team also required that every incident be "backed up by at least two independent sources"; "uncorroborated incidents claimed by one single source" were not included in the report.[66] In other words, "different reports on the same incident and based on the same primary source would not constitute corroboration by a separate source."[67] Each paragraph describing an incident included a footnote reference "identifying the primary and secondary sources of the information reported."[68]

The team was also candid regarding its standard of proof. It acknowledged that because the "primary objective ... was to 'gather basic information on incidents uncovered,' the level of evidence required was naturally lesser than would be expected from a case brought before a criminal court."[69] The team therefore utilized a "reasonable suspicion" standard, rather than more rigorous levels of proof such as "a preponderance of the evidence" or "beyond a reasonable doubt".[70]

The final report concluded that the vast majority of the 617 incidents described in the survey constituted "crimes under international law, if judicially investigated and proven," including war crimes and crimes against humanity. It also found that "whether the many serious acts of violence committed against Hutus in 1996 and 1997 constitute crimes of genocide can only be decided by a competent court."[71]

---

[64] Id. at para. 102.
[65] Id. at paras. 8, 102
[66] Id. at para. 10.
[67] Id.
[68] Id. at para. 106.
[69] Id. at para. 7.
[70] Reasonable suspicion is defined as "necessitating a reliable body of material consistent with other verified circumstances tending to show that an incident or event did happen." See id. at para. 7.
[71] Id. at para. 125.

Criticisms of the Mapping Exercise

While the mapping exercise applied a transparent and systematic methodology to its work that mitigated against some of the problems that have plagued other fact-finding initiatives, the mapping approach did not insulate against others. Some of these issues were reflected in criticism presented by the countries implicated in the document.

As required by the terms of reference, a draft of the report was transmitted for comment to the Congolese government. The draft does not appear to have been sent to the governments of Rwanda, Burundi, Uganda, and Angola, which were central actors in the conflict and were mentioned repeatedly in the report as perpetrating gross violations of human rights and humanitarian law. Instead, it appears they only became aware of the draft report's contents after they were leaked to the press.[72]

The Congolese response to the mapping exercise was generally supportive.[73] The government did criticize several aspects of the document, however, including the report's short timeframe, its repetitiveness, and the omission of many human rights violations, in particular, those committed by MONUC. It queried the basis on which sources were deemed independent, such that they were sufficient to verify abuses. The Congolese government also objected to the mapping team's failure to consult government sources.

The other countries voiced serious objections to the content and methodology of the report. Angola complained in a July 2010 letter to Ban Ki-Moon that the accusations made against Angolan forces were "foolish and slanderous insinuations" based on "unproven assertions, in particular by organizations or sources with a proven track record of anti-Angola attitudes."[74] Burundi questioned several of the factual

---

[72] *Mapping Report, supra* note 48, at para. 93; Colum Lynch, *UN waters down genocide charges against Rwandan forces in Congo*, FOREIGN POLICY, October 1, 2010, available at http://turtlebay.foreignpolicy.com/posts/2010/10/01/un_waters_down_genocide_charges_against_rwandan_forces_in_congo.

[73] The DRC's Ambassador to the United Nations, Ileka Atoki penned an op-ed in the *Huffington Post* stating that the Congolese government found the mapping exercise to be "detailed and credible, and we welcome its publication." Ileka Atoki, *Justice for the Victims in Congo*, HUFFINGTON POST, October 1, 2010, available at http://www.huffingtonpost.com/amb-ileka-atoki/post_976_b_746003.html; Observations of the Congolese government on the DRC mapping project August 2010, available at http://www.ohchr.org/Documents/Countries/ZR/DRC_Report_Comments_DRC.pdf.

[74] Letter from Angolan Minister of External Relations to UN Secretary General, Ban Ki-Moon, July 30, 2010, available at http://www.ohchr.org/Documents/Countries/ZR/DRC_Report_Comments_Angola.pdf.

assertions made by the mapping team. For instance, in contrast to the report's claims, it denied that its forces formed a coalition with the Rwandan army and Rwandan-backed militias.[75] Burundi also denied claims in the report that Rwandan and Ugandan troops used Burundi territory to launch attacks on the DRC.[76]

Uganda rejected the mapping exercise in its entirety.[77] It called the report a "compendium of rumors deeply flawed in methodology, sourcing, and standard of proof." It complained about reliance upon unspecified NGOs and allegations of criminal conduct by Ugandan troops, which it claimed were not present at those locations. The Ugandan government also noted that the team did not contact any Ugandan officials during its two years of work. It alleged that the team ignored progress made in improving relations between the DRC and its neighbors, and argued the mapping exercise undermined those relations. It further noted that these "sinister tactics" could impact the work of Ugandan forces taking part in UN peacekeeping missions. Pointedly, it charged that the purpose of the report was to accuse regional forces of committing a "reverse genocide" against Hutus in order to cover up the UN's failure to stop the 1994 genocide of Tutsis in Rwanda.

The most notable response to the report came from the Rwandan government (GoR) which issued a 28-page critique of the mapping exercise.[78] The GoR claimed that information was "collected through politicized NGOs at the hands of unnamed investigators," and relied "on blatant hearsay from unnamed witnesses, about unidentified victims, and leveled against unnamed perpetrators." The GoR was also concerned that the team rendered "legal qualifications of crimes, yet no such requirement is found in the Terms of Reference." What most disturbed the GoR, however, was that the "historical and political context presented in The Draft Mapping Report deals exclusively with internal Congolese political dynamics." It said little about the Rwandan genocide, the exploitation of humanitarian aid by the ex-FAR and

[75] Letter from the Burundi Ministry of External Affairs and International Cooperation to Ban Ki-Moon, September 21, 2010, available at http://www.ohchr.org/Documents/Countries/ZR/DRC_Report_Commetnts_Burundi.pdf.

[76] Id.

[77] Uganda's Position on the Draft DRC Mapping Exercise Report, September 30, 2010, available at http://www.ohchr.org/Documents/Countries/ZR/DRC_Report_Comments_Uganda.pdf.

[78] Official Government of Rwanda Comments on the Draft UN Mapping Report on the DRC, September 30, 2011, available at http://www.gov.rw/IMG/pdf/DRC_Report_Comments_Rwanda.pdf.

Interwahame, the subsequent launching of attacks into Rwanda by Hutu militants from within refugee camps in the DRC, and the long-standing discrimination and persecution of Tutsis in the region. The report suggested that the GoR committed genocide against Hutus in the DRC, yet the report omitted that the GoR had repatriated more than 1.5 million Hutus at the time of the events described in the report, which would negate a charge of genocide.

While many of these complaints lack merit, there are several valid points raised in the country responses. Several governments objected to the mapping team's reliance on organizations they perceived to be biased. It is beyond the scope of this case study to assess the credibility of the organizations consulted by the mapping team. However, while the report does provide a list of NGOs contacted, it does not specify the selection criteria for these organizations. The report also does not include information as to how the team specifically applied the "admiralty scale" to individual organizations to assess credibility and veracity of source material. These concerns were heightened by the failure of the mapping team to consult with governmental officials from neighboring countries. Similarly, omitting the names of the mapping team members contributed to the perception that the team was biased.

Nevertheless, despite the legitimate criticisms, what differentiates the mapping report from the other case studies is the extent to which the mapping team acknowledged its limitations and qualified its work as a result. For example, at the beginning of the report, the team remarked that "the Mapping Exercise remains necessarily incomplete and can in no case reconstruct the complexity of each situation …"[79] In another section, with regards to assessing casualty figures, the team noted that

> It is very hard to determine how many people died in the first few months of the conflict. Every community has its own version of the facts and its own estimate of the number of victims. Furthermore, killing sprees often occurred at very heavily dispersed sites that are hard to access even now. Where it is possible to visit these sites, it is rare to find first hand witnesses to the events.[80]

The team also took into account the comments it received from the GoR regarding the charges of genocide. According to journalist, Colum Lynch, who reviewed both the draft and final versions of the report,

---

[79] *Mapping Report, supra* note 48, at para. 9.
[80] Id. at para. 155.

"[i]nstead of stating whether crimes had been committed, the final report leaves it to a court to definitively decide."[81] The final version also contains "a far more detailed and robust set of countervailing legal arguments," as well as qualifying language such as the terms "alleged," "suggests," "apparent," and "if proven in a court of law." The willingness of the mapping team to acknowledge its limitations and to modify its work in response to criticism stands in marked contrast to many NGO fact-finding initiatives.

Although the DRC mapping exercise was not without flaws, it serves as a potential model for fact-finding. In particular, the drafting and publication of a detailed terms of reference, clear and transparent guidelines for evaluating evidence, criteria for selection of incidents, a defined standard of proof, the listing of source material, candid acknowledgment of the limitations in its work, and the qualification of conclusions when warranted all serve as exemplary practices to be emulated by NGOs and future fact-finding missions.

[81] See Lynch, *supra* note 72.

Case Study 4: The Work of Amnesty International and Human Rights Watch: Evidence from Colombia (1988–2004) – Conflict Analysis Resource Center/University of London

Researchers from the Conflict Analysis Resource Center (CERAC) and the University of London tracked the output of Amnesty International and Human Rights Watch for a sixteen year period (1988–2004) in a single country: Colombia.[82] CERAC also tracked more than 21,000 events perpetrated by left-wing guerrillas, right-wing paramilitaries, and government forces.[83] The organization built its data set off of information from local NGO reports and periodicals, local newspapers, government sources, and primary source interviews.[84]

CERAC analyzed AI's and HRW's special reports on Colombia and sections of annual reports devoted to the country, and conducted a quantitative analysis of the extent and consistency of their coverage.[85] CERAC focused on Colombia because AI and HRW both have high profiles in that country, devote substantial resources in response to the conflict, and hold influence with wealthier countries that give aid to Colombia.[86] CERAC's report is one of the few comprehensive (and long-term) analyses of NGO methodology, and highlights concerns about relying at face value on information from these organizations.

In particular, CERAC focused on the problem of transparency. CERAC notes that, optimally, a human rights report should clearly define a discrete group of variables to cover "regularly and systematically" and define how those variables are measured and sourced.[87] The report concludes that AI and HRW have no systematic approach. Rather, these organizations frequently changed what variables they chose to measure, and revealed sources for less than one-fourth of their information.[88] For example, CERAC found that while HRW had definitions for "political assassinations" and "massacres," those

---

[82] Ballesteros, Andres, Jorge A. Restrepo, Michael Spagat, and Juan F. Vargas, Conflict Analysis Resource Center and the University of London, *The Work of Amnesty International and Human Rights Watch: Evidence from Colombia* 2–3 (2007), available at http://www.ngo-monitor.org/data/images/File/evidencefromcolumbia_feb2007.pdf.

[83] Id. at 5–6.

[84] Id. at 6.

[85] Id. at 5.

[86] Id. at 2–3.

[87] Id. at 7.

[88] Id.

definitions varied from report to report.[89] In some years, HRW included combatants in their political assassinations figures, and in other years it excluded them.[90] AI, in some years, included killings by guerrillas, and in some years it did not, creating a wide variation in the statistics from year to year.[91] In addition, HRW and AI grossly overestimated the number of massacres. For example, AI claimed that "hundreds" of massacres happened in a particular year, demonstrating a variable understanding of the (usually large-scale) term.[92]

The CERAC report also highlighted quantitative problems in HRW's and AI's reporting. CERAC noted that each year, both organizations issued an almost automatic statement that the conflict had intensified, even as the conflict in fact, waxed and waned during the time period studied.[93] The report stated that both organizations reported particularly poorly on the actions of paramilitaries, almost entirely ignoring any fluctuation in activity level from year to year.[94] In many of its statistics, AI failed to distinguish between paramilitary groups and armed opposition groups, while HRW was sometimes more discerning.[95]

Another issue was the inconsistent figures provided for internally displaced persons (IDPs), probably due to disparate sourcing. Some sources required IDPs to officially identify themselves as such. Others used a different metric for classifying when IDP status terminates. AI and HRW would often mix these sources without attribution, causing confusion.[96] In 2002, for instance, AI reports cited four different figures for IDPs, which ranged from between 720,000 to 3,000,000.[97]

CERAC found, however, that AI and HRW had better sourcing and greater reliability when describing specific events in the conflict (rather than presenting quantitative information). In fact, in the case of at least three massacres, AI and HRW credibly shifted blame to the

---

[89] Id. at 8.
[90] Id. at 12.
[91] Id.
[92] Id. at 15.
[93] Id. at 11.
[94] Id.
[95] Id. at 16–17.
[96] Id. at 17. Adam Roberts discusses similar problems with inconsistent definitions of "civilian war casualties" and the difficulty finding reliable statistics. See Roberts, Adam, *Lives and Statistics: Are 90% of War Victims Civilians?*, 52 SURVIVAL 115, 116–18 (2010), available at http://www.iiss.org/publications/survival/survival-2010/year-2010-issue-3/lives-and-statistics-are-90-of-war-victims-civilians/.
[97] Ballesteros, *supra* note 82, at 17.

government after others had initially blamed the paramilitaries.[98] Also, both organizations produced almost identical information about collusion between the government and the paramilitaries.[99]

Some of these findings suggest a bias against the government relative to the guerrillas. HRW acknowledged that it focused more attention on government institutions:

> [HRW focused on] institutionalized human rights problems in Colombia, such as those created by the civilian and military justice systems, impunity, and the government's failure to protect vulnerable sectors of the population from violence by state and private actors. We worked … to press the Colombian government to live up to its international human rights obligations. At the same time, we called on guerrillas to cease violating international humanitarian law.[100]

AI, in its response to CERAC, noted that its primary concern was the actions of the government: "[F]or strategic reasons AI's focus has to be on changing government policy. They are the signatories to international human rights treaties and should hold a monopoly of power. As such, they will continue to be the main, but not exclusive, focus of AI's work."[101] In the AI statute, however, the organization states that it "addresses governments, intergovernmental organizations, armed political groups, companies and other non-state actors. … It systematically and impartially researches the facts of individual cases and patterns of human rights abuses."[102] It would appear, therefore, that its over-emphasis on actions of the Colombian government was not in keeping with the mandate of the organization.

In response to the CERAC study, AI asserted that its mandate was not to make "detailed quantifiable claims" or establish a data set that can be used from country to country.[103] HRW issued a harsher critique to CERAC's report, calling its criticisms "nonsense" with "a superficial

---

98 Id. at 19.

99 Id. at 20–21.

100 Id. at 22.

101 Amnesty International, *Amnesty International response to Andrés Ballesteros, Jorge A. Restrepo, Michael Spagat, Juan F. Vargas,* The Work of Amnesty International and Human Rights Watch: Evidence from Colombia, *CERAC, Colombia, February 2007* (2007), available at http://www.amnesty.org/en/library/asset/AMR23/006/2007/en/83aa83aa-d399-11dd-a329-2f46302a8cc6/amr230062007en.html.

102 Amnesty International, *Statute of Amnesty International,* available at http://www.amnesty.org/en/who-we-are/accountability/statute-of-amnesty-international (last visited Jan. 9, 2011).

103 Id.

veneer of academic rigor."[104] HRW argued that many of its claims—such as placing emphasis on government-paramilitary ties—came from information that cannot be definitely qualified in percentage terms.[105]

Although both of these organizations claimed that their focus is more qualitative than quantitative, AI and HRW presented quantitative information in their reports on Colombia. Moreover, the quantitative information is also used to influence government policy and public opinion. As a result, it should not be insulated from criticism and analysis, simply because these organizations chose to place more focus on qualitative data. Careful and consistent standards and methodologies must be applied to all information presented to the public, not just that which is deemed more important.

The quantitative and qualitative inconsistencies in the HRW and Amnesty publications detailed by CERAC were not just found in the organizations' reporting on Colombia. As the next case study discusses, similar problems were found in reports issued on the 2006 Lebanon War between Israel and Hezbollah.

---

[104] Vivanco, Jose Miguel, *HRW Response to CERAC Charges about our Colombia Work* (2007), available at http://www.hrw.org/en/news/2007/03/15/hrw-response-cerac-charges-about-our-colombia-work.

[105] Id.

Case Study 5: Human Rights Watch and the Lebanon War (2006)

Human Rights Watch (HRW) has published numerous reports claiming expertise regarding the Arab-Israeli conflict, and this NGO was particularly active during the 2006 war between Hezbollah (the Iranian-backed Shi'ite "Party of God" based in Lebanon) and the Israel Defense Forces. The war began when Hezbollah launched a cross-border attack from its bases in Lebanon into Israel on July 12, killing eight Israeli soldiers and abducting two.[106] The initial Israeli response was a major air campaign, followed by ground attacks which targeted Hezbollah strongholds in southern Lebanon and certain neighborhoods of Beirut.[107] The fighting lasted 34 days, during which Hezbollah launched an estimated 3,970 Katyusha rockets on military and civilian targets in Israel, including the city of Haifa, killing 162 Israelis and wounding 4,000.[108] Approximately 1,000 Lebanese were reported killed and 4,000 wounded.[109] Hundreds of thousands of civilians on both sides of the border were displaced internally.

From the outset, HRW took an active role commenting on the conflict, issuing more than 40 publications, including lengthy reports, press releases, op-eds, letters, and other public statements. On July 16, 2006, four days after the start of the fighting, HRW issued a press release alleging that Israel failed to "take all feasible precautions to protect civilians" in targeting Hezbollah installations.[110] In the next week, HRW accused Israel of committing war crimes against Lebanese civilians.[111] On August 2, 2006, HRW issued a 49-page publication entitled *Fatal Strikes: Israel's Indiscriminate Attacks Against Civilians in Lebanon*. The report purported to document "serious violations of international humanitarian law (the laws of war) by Israel Defense

---

[106] Kalb, Marvin, and Carol Saivetz, Harvard University Kennedy School of Government, *The Israeli-Hezbollah War of 2006: The Media as a Weapon in Asymmetrical Conflict* 8 (2006).

[107] Id.

[108] *The Interim Winograd Report* (April 2007), available at http://www.vaadatwino.org.il/pdf/???%20????.pdf (Hebrew).

[109] Id.

[110] Human Rights Watch, *Israel: Investigate Attack on Civilians in Lebanon* (July 16, 2006), available at http://www.hrw.org/en/news/2006/07/16/israel-investigate-attack-civilians-lebanon.

[111] Human Rights Watch, *Israel/Lebanon: Israel Responsible for Qana Attack* (July 29, 2006), available at http://www.hrw.org/en/news/2006/07/29/israellebanon-israel-responsible-qana-attack.

Forces (IDF) in Lebanon between July 12 and July 27, 2006, as well as the July 30 attack in Qana."

Methodology of Fatal Strikes

The claims in *Fatal Strikes* were almost entirely derived from interviews with Lebanese located in areas controlled by Hezbollah. According to the "Acknowledgments" section, the report was based on "research conducted in Beirut, Qana, Srifa, and Tyre, Lebanon, from July 12 to August 1, 2006." Its findings were based "primarily on investigations by Human Rights Watch researchers, who have been in Beirut since the onset of the conflict and traveled for two days to Lebanon's South." HRW claimed that it "carefully corroborat[ed] and cross-check[ed] [witness] accounts with international aid workers, international and local journalists, medical professionals, local officials, as well as information from the IDF," though no information was provided on how such corroboration and cross-checking was conducted.

The methodology section also included an explanatory note that "[s]ecurity conditions did not permit on-site visits to many of the villages or other sites where civilian casualties are documented in this report, but in all cases Human Rights Watch located eyewitnesses to attacks." HRW does not disclose how it located such eyewitnesses, established their credibility, nor how incidents were selected for inclusion in the report. HRW also noted that

> [i]n a small minority of cases, Human Rights Watch researchers in Lebanon could locate witnesses only in Hezbollah-controlled camps for displaced persons in Beirut. Hezbollah controls an estimated seventy of the 120 schools currently housing the displaced. On such occasions, Hezbollah officials often insisted that Human Rights Watch researchers not ask questions about the location of Hezbollah militants because such information, wherever Hezbollah might be located, was of military value. These conditions limited Human Rights Watch's ability to make a legal determination regarding whether the target in question was legitimate.[112]

HRW does not say why this disclaimer only applied to witnesses in displaced persons camps in Beirut. It was widely reported that Hezbollah was in complete control of Southern Lebanon at the time of

[112] Human Rights Watch, *Fatal Strikes: Israel's Indiscriminate Attacks Against Civilians in Lebanon* 9 (2006), available at http://www.hrw.org/en/reports/2006/08/02/fatal-strikes.

HRW's research.[113] Therefore, it is not possible to establish the extent to which HRW researchers were shadowed by Hezbollah operatives during its two days of interviews in the area or whether those interviewed had connections to the terror organization.

The Acknowledgments section lists fourteen HRW staffers who worked on the report, including HRW's Executive Director Kenneth Roth. The authors of the report included HRW's Emergencies Director, Peter Bouckaert; Nadim Houry, the Lebanon and Syria researcher in the Middle East Division; and Lucy Mair, researcher for Israel and the Occupied Palestinian Territories. A consultant to HRW, Jonathan Fox, "contributed additional research from northern Israel and contacts with the Israel Defense Forces," and Fred Abrahams, senior emergencies researcher "coordinated the research effort and did additional research from New York." Sarah Leah Whitson, executive director of HRW's Middle East and North Africa division; Wilder Tayler, legal and policy director; Iain Levine, program director; and Ken Roth are listed as editors. Steve Goose, "executive director of the arms division and other members of the arms division staff provided input and analysis," and associates Assef Ashraf, Thodleen Desssources, Tarek Radwan, and Leeam Azulay-Yagev "greatly assisted with research and administrative support."[114]

Claims of Indiscriminate Attacks

Fatal Strikes was harshly critical of Israel, claiming that the IDF "consistently launched artillery and air attacks with limited or dubious military gain but excessive civilian cost." HRW also alleged that in "dozens of attacks, Israeli forces struck an area with no apparent military target." HRW concluded that there was a "systematic failure by the IDF to distinguish between combatants and civilians" and that "the extent of the pattern and the seriousness of the consequences indicate the commission of war crimes." Even more controversially, the report alleged that HRW had "found no cases in which Hizbullah deliberately used civilians as shields to protect them from retaliatory IDF attack."[115]

---

[113] See, e.g. Kalb and Saiyetz *supra* note 106; Anderson Cooper, Hezbollah Remains Secretive Organization, *Anderson Cooper 360 on CNN*, Aug. 9, 2006.

[114] *Fatal Strikes*, "Acknowledgments," *supra* note 112.

[115] Dershowitz, Alan, *First Word: What is 'Human Rights Watch' watching?*, JERUSALEM POST, Aug. 26, 2006, available at http://www.jpost.com/Opinion/Columnists/Article.aspx?id=32731.

The report did not investigate the thousands of indiscriminate rocket attacks launched by Hezbollah at Israeli population centers, the origins of these weapons, or associated war crimes and human rights violations.

Criticisms of Fatal Strikes

HRW was intensely criticized for its claims in *Fatal Strikes*, and critics raised several specific methodological problems with HRW's work, including a blatant disregard of sources that ran counter to a particular narrative, reliance on unverifiable eyewitness testimony, disproportionate focus on one party in the conflict, the rush to conclusions, improper application of international law, and potential pre-existing bias by researchers.

Henry Steiner, Philip Alston, and Ryan Goodman summarize some of these criticisms in their book *International Human Rights in Context: Law, Politics and Morals*. They refer to articles in *The New Republic* and the *Jerusalem Post* claiming that HRW's Lebanon reporting destroyed the organization's credibility.[116] Specifically, they quote Professor Alan Dershowitz: "When it comes to Israel and its enemies, Human Rights Watch cooks the books about facts, cheats on interviews, and puts out predetermined conclusions that are driven more by their ideology then by evidence."[117]

Dershowitz, in particular, challenged HRW's claim that it found "no cases in which Hizbullah deliberately used civilians as shields to protect them from retaliatory IDF attack." He also criticized HRW for relying solely on Lebanese testimony, while at the same time failing to acknowledge that the entire interview environment was controlled by Hezbollah.[118] In contrast to charges made by HRW, Dershowitz provided evidence of the use of human shields by Hezbollah from six media sources and a United Nations press release. For example, he cites a *New York Times* article quoting a Lebanese villager that "Hezbullah … are shooting from between our houses."[119]

---

[116] Steiner, Henry J., Philip Alston and Ryan Goodman, INTERNATIONAL HUMAN RIGHTS IN CONTEXT: LAW POLITICS AND MORALS 1422 (3d ed. 2008).

[117] Id.

[118] As discussed, HRW mentioned that in some cases, it interviewed witnesses in camps controlled by Hezbollah in Beirut. The organization said nothing, however, regarding the near complete control of Hezbollah over Southern Lebanon and how that impacted its work. See *Fatal Strikes, supra* note 112.

[119] Id.

Aryeh Neier, the former executive director of HRW, rejected Dershowitz's criticisms because, among other reasons, the sources cited by Dershowitz referred to events that were not reported on by HRW.[120] This attempted justification highlights the methodological issue of how events were chosen by HRW for inclusion in their reports. The omission of these examples by HRW appears to reflect a choice to include only those incidents where HRW did not find evidence of Hezbollah shielding, despite the existence of several incidents that are inconsistent with the organization's conclusions.

Neier also argued that "the fact that Hezbollah fighters mingled with the civilian population in some places does not mean that all attacks on civilians were justified."[121] In addition to faulty logic in this statement (Dershowitz did not claim that all attacks were justified), the admission by Neier that Hezbollah fighters mixed with civilians, itself went far beyond HRW's brief acknowledgement that Hezbollah "occasionally did store weapons" near populated areas.[122]

William Arkin, a former senior military analyst at HRW who conducted an independent analysis of the war (discussed later in this chapter), also vociferously disputed the conclusions of HRW in *Fatal Strikes* as well as claims made by Amnesty International. In particular, he challenged their excessive reliance on Lebanese sources:

> The prominent international human rights organizations which investigated damage to the civilian infrastructure in Lebanon further reported that they found little or no evidence of previous Hezbollah presence where attacks took place, suggesting Israeli intent to destroy Lebanon's infrastructure and economy as well as gross neglect and lack of discrimination in attacks, even against legitimate targets.
>
> The problem with this dominant and conventional accounting of damage is that most of it is grossly exaggerated, misleading, or patently false. Based upon on-the-ground inspections, discussions with Israeli and Lebanese officials, imagery analysis, and a close reading of government and international organization materials, a good majority of the reports of damage in Lebanon are incorrect or downright fraudulent.[123]

---

[120] Neier, Aryeh, *The Attack on Human Rights Watch*, N.Y. REVIEW OF BOOKS, Nov. 2, 2006, at 6–7.

[121] Id. at 6.

[122] Human Rights Watch, *Fatal Strikes, supra* note 112, at 3 (2006).

[123] William M. Arkin, "Divining Victory - Airpower in the 2006 Israel-Hezbollah War," Air University Press 76 (2007), available at http://www.4shared.com/document/NRfziHeq/Divining_Victory_-_Airpower_in.html. Arkin further states that "[t]here is no evidence that Israel intentionally attacked any proscribed medical facilities,

> ...
> Even in cases where Israel did attack or damage many objects, the Lebanese government, news media, and many nongovernmental organizations (NGO) consistently described things as having been "destroyed" when they were not destroyed or only peripherally damaged.[124]

Bar Ilan University Professor Abraham Bell, a strong critic of HRW's reporting in Lebanon, accused the organization of a disproportionate focus on purported Israeli violations. He noted that *Fatal Strikes* accused Israel of war crimes in 21 incidents while only briefly acknowledging that in the same period, Hezbollah launched 1,300 indiscriminate attacks on Israeli civilians.[125] Bell also accused the organization of rushing to conclusions, noting two incidents in particular. In one, Kenneth Roth, HRW's Executive Director, alleged in a July 31, 2006 *New York Sun* op-ed that Israel had killed 42 civilians in the Lebanese village of Srifa. Three days later, HRW's *Fatal Strikes* placed the number at 23.[126]

A second incident involved an Israeli airstrike in the town of Qana on July 30, 2006. HRW issued a press release a few hours after the incident accusing Israel of killing at least 54 civilians in Qana in "an indiscriminate bombing campaign."[127] As mentioned in Chapter Two, HRW based the casualty number solely on the testimony of a Lebanese resident whose affiliations with Hezbollah were unknown, and ignored an official statement issued that same day by the Lebanese Red Cross reporting 28 casualties.[128] Although HRW later repeated the correct casualty figure of 28, the original claim of 54 remains on its website.[129]

These issues are examined by Bell in more detail in a study co-authored with Gerald Steinberg, entitled "Methodologies for NGO

---

no real proof that it 'targeted' ambulances (and certainly not because they were ambulances engaged in protected activity), no evidence that it targeted mosques or other religious structures, and there were no intentional attacks on schools. The Qreitem 'Old Lighthouse' in Beirut was attacked because it housed radar and observation posts used to target Israeli ships. Grain silos were hit incidental to attacking a naval base exclusively used by Hezbollah." Id. at 76–7.

[124] Id. at 77.

[125] Bell, Abraham, Human Rights Watch has some explaining to do, Opinio Juris, September 1, 2006, available at http://opiniojuris.org/2006/09/01/human-rights-watch-has-some-explaining-to-do/.

[126] Id.

[127] Id.

[128] Murphy, Kim, *Officials Say 28 Died in Qana, Not 54*, L.A. Times, Aug. 4, 2006, available at http://articles.latimes.com/2006/aug/04/world/fg-qana4.

[129] Id.

Human Rights Fact-Finding in Modern Warfare: The 2006 Lebanon War as a Case Study."[130] The study examines the publications of HRW and Amnesty International on the war from both a quantitative and a qualitative perspective. The study found "a widespread pattern of methodological failures, including opacity of research procedures, gaps between the available evidence and the conclusions stated, distortion of evidence, use of unverifiable and apparently unreliable evidence, improper application of legal standards, bias, and non-responsiveness to criticism." In particular, the study analyzed "seven significant events and battle areas allegedly involving civilian casualties," including incidents in Srifa, Qana, Bint Jbeil, and Marwahim.

In the analysis, HRW publications regarding these seven central incidents were found be "highly partisan," and the NGOs factual claims varied "substantially from the initial reports through the later statements." The study also found that claims "generally echoed the Lebanese/Hezbollah characterizations and figures during and after the war."[131] Indeed, in "nearly every case, [HRW's] initial estimation of Lebanese casualties was exaggerated," and "the lack of reliable sources of information [was] prominent."[132] In one example, the study notes that a 249-page HRW report, *Why They Died*, relied solely on casualty figures provided by Hezbollah, even though there was a wide discrepancy among many sources regarding the actual number.[133] Overall, the study concludes that "[HRW's] reports were closer to unverified claims than researched conclusions."[134]

The Intelligence and Terrorism Information Center at the Center for Special Studies (ITIC) in Israel, headed by Dr. Reuven Erlich, further impugned HRW's claims and sourcing. In December 2006, the Center issued a 61-page report documenting "Hezbollah's consistent pattern of intentionally placing its fighters and weapons among civilians."[135]

---

[130] Bell, Abraham and Gerald M. Steinberg, *Methodologies for NGO Human Rights Fact-Finding in Modern Warfare: The 2006 Lebanon War as a Case Study*, Report to the Israel Science Foundation, October 2011.

[131] Id. at 30.

[132] Id. at 30–1.

[133] Id. at 26–7. HRW's reliance on Hezbollah figures stands out in comparison to the DRC Mapping Exercise which specifically acknowledged the difficulty reporting on casualty figures: "It is very hard to determine how many people died in the first few months of the conflict. Every community has its own version of the facts and its own estimate of the number of victims." See *supra* note 54.

[134] Id. at 31.

[135] Intelligence and Terrorism Information Center at the Center for Special Studies, *Hezbollah's use of Lebanese civilians as human shields: the extensive military*

The report compiled Israeli military intelligence information and other sources, including photographs from the Israeli Air Force and Israeli ground troops, television footage of Hezbollah public statements, testimony from Hezbollah detainees, captured Hezbollah documents, and Israeli radar information.[136] The report discredited many of the accusations made by HRW in *Fatal Strikes* (as well as AI reports) by listing "specific instances of Hezbollah activity in areas HRW claims there was no Hezbollah presence."[137]

For example, in *Fatal Strikes*, HRW claimed Israel committed an indiscriminate attack by killing four civilians in the Lebanese village of Bint Jbeil. In support of its allegation that the Israeli airstrike was not aimed at a military objective, HRW relied on an eyewitness who stated that "there was no fighting taking place in the village—there was no one but civilians."[138] In contrast, the ITIC study provided documentary evidence showing that Bint Jbeil was a Hezbollah stronghold. An aerial photograph showed 20 Hezbollah bases and five weapons storehouses within the village, and other documentation revealed that more than 60 Hezbollah operatives were stationed there.[139] It also showed that much of the weaponry was stored in civilian residential buildings.[140] Finally, ITIC reported that more than 87 rockets had been fired on Israel from within village homes, 109 from within a 200 meter radius of the village, and 136 within a 500 meter radius of the village.[141] The ITIC report contains many more examples directly contradicting HRW's claims.

Another critique of HRW's work centered on potential pre-existing bias by the authors of *Fatal Strikes*. As HRW's reports were published during and immediately after the conflict, Gerald Steinberg noted that several of HRW's Mideast and North Africa Division staffers had

---

infrastructure positioned and hidden by Hezbollah in populated areas. From within the Lebanese towns and villages deliberate rocket attacks were directed against civilian targets in Israel (Dec. 5, 2006), (hereinafter "ITIC Report") available at http://www.terrorism-info.org.il/malam_multimedia/English/eng_n/html/human_shields.htm.

136 Id.

137 Id. See also Mandel, Sarah, NGO Monitor, *Experts or Ideologues? A Systematic Analysis of Human Rights Watch's Focus on Israel* (2009); Myre, Greg, *Offering Video, Israel Answers Critics on War*, N.Y. Times, Dec. 5, 2006, available at http://www.nytimes.com/2006/12/05/world/middleeast/05mideast.html?_r=1&hp&ex=1165294800&en=8118d4b5432dffa0&ei=5094&partner=homepage&oref=slogin.

138 *Fatal Strikes*, *supra* note 112.

139 *ITIC Report*, *supra* note 135, at Part 2, p. 77, Appendix 1.

140 Id.

141 Id. at Part 2.

backgrounds in pro-Palestinian advocacy. One such individual was Lucy Mair, HRW's researcher for Israeli/Palestinian issues at the time, who had published anti-Israel propaganda in platforms such as the "Electronic Intifada."[142] The inclusion of such individuals in an investigation of Israeli "war crimes" would present a conflict of interest and raised questions regarding the objectivity of the organization in carrying out its work. It is for this reason that the Lund-London Guidelines, for instance, advises that a "mission's delegation should comprise individuals who are and are seen to be unbiased."[143]

Why They Died

The methodological problems highlighted after the release of *Fatal Strikes* largely remained in HRW's September 2007 follow-up publication, *Why They Died: Civilian Casualties in Lebanon during the 2006 War*.[144] In *Why They Died*, HRW belatedly acknowledged that Hezbollah "violated the prohibition against unnecessarily endangering civilians when they took over civilian homes in the populated village, fired rockets close to homes, and drove through the village in at least one instance with weapons in their cars," but concludes that this conduct did not constitute human shielding because it was not "purposeful."[145] HRW did not explain how these actions were not "purposeful." HRW also did not clarify why it employed a more narrow definition for "human shielding" in the Lebanon conflict than it employed in other conflicts such as Sri Lanka, Somalia, Chechnya, and elsewhere.[146]

Like *Fatal Strikes*, *Why They Died* accepted uncorroborated or contradictory indicators regarding the combatant status of casualties. HRW appears, at first, to classify decedents as civilians or combatants based on whether there were Hezbollah "martyr" posters issued in their

---

[142] Steinberg, Gerald M., *Ken Roth's blood libel*, JERUSALEM POST, August 26, 2006, available at http://fr.jpost.com/servlet/Satellite?cid=1154525949034&pagename=JPArticle%2FShowFull.

[143] Raoul Wallenberg Institute of Human Rights and Humanitarian Law, *Guidelines on International Human Rights Fact-Finding Visits and Reports (The Lund-London Guidelines)*, ¶8 (2009), available at http://www.factfindingguidelines.org/guidelines.html.

[144] Human Rights Watch, *Why They Died: Civilian Casualties in Lebanon during the 2006 War* (2007), available at http://www.hrw.org/en/reports/2007/09/05/why-they-died.

[145] Id. at 55.

[146] Mandel, *supra* note 137, at 38–40.

honor.[147] But, at other times, when a decedent did appear on a "martyr" poster, HRW concludes that "an association [with Hezbollah] alone does not establish combatant status."[148] In one instance, when pictures of decedents holding automatic weapons appeared on the "martyr" posters, HRW solely relies on villager claims that the men were not fighters and that the images of weapons were computer generated.[149]

At the same time that HRW credited Lebanese claims, it discounted evidence from the Israeli side, even when hard documentary and photographic evidence was available. In one specific example, the authors of *Why They Died* explain that they excluded consideration of video material from the Israeli government, showing "Hezbollah fighters firing rockets from what appear to be civilian structures," because the footage did not show if there were civilians in the structure at the time of the firing.[150]

Why They Died did, however, retract many of the claims made in *Fatal Strikes*, as well as many public statements made by Ken Roth, Peter Bouckaert, and Sarah Leah Whitson. Yet, these retractions were issued more than a year after the original claims, and *Fatal Strikes* remains on HRW's website despite the inaccuracies. In addition, these corrections, while incomplete, are sufficient to highlight the systematic failures of HRW's minimal research methodology.

One such example involved Israeli airstrikes on the town of Srifa. On July 19, 2006, Israel struck targets, killing several people. *Fatal Strikes* claimed 26 civilians were killed in the attack (though another section of the report said 19), while an op-ed published by Ken Roth two days earlier claimed that 42 civilians were killed. Op-eds penned by both Peter Bouckaert and Sarah Leah Whitson in August 2006 claimed 26 and 19 casualties, respectively. HRW alleged that these deaths were the result of an indiscriminate attack by Israel and evidence of Israeli war crimes. *Why They Died* revised these claims alleging that 26 civilians were not in fact killed at Srifa as reported, but rather, there were 17 combatant and five civilian casualties.[151]

---

147 Human Rights Watch, *Why They Died*, *supra* note 144, at 26. ("The information collected by Human Rights Watch researchers from cemeteries and 'martyr' posters proved important in corroborating whether an individual was a civilian, combatant, or Hezbollah official.")

148 Id. at 84.

149 Id. at 133.

150 Id. at 53–54.

151 Human Rights Watch, *Why They Died*, *supra* note 144, at 18; see also Bell and Steinberg, *supra* note 130 at 31–39.

In addition to several corrections, *Why They Died* provides more information regarding HRW's research practices. HRW claimed that in order to achieve accuracy and corroboration, the team members conducted interviews in as private a setting as possible, "separately and independently" from other witnesses and with the same set of questions where possible.[152] HRW noted that there was an Arabic-speaking researcher present at each interview (though HRW does not indicate if that researcher was a local Lebanese or had affiliations with Hezbollah).

Despite emphasizing its standards for corroborating witness statements, HRW did not find a single instance (outside of one episode in an earlier report) "where witnesses deliberately tried to mislead us on whether casualties were civilian or militants."[153] HRW states that it determined the number of civilians killed in each town before interviewing local officials, family members, or eyewitnesses.[154] But it is unclear how HRW made this calculation, and based on the many inconsistencies and factual errors, HRW does not explain why this is a suitable methodology.[155] Moreover, while journalists were under restrictions due to tight Hezbollah control of southern Lebanon, HRW does not acknowledge the restrictions in the area or whether its team was shadowed by Hezbollah "minders" as other researchers have reported.[156]

Alternative Analysis on Lebanon

William Arkin, an independent researcher and former senior military analyst for Human Rights Watch, conducted an independent analysis of the Lebanon War while serving as the military advisor to a UN fact-finding mission, entitled "Divining Victory: Airpower in the 2006 Israel-Hezbollah War," published in August 2007. The study

---

[152] Human Rights Watch, *Why They Died*, *supra* note 144, at 24–25. The report unfortunately does not indicate what set of questions were asked.

[153] Id. at 28.

[154] Id. at 24.

[155] See for example errors in HRW's reporting on incidents in Srifa and Qana, *supra*.

[156] See, e.g., CNN Transcripts, *CNN Reliable Sources: Coverage of the Mideast Conflict* (July 23, 2006), available at http://edition.cnn.com/TRANSCRIPTS/0607/23/rs.01.html. (CNN's Nic Robertson: "[I]n the southern suburbs of Beirut that Hezbollah controls, the only way we can get into those areas is with a Hezbollah escort… [Y]ou have to point out to the audience and let them know that this was a guided tour by Hezbollah press officials along with security, that it was a very rushed affair.")

contradicted many of HRW's claims, while applying much more rigorous methodological standards.

Arkin begins his study with a five-page methodology detailing his working methods and sources consulted.[157] He appears to be careful to have consulted and analyzed both Lebanese and Israeli sources, in addition to numerous UN documents and media reports. He also took extensive time to map and understand the Lebanese terrain. Despite his months-long effort, Arkin is candid to admit that his report is "still quite flawed" based on the difficulty in gaining access to military data. In contrast to many NGO fact-finding missions that often fail to acknowledge that there is much they do not know, Arkin was careful not to speculate or assert unverifiable claims. Importantly, Arkin was also clear that the purpose of his study was to provide a "quick look" rather than a comprehensive accounting in order to "enhance both professional military education and planning, both inside and outside the military." Often, NGO fact-finding reports fail to acknowledge this critical distinction.

Substantively, Arkin's survey differed greatly from HRW's reporting and analysis on the conflict. Unlike HRW's emphasis on anecdotal suffering derived from brief on-site surveys and interviews, Arkin was "mindful that images of bomb damage and enumerations of a relentless effort could also end up conveying exactly the opposite of the actual meaning." Indeed, he writes, "divining Israeli and Hezbollah intent through examining destruction on the ground … can, if one is not careful, convey a much distorted picture."[158]

Arkin also pointed out the NGOs' one-sided characterization of the war and the downplaying of Hezbollah fighting out of civilian areas: "Virtually absent [from portrayals of the conflict was how entrenched] Hezbollah, an organization that managed to fire over 4,000 rockets and projectiles at 160 Israeli settlements, towns, and cities (and over 1,000 powerful antitank missiles inside Lebanon!) … was in the country's civilian fabric." Nevertheless, "when human rights organizations and much of the international community showed up or commented, they seemed to act as if the force Israel was battling was nonexistent."[159]

In fact, Arkin provides extensive evidence of how Hezbollah embedded and operated out of civilian areas.[160] Arkin notes that Hezbollah kept a force of "3000 'reservists' nevertheless drawn from home villages,

---

[157] Arkin, *supra* note 123, at xiv–xviii.
[158] Id. at xviii.
[159] Id. at n. 102.
[160] See, e.g., id. at 24–7, 47–9, 86.

[who] kept their weapons at home." Hezbollah also maintained "arms caches and supply and support bases dispersed down to the house level."[161] Moreover, Hezbollah "base structure was almost exclusively and intrinsically integrated into otherwise normal civilian homes and structures. In Beirut, Hezbollah commandeered entire civilian neighborhoods and built military and political offices and bases in and amongst civilian buildings. In the south, Hezbollah's military infrastructure was intentionally situated in and around densely populated areas."[162] Details such as these render HRW's claims that it found "no cases in which Hizbullah deliberately used civilians as shields to protect them from retaliatory IDF attack" to be entirely without credibility.[163]

Although Arkin characterized the Israeli operation to be excessive and ineffective, he also took issue with characterizations that Israel engaged in indiscriminate attacks. He notes that while "gross destruction was visited upon Hezbollah's stronghold in south Beirut, ... that destruction was still undertaken with precision, as is evidenced by its coexistence with vast untouched areas of the city. Israel indeed made decisions and took steps to limit civilian harm."

Arkin's work was conducted over the course of many months (not just two weeks as in the case of HRW's *Fatal Strikes*) and relied on sources from all parties in the conflict; he did not simply rely upon interviews of Lebanese from Hezbollah-controlled areas. He provided an unbiased narrative of the conflict and did not cherry-pick incidents simply to bolster allegations of Israeli war crimes. Arkin also recommended that analyzing the war and civilian damage must be done in context and in comparison to other conflicts in order to assess damage and liability.[164] He argues for the particular importance of including the complexity of the conflict when dealing with an enemy that is "intentionally embedded within civilian structures and civil society."[165] Arkin's restraint in making broad fact-finding claims that could not be clearly demonstrated by credible evidence, and his refusal to issue sweeping legal conclusions under these circumstances stands in marked contrast to HRW's highly problematic methodology.

[161] Id. at 26.

[162] Id. at 27.

[163] For instance, in supporting its claims of indiscriminate Israeli attacks in Fatal Strikes, HRW quoted an eyewitness that in the Lebanese town of Bint Jbail, "there was no fighting taking place in the village – there was no one but civilians." In contrast, Arkin repeatedly refers to the town as a "Hezbollah Center". See Arkin, *supra* note 123, at 47.

[164] Id. at 102–3.

[165] Id.

CHAPTER FIVE

ANALYSIS AND CONCLUSIONS

The standardization of human rights fact-finding methodology is both very complex and also necessary to ensure that reports maintain a basic level of reliability. As Dermot Groome writes, "it is true that human rights investigation does present a number of unique obstacles to the investigator ... this does not preclude a set of standards to which investigators should aspire."[1] The continued absence of standards in an ever-increasing field of human rights groups casts doubt on the relevancy and legitimacy of reports from the entire NGO sector.[2] Before governments and the international community are able to treat such reports as credible, NGOs must develop "universally applicable minimal standards of due process" in order to conduct investigations and then evaluate fact-finding and reporting methodology according to a basic practice standard.[3]

Such guidelines can be generated by the NGO community, broadly defined, or by an independent panel whose members can be chosen in consultation with that community, in cooperation with legal, military, medical and other experts. NGOs have expressed concern about having their independence or flexibility curbed by the entities they monitor, and efforts to establish standards dictated by governments or politically-based bodies such as the United Nations would be problematic.[4] Robert Charles Blitt suggests that the creation of baseline fact-finding standards "ought to be advanced by a representative consortium of leading [human rights organizations], working together with independent academic and judicial figures having expertise in international

---

[1] Groome, Dermot, The Handbook of Human Rights Investigation: A Comprehensive Guide to the Investigation and Documentation of Violent Human Rights Abuses 255 (2000); see also Blitt, *infra* note 2, at 349.

[2] Blitt, Robert Charles, *Who will watch the watchdogs? Human rights Nongovernmental Organizations and the case for regulation*, 10 Buff. Hum. Rts. L. Rev. 261, 339 (2004), available at http://www.ngo-monitor.org/data/images/File/SSRN-id753487.pdf.

[3] Franck, Thomas M. and H. Scott Fairley, *Procedural Due Process in Human Rights Fact-Finding by International Tribunals*, 74 Am. J. Int'l L. 308, 309 (1980).

[4] See Blitt, *supra* note 2, at 349.

law, human rights and regulatory systems."[5] He notes that human rights NGOs that agree to a set of standards will be imbued with a greater international influence, while organizations that fail to adopt the standards will lose the halo effect that previously helped to shield NGOs from criticisms.[6]

The key to establishing workable guidelines for human rights investigations, particularly in the context of military conflict, is to find a middle ground between overstandardization and the current situation in which there are no baseline standards at all. The basic concept of fact-finding is built on the necessity of collecting accurate and complete information, and on this basis, the importance of systematic and professional criteria cannot be understated.[7] At the same time, given the varying contexts and circumstances in different conflicts and regions, some flexibility is required. As in the case of the Lund-London Guidelines, useful guidelines must allow for an appropriate level of interpretation and adaptation.

In this process, human rights NGOs must consistently and clearly explicate and delineate the boundary between the fact-finding and advocacy roles of any investigation. Fact-finding for armed conflicts requires professional expertise regarding the issues under investigation, including detailed knowledge of relevant weapons and technology, the geographical setting and language skills. The tasks of the on-the-ground investigators must be narrowly defined to ensure their objectivity, and prevent existing ideologies or biases from pre-determining the focus and contents of the research activities.[8] In contrast to some of the examples examined above in the case studies, such professionalism and objectivity will help shield the NGO from charges of selection bias and exaggeration, and give their reports greater influence.[9] In addition, the investigator should provide his or her assessment of a witness's credibility and the factors that led to that conclusion, to enable readers to understand and weigh the veracity of statements accordingly.[10]

---

[5] Id. at 392.

[6] Id. at 397.

[7] See, e.g., International Counsel on Human Rights Policy, *Crime, Public Order, and Human Rights* 118 (2003), available at http://www.ichrp.org/files/reports/8/114_report_en.pdf; Schultz, Norman, Conflict Research Consortium, *Fact-Finding* (2004), available at http://www.beyondintractability.org/essay/fact-finding/.

[8] Groome, *supra* note 1, at 40; see also Blitt, *supra* note 2, at 349.

[9] Groome, *supra* note 1, at 255; see also Blitt, *supra* note 2, at 346.

[10] Groome, *supra* note 1, at 387; see also Blitt, *supra* note 2, at 349.

Dermot Groome provides sample questions that an investigator can address in the report: "Did the investigator undertake preliminary and/or comprehensive interviews; what steps were taken to ascertain the credibility and reliability of witnesses; did the investigator ensure separate interviews and maintain a 'healthy suspicion' of witnesses; and finally, did the investigator not divulge specific facts about the case to the witness?"[11] With such information, the NGO reports will be able to state the bases for factual assertions. Evaluations and opinions can then be placed in a conclusions section, or in a separate publication altogether.

As shown in this work, such guidelines for human rights reporting are far from the current practice, in which NGO reports often fail to include the most basic explanations of their methodology, including team composition, mandate, and how witnesses were selected and interviewed. Without standards and without disclosure, fact-finding will continue to be an unsupervised venture with little distinction between established human rights entities and any other third party. Most significantly, without such basic changes, governments, international organizations, academics, and journalists will give less weight to human rights reports, meaning that major and real violations will go unaddressed.

Proposals such as the Lund-London Guidelines have paved the way for standardization and contain more comprehensive practice guidelines than current internal standards presented by Amnesty International, Human Rights Watch, and other major NGOs—many of whom have no clear explanation of their practices at all. International NGOs worked together to agree on standards for financial accountability and humanitarian duties, and the same level of cooperation can be reached for fact-finding as well. Until then, the international community has no clear baseline by which NGO reliability can be judged.

[11] Groome, *supra* note 1, at 175.

APPENDICES

Proclamation of Teheran, Final Act of the International Conference on Human Rights

Teheran, 22 April to 13 May 1968, U.N. Doc. A/CONF. 32/41 at 3 (1968)

The International Conference on Human Rights,
Having met at Teheran from April 22 to May 13, 1968 to review the progress made in the twenty years since the adoption of the Universal Declaration of Human Rights and to formulate a programme for the future,
Having considered the problems relating to the activities of the United Nations for the promotion and encouragement of respect for human rights and fundamental freedoms,
Bearing in mind the resolutions adopted by the Conference,
Noting that the observance of the International Year for Human Rights takes place at a time when the world is undergoing a process of unprecedented change,
Having regard to the new opportunities made available by the rapid progress of science and technology,
Believing that, in an age when conflict and violence prevail in many parts of the world, the fact of human interdependence and the need for human solidarity are more evident than ever before,
Recognizing that peace is the universal aspiration of mankind and that peace and justice are indispensable to the full realization of human rights and fundamental freedoms, Solemnly proclaims that:

1. It is imperative that the members of the international community fulfill their solemn obligations to promote and encourage respect for human rights and fundamental freedoms for all without distinctions of any kind such as race, colour, sex, language, religion, political or other opinions;
2. The Universal Declaration of Human Rights states a common understanding of the peoples of the world concerning the inalienable and inviolable rights of all members of the human family and constitutes an obligation for the members of the international community;
3. The International Covenant on Civil and Political Rights, the International Covenant on Economic, Social and Cultural Rights, the Declaration on the Granting of Independence to Colonial Countries

and Peoples, the International Convention on the Elimination of All Forms of Racial Discrimination as well as other conventions and declarations in the field of human rights adopted under the auspices of the United Nations, the specialized agencies and the regional intergovernmental organizations, have created new standards and obligations to which States should conform;

4. Since the adoption of the Universal Declaration of Human Rights the United Nations has made substantial progress in defining standards for the enjoyment and protection of human rights and fundamental freedoms. During this period many important international instruments were adopted but much remains to be done in regard to the implementation of those rights and freedoms;

5. The primary aim of the United Nations in the sphere of human rights is the achievement by each individual of the maximum freedom and dignity. For the realization of this objective, the laws of every country should grant each individual, irrespective of race, language, religion or political belief, freedom of expression, of information, of conscience and of religion, as well as the right to participate in the political, economic, cultural and social life of his country;

6. States should reaffirm their determination effectively to enforce the principles enshrined in the Charter of the United Nations and in other international instruments that concern human rights and fundamental freedoms;

7. Gross denials of human rights under the repugnant policy of apartheid is a matter of the gravest concern to the international community. This policy of apartheid, condemned as a crime against humanity, continues seriously to disturb international peace and security. It is therefore imperative for the international community to use every possible means to eradicate this evil. The struggle against apartheid is recognized as legitimate;

8. The peoples of the world must be made fully aware of the evils of racial discrimination and must join in combating them. The implementation of this principle of non-discrimination, embodied in the Charter of the United Nations, the Universal Declaration of Human Rights, and other international instruments in the field of human rights, constitutes a most urgent task of mankind at the international as well as at the national level. All ideologies based on racial superiority and intolerance must be condemned and resisted;

9. Eight years after the General Assembly's Declaration on the Granting of Independence to Colonial Countries and Peoples the

problems of colonialism continue to preoccupy the international community. It is a matter of urgency that all Member States should co-operate with the appropriate organs of the United Nations so that effective measures can be taken to ensure that the Declaration is fully implemented;

10. Massive denials of human rights, arising out of aggression or any armed conflict with their tragic consequences, and resulting in untold human misery, engender reactions which could engulf the world in ever growing hostilities. It is the obligation of the international community to co-operate in eradicating such scourges;

11. Gross denials of human rights arising from discrimination on grounds of race, religion, belief or expressions of opinion outrage the conscience of mankind and endanger the foundations of freedom, justice and peace in the world;

12. The widening gap between the economically developed and developing countries impedes the realization of human rights in the international community. The failure of the Development Decade to reach its modest objectives makes it all the more imperative for every nation, according to its capacities, to make the maximum possible effort to close this gap;

13. Since human rights and fundamental freedoms are indivisible, the full realization of civil and political rights without the enjoyment of economic, social and cultural rights is impossible. The achievement of lasting progress in the implementation of human rights is dependent upon sound and effective national and international policies of economic and social development;

14. The existence of over seven hundred million illiterates throughout the world is an enormous obstacle to all efforts at realizing the aims and purposes of the Charter of the United Nations and the provisions of the Universal Declaration of Human Rights. International action aimed at eradicating illiteracy from the face of the earth and promoting education at all levels requires urgent attention;

15. The discrimination of which women are still victims in various regions of the world must be eliminated. An inferior status for women is contrary to the Charter of the United Nations as well as the provisions of the Universal Declaration of Human Rights. The full implementation of the Declaration on the Elimination of Discrimination against Women is a necessity for the progress of mankind;

16. The protection of the family and of the child remains the concern of the international community. Parents have a basic human right to

determine freely and responsibly the number and the spacing of their children;
17. The aspirations of the younger generation for a better world, in which human rights and fundamental freedoms are fully implemented, must be given the highest encouragement. It is imperative that youth participate in shaping the future of mankind;
18. While recent scientific discoveries and technological advances have opened vast prospects for economic, social and cultural progress, such developments may nevertheless endanger the rights and freedoms of individuals and will require continuing attention;
19. Disarmament would release immense human and material resources now devoted to military purposes. These resources should be used for the promotion of human rights and fundamental freedoms. General and complete disarmament is one of the highest aspirations of all peoples;

Therefore,
The International Conference on Human Rights,

1. Affirming its faith in the principles of the Universal Declaration of Human Rights and other international instruments in this field,
2. Urges all peoples and governments to dedicate themselves to the principles enshrined in the Universal Declaration of Human Rights and to redouble their efforts to provide for all human beings a life consonant with freedom and dignity and conducive to physical, mental, social and spiritual welfare.

UN General Assembly Resolution 35/176 Alternative approaches and ways and means within the United Nations system to improve the effective enjoyment of human rights and fundamental freedoms

(96th plenary meeting, December 15, 1980)

The General Assembly,

Recalling the responsibility entrusted by the Charter of the United Nations for ensuring universal respect for human rights and fundamental freedoms,

Noting the growing awareness of the international community of the need to ensure effective promotion and protection of human rights,

Also recalling the experience acquired by the United Nations in pursuing the goal of the promotion and protection of human rights, *inter alia*, through the use of fact-finding missions, in cases in which mass and flagrant violations of human rights have been recognized,

1. *Considers* that the question of the establishment of bodies entrusted with fact-finding missions and the extent to which they may enhance the promotion and prot ection of human rights requires serious consideration;
2. *Requests* the Commission on Human Rights to discuss this question at its thirty-seventh session under the item entitled "Further promotion and encouragement of human rights and fundamental freedoms, including the question of the programme and methods of the work of the Commission: alternative approaches and ways and means within the United Nations system for improving the effective enjoyment of human rights and fundamental freedoms."

Belgrade Minimal Rules of Procedure for International Human Rights Fact-Finding Missions

Adopted at the Belgrade Session of the International Law Association in 1980

I. Terms of Reference (Mandate)

1. The organ of an organization establishing a fact finding mission should set forth objective terms of reference which do not prejudge the issues to be investigated. These terms should accord with the instrument establishing the organization.
2. The resolution authorizing the mission should not prejudge the mission's work and findings.
3. While terms of reference should not unduly restrict the mission in the investigation of the subject and its context, they should be so specific as to indicate the nature of the subject to be investigated.

II. Selection of Fact Finders

4. The fact finding mission should be composed of persons who are respected for their integrity, impartiality, competence and objectivity and who are serving in their personal capacities.
5. Where the mandate of the mission concerns one or several specific states, in order to facilitate the task of the mission, the government or governments concerned, whenever possible, should be consulted in regard to the composition of the mission.
6. Any person appointed a member of the fact finding mission should not be removed from membership except for reasons of incapacity or gross misbehaviour.
7. The chairman and the rapporteur of the fact finding mission should not be replaced during the term of the mission except for reasons of incapacity or gross misbehaviour.
8. Once a fact finding mission has been established and its chairman and members appointed, no persons should be added to the mission as members except to fill vacancies in the mission.

III. Collection of Evidence

9. At the commencement of the mission, all material relevant to the purpose of the mission should be made available to it, with the assistance of the organization concerned.

10. Fact finding missions should operate with staff sufficient to permit the independent collection of data and should be assisted by such independent experts as the mission may deem necessary.
11. Fact finding missions may invite the submission of evidence that is in writing and contains specific statements of fact that are in their nature verifiable.
12. The state concerned should have an opportunity to comment in writing on data referred to in paragraph 10 and statements referred to in paragraph 11.
13. Both the petitioners, such as states, non–governmental organizations, or groups of individuals, and the states concerned may present lists of witnesses to the fact finding mission. The fact finding mission should make its own determination as to which witnesses it will hear.
14. Petitioners ought ordinarily to be heard by the fact finding mission in public session with an opportunity for questioning by the states concerned.
15. The fact finding mission shall in advance require the state concerned to provide adequate guarantee of non–retaliation against individual petitioners, witnesses and their relatives.
16. In case a guarantee, as referred to in paragraph 15, is provided to the satisfaction of the fact finding mission, the latter should, on hearing witnesses, either provide an opportunity for the state concerned to be present and to question witnesses, or make available to the state concerned a record of the witnesses' testimony for comment.
17. The fact finding mission may withhold information which, in its judgment, may jeopardize the safety or well–being of those giving testimony, or of third parties, or which in its opinion is likely to reveal sources.
18. On the basis of data generated by its staff, written statements, and testimony of witnesses, the fact finding mission should make its own determination as to whether it needs to conduct an on–site inspection.

IV. The On–Site Investigation

19. The fact finding mission should draw up its programme of work, including the list of witnesses it wishes to interview at the site of the investigation, places it wishes to visit, and the sequence, timing and location of its activities on the site.
20. The fact finding mission may operate as a whole or in smaller groups assigned to conduct specific parts of the investigation.

21. The fact finding mission should insist on interviewing any persons it deems necessary, even if incarcerated.

V. Final Stage

22. After conclusion of the on–site investigation, members of the fact finding mission should draw up a set of preliminary findings and submit these, together with supplementary questions where appropriate, to the state concerned, giving it an opportunity, within a reasonable time, to present comments and/or to rectify the matter investigated.
23. A final report shall be prepared by the chairman reflecting the consensus of the fact finding mission. In the absence of a consensus, the mission's report should contain the findings of the majority as well as any views of dissenting members.
24. In case a decision is made to publish the report, it should be published in its entirety.
25. The Organization establishing the fact finding mission should keep under review the compliance of states with their undertaking regarding non–reprisal against petitioners, witnesses, their relatives and associates.

UN General Assembly Resolution 46/59
Declaration on Fact-finding by the United Nations in the Field of the Maintenance of International Peace and Security

(67th plenary meeting, December 9, 1991)

The General Assembly,

Recalling its resolutions 43/170 of 9 December 1988, 44/37 of 4 December 1989 and 45/44 of 28 November 1990,

Taking note of the report of the Special Committee on the Charter of the United Nations and on the Strengthening of the Role of the Organization, which met in New York from 4 to 22 February 1991 and completed a draft Declaration on Fact-finding by the United Nations in the Field of the Maintenance of International Peace and Security,

Convinced that the adoption of the draft Declaration will contribute to strengthening the role of the United Nations and enhancing its effectiveness in maintaining international peace and security,

Considering the need to ensure a wide dissemination of the text of the Declaration,

Considering the Declaration to be an important and concrete contribution of the Special Committee to the United Nations Decade of International Law,

1. *Approves* the Declaration on Fact-finding by the United Nations in the Field of the Maintenance of International Peace and Security, the text of which is annexed to the present resolution;
2. *Expresses* its appreciation to the Special Committee on the Charter of the United Nations and on the Strengthening of the Role of the Organization for its important contribution to the elaboration of the text of the Declaration;
3. *Requests* the Secretary-General to inform the Governments of the States Members of the United Nations or members of specialized agencies, and the Security Council, of the adoption of the Declaration;
4. *Urges* that all efforts be made so that the Declaration becomes generally known and fully implemented.

ANNEX

Declaration on Fact-finding by the United Nations in the Field of the Maintenance of International Peace and Security

The General Assembly,

Recalling the Declaration on Principles of International Law concerning Friendly Relations and Cooperation among States in accordance with the Charter of the United Nations, the Manila Declaration on the Peaceful Settlement of International Disputes, the Declaration on the Enhancement of the Effectiveness of the Principle of Refraining from the Threat or Use of Force in International Relations, the Declaration on the Prevention and Removal of Disputes and Situations Which May Threaten International Peace and Security and on the Role of the United Nations in this Field, and their provisions regarding fact-finding,

Emphasizing that the ability of the United Nations to maintain international peace and security depends to a large extent on its acquiring detailed knowledge about the factual circumstances of any dispute or situation, the continuance of which might threaten the maintenance of international peace and security (hereinafter, "disputes or situations"),

Recognizing that the full use and further improvement of the means for fact-finding of the United Nations could contribute to the strengthening of the role of the United Nations in the maintenance of international peace and security and promote the peaceful settlement of disputes, as well as the prevention and removal of threats to peace,

Desiring to encourage States to bear in mind the role that competent organs of the United Nations can play in ascertaining the facts in relation to disputes or situations,

Recognizing the particular usefulness of fact-finding missions that the competent United Nations organs may undertake in this respect,

Bearing in mind the experience and expertise acquired by the United Nations in the field of fact-finding missions,

Recognizing the need for States, in exercising their sovereignty, to cooperate with the relevant organs of the United Nations as regards fact-finding missions undertaken by them,

Seeking to contribute to the effectiveness of the United Nations, with a view to enhancing mutual understanding, trust and stability in the world,

Solemnly declares that:

I

1. In performing their functions in relation to the maintenance of international peace and security, the competent organs of the

United Nations should endeavour to have full knowledge of all relevant facts. To this end they should consider undertaking fact-finding activities.

2. For the purpose of the present Declaration fact-finding means any activity designed to obtain detailed knowledge of the relevant facts of any dispute or situation which the competent United Nations organs need in order to exercise effectively their functions in relation to the maintenance of international peace and security.

3. Fact-finding should be comprehensive, objective, impartial and timely.

4. Unless a satisfactory knowledge of all relevant facts can be obtained through the use of the information-gathering capabilities of the Secretary-General or other existing means, the competent organ of the United Nations should consider resorting to a fact-finding mission.

5. In deciding if and when to undertake such a mission, the competent United Nations organs should bear in mind that the sending of a fact-finding mission can signal the concern of the Organization and should contribute to building confidence and defusing the dispute or situation while avoiding any aggravation of it.

6. The sending of a United Nations fact-finding mission to the territory of any State requires the prior consent of that State, subject to the relevant provisions of the Charter of the United Nations.

II

7. Fact-finding missions may be undertaken by the Security Council, the General Assembly and the Secretary-General, in the context of their respective responsibilities for the maintenance of international peace and security in accordance with the Charter.

8. The Security Council should consider the possibility of undertaking fact-finding to discharge effectively its primary responsibility for the maintenance of international peace and security in accordance with the Charter.

9. The Security Council should, wherever appropriate, consider the possibility of providing in its resolutions for recourse to fact-finding.

10. The General Assembly should consider the possibility of undertaking fact-finding for exercising effectively its responsibilities under the Charter for the maintenance of international peace and security.

11. The General Assembly should, wherever appropriate, consider the possibility of providing for recourse to fact-finding in its resolutions relevant to the maintenance of international peace and security.
12. The Secretary-General should pay special attention to using the United Nations fact-finding capabilities at an early stage in order to contribute to the prevention of disputes and situations.
13. The Secretary-General, on his own initiative or at the request of the States concerned, should consider undertaking a fact-finding mission when a dispute or a situation exists.
14. The Secretary-General should prepare and update lists of experts in various fields who would be available for fact-finding missions. He should also maintain and develop, within existing resources, capabilities for mounting emergency fact-finding missions.
15. The Security Council and the General Assembly should, in deciding to whom to entrust the conduct of a fact-finding mission, give preference to the Secretary-General, who may, inter alia, designate a special representative or a group of experts reporting to him. Resort to an *ad hoc* subsidiary body of the Security Council or the General Assembly may also be considered.
16. In considering the possibility of undertaking a fact-finding mission, the competent United Nations organ should bear in mind other relevant fact- finding efforts, including those undertaken by the States concerned and in the framework of regional arrangements or agencies.
17. The decision by the competent United Nations organ to undertake fact- finding should always contain a clear mandate for the fact-finding mission and precise requirements to be met by its report. The report should be limited to a presentation of findings of a factual nature.
18. Any request by a State to a competent organ of the United Nations for the sending of a United Nations fact-finding mission to its territory should be considered without undue delay.

III

19. Any request by a competent organ of the United Nations for the consent of a State to receive a fact-finding mission within its territory should be given timely consideration by that State. That State should inform the organ of its decision without delay.
20. In the event a State decides not to admit a United Nations fact-finding mission to its territory, it should, if it deems it appropriate, indicate the reasons for its decision. It should also keep the possibility of admitting the fact-finding mission under review.

21. States should endeavour to follow a policy of admitting United Nations fact-finding missions to their territory.
22. States should cooperate with United Nations fact-finding missions and give them, within the limits of their capabilities, the full and prompt assistance necessary for the exercise of their functions and the fulfilment of their mandate.
23. Fact-finding missions should be accorded all immunities and facilities needed for discharging their mandate, in particular full confidentiality in their work and access to all relevant places and persons, it being understood that no harmful consequences will result to these persons. Fact-finding missions have an obligation to respect the laws and regulations of the State in which they exercise their functions; such laws and regulations should not however be applied in such a way as to hinder missions in the proper discharge of their functions.
24. The members of fact-finding missions, as a minimum, enjoy the privileges and immunities accorded to experts on missions by the Convention on the Privileges and Immunities of the United Nations. Without prejudice to their privileges and immunities, members of fact-finding missions have an obligation to respect the laws and regulations of the State in the territory in which they exercise their functions.
25. Fact-finding missions have an obligation to act in strict conformity with their mandate and perform their task in an impartial way. Their members have an obligation not to seek or receive instructions from any Government or from any authority other than the competent United Nations organ. They should keep the information acquired in discharging their mandate confidential even after the mission has fulfilled its task.
26. The States directly concerned should be given an opportunity, at all stages of the fact-finding process, to express their views in respect of the facts the fact-finding mission has been entrusted to obtain. When the results of fact-finding are to be made public, the views expressed by the States directly concerned should, if they so wish, also be made public.
27. Whenever fact-finding includes hearings, appropriate rules of procedure should ensure their fairness.

IV

28. The Secretary-General should monitor the state of international peace and security regularly and systematically in order to provide early warning of disputes or situations which might threaten international

peace and security. The Secretary-General may bring relevant information to the attention of the Security Council and, where appropriate, of the General Assembly.
29. To this end, the Secretary-General should make full use of the information-gathering capabilities of the Secretariat and keep under review the improvement of these capabilities.

V

30. The sending of a United Nations fact-finding mission is without prejudice to the use by the States concerned of inquiry or any similar procedure or of any means of peaceful settlement of disputes agreed by them.
31. Nothing in the present Declaration is to be construed as prejudicing in any manner the provisions of the Charter.

Rules of the International Humanitarian Fact-Finding Commission

(adopted on July 8, 1992, in Berne and amended on March 11, 2003, in Geneva)

Table of Contents:

PREAMBLE

The Commission:
Having regard to Protocol I Additional to the Geneva Conventions of 1949 for the protection of the victims of armed conflicts, hereinafter referred to as "the Protocol",
Bearing in mind its competence in respect of enquiry as well as of good offices, recognised for the purpose of obtaining the observation of the principles and rules of international law applicable in armed conflict,
Convinced of the need to take all appropriate initiatives as necessary in cooperation with other international bodies, in particular the United Nations, with the purpose of carrying out its functions in the interest of the victims of armed conflict,

Acting under article 90 of the Protocol,
Adopts the present Rules:

PART I – ORGANISATION OF THE COMMISSION

Chapter I – Members of the Commission

Rule 1 – Independence and Solemn Declaration

1. In the performance of their functions, the Members of the Commission (hereinafter referred to as the "Members") shall accept no instructions from any authority or person whatsoever and serve in their personal capacity.
2. Before taking up his duties, each Member shall make the following solemn declaration: "I will exercise my functions as a Member of this Commission impartially, conscientiously and in accordance with the provisions of the Protocol and these Rules, including those concerning secrecy".

Rule 2 – Availability

Unless prevented by serious reasons duly justified to the President, Members shall at all times be able to respond to a call by the President or, as the case may be, by the Head of a Chamber in order to ensure the accomplishment of the Commission's functions under the Protocol.

Rule 3 – Incompatibilities

During their term of office, Members shall not engage in any occupation or make any public statement that may cast a legitimate doubt on their morality and impartiality required by the Protocol. In case of doubt, the Commission shall decide on the proper measures to take.

Rule 4 – Resignation

1. The resignation of a Member shall be addressed to the President, who shall communicate it without delay to the secretariat of the Commission (hereinafter referred to as the "Secretariat"). The Secretariat shall register the resignation under Rule 37 (1).
2. The President shall address his resignation to the first Vice-President.
3. The resignation shall take effect on the day of its registration by the Secretariat who shall without delay inform the Members of the date.

Rule 5 – The Filling of Casual Vacancies

1. The Commission shall ensure that each candidate possesses the qualifications required by article 90 of the Protocol and that, in the Commission as a whole, equitable geographical representation is maintained.
2. In the absence of a consensus among the Members, the following provisions shall apply:
a. When no candidate obtains in the first ballot the majority required, a second ballot, restricted to the two candidates who obtained the highest number of votes, shall be taken.
b. If the second ballot is inconclusive and a majority vote of Members present is required, a third ballot shall be taken in which votes may be cast for any eligible candidate. If the third ballot is inconclusive, the next ballot shall be restricted to the two candidates who obtained the highest number of votes in the third ballot and so on, with unrestricted and restricted ballots alternating, until a Member is elected.
c. The elections referred to in this Rule shall be held by secret ballot. Election shall be by a majority of the Members present.
3. A Member elected under this Rule shall serve for the remainder of the term of his predecessor.

Chapter II - Presidency and Precedence

Rule 6 – Election of the President and Vice-Presidents

1. The Commission shall elect from among its Members a President as well as three Vice-Presidents who together shall constitute the Bureau.
2. The President and the Vice-Presidents shall be elected for a term of 2 years. They may be reelected.
However, the term of office of the President or of a Vice-President shall end if he ceases to be a Member.
3. If the President or a Vice-President ceases to be a Member or resigns his office of President or Vice-President before its normal expiry, the Commission may elect a successor for the remainder of the term of that office.
4. The elections referred to in this Rule shall be held by secret ballot. Election shall be by a majority of the Members.

Rule 7 – Precedence

1. The Vice-Presidents shall take precedence as first, second and third Vice-Presidents after the President according to the duration of their term of office.

2. Vice-Presidents having the same length of time in office shall take precedence according to age.
3. The Members shall take precedence after the President and Vice-Presidents according to the duration of their term of office.
4. Members having the same length of time in office shall take precedence according to age.

Rule 8 – Functions of the President

1. The President shall chair the meetings of the Commission and perform all other functions conferred upon him by the Protocol, these Rules and by the Commission.
2. In exercising his functions, the President shall remain under the authority of the Commission.
3. The President may delegate some of his functions to either Vice-President.
4. In co-operation with the Vice-Presidents and the Secretariat, the President shall take the necessary measures to ensure that the functions of the Commission can be exercised at all times and expeditiously.

Rule 9 – Temporary Replacement of the President

The first Vice-President shall take the place of the President if the presidency is vacant or the President is prevented from carrying out his duties, especially if, in the case of an enquiry, he is a national of a party to the conflict. The second Vice-President shall replace the first Vice-President if the latter is prevented from carrying out his duties or if the office of first Vice-President is vacant. The third Vice-President shall replace the second Vice-President if the latter is prevented from carrying out his duties or if the office of second Vice-President is vacant.

Rule 10 – Replacement of the President and Vice-Presidents

If the President and Vice-Presidents are at the same time prevented from carrying out their duties or if their offices are vacant at the same time, the duties of President shall be carried out by another Member according to the order of precedence established by Rule 7.

PART II – WORKING OF THE COMMISSION

Chapter I – Seat of the Commission, Secretariat and Languages

Rule 11 – Seat of the Commission

The seat of the Commission shall be in Berne, Switzerland.

Rule 12 – Secretariat

The functions of the Secretariat of the Commission shall be assumed by the Depositary State of the Geneva Conventions and the Protocol.

Rule 13 – Languages

The official and working languages of the Commission shall be English and French.

Chapter II - Meetings of the Commission

Rule 14 – Holding of Meetings

1. The Commission shall hold such meetings as it considers necessary to perform its functions. It shall meet at least once a year. The Commission shall also meet if at least one third of the Members so request or the Bureau so decides.
2. The Commission shall hold its meetings at its seat, unless the Commission or the Bureau decides otherwise.
3. Commission meetings shall be convened at dates set by the Commission or by the Bureau.
4. The Secretariat shall notify the Members of the date, time and place of each Commission meeting. Whenever possible, such notification shall be given at least six weeks in advance.

Rule 15 – Agenda

1. Following consultation with the President, the Secretariat shall transmit a draft agenda to the Members of the Commission, whenever possible at least six weeks before a meeting.
2. The agenda shall be adopted by the Commission at the beginning of the meeting.

Rule 16 – Documentation

The Secretariat shall transmit to the Members the working documents relating to the different agenda items, whenever possible at least four weeks in advance.

Rule 17 – Quorum

Eight Members shall constitute a quorum.

Rule 18 – Privacy of Meetings

1. The Commission shall meet in camera. Its deliberations shall remain confidential.

2. Apart from Members, only members of the Secretariat, interpreters and persons assisting the Commission may attend its meetings, unless the Commission determines otherwise.

Rule 19 – Hearings

The Commission may hear any person whom it considers to be in a position to assist it in the performance of its functions.

PART III – ENQUIRIES

Chapter I – Enquiry Request

Rule 20 – Lodging the Request

1. The request for an enquiry shall be addressed to the Secretariat.
2. It shall state the facts that, in the opinion of the requesting party, constitute a grave breach or a serious violation, as well as the date and the place of their occurrence.
3. It shall list the evidence the requesting party wishes to present in support of its allegations.
4. It shall name the authority to which all communications concerning the enquiry shall be addressed, as well as the most expedient means of contacting that authority.
5. Where applicable and to the extent possible, it shall contain, in the enclosure, the original or a certified copy of any document cited in the list of evidence.
6. If the Commission receives a request for an enquiry under article 90(2)(d), and the consent of the other party or parties concerned has not yet been indicated, the Commission shall refer the request to that party or those parties with a request that it or they indicate its or their consent.

Rule 21 – Examination of the Request for an Enquiry

1. On receiving a request for an enquiry, the President shall without delay advise the interested party or parties of it. He shall send them, as soon as possible, a copy of the request as well as its enclosures and, subject to Rule 20(6), advise them of their right to submit, within a fixed time period, their observations concerning the admissibility of the request. The setting of that time limit does not however prevent the Commission from opening the enquiry at once.

2. The Commission may ask the requesting party to supply additional information within a fixed time limit.
3. If the competence of the Commission is contested, the latter shall decide by means of speedy consultation.
4. The Commission shall inform the requesting party if the request does not meet the conditions described in Rule 20, or if an enquiry cannot be conducted for any other reason.
5. All parties to the conflict shall be informed of the Commission's decision to open an enquiry.
6. If, in the course of an enquiry, the requesting party communicates to the Commission the withdrawal of its request, the Chamber shall cease its enquiry only with the consent of the other parties to the conflict. The withdrawal does not affect the payment of the costs of the enquiry in accordance with article 90 (7) of the Protocol.

Rule 22 – Expenses of the Enquiry

The President, in consultation with the Secretariat, shall determine the amount to be advanced by the requesting party to cover the expenses of the enquiry.

Chapter II – The Chamber

Rule 23 – Formation of the Chamber

Unless the interested parties agree otherwise, the following provisions apply:
a. The President shall appoint, after consultation with the Bureau and the parties to the conflict, and on the basis of equitable geographical representation, five Members of the Chamber, not nationals of any party to the conflict.
b. The President shall invite the parties concerned to appoint, within a fixed time period, two additional persons, not nationals of any party to the conflict, as *ad hoc* Members of the Chamber.
c. If one or both of the *ad hoc* Members have not been appointed within the time limit set under Rule 23(b), the President shall immediately make the appointments necessary to fill the seats of the Chamber.
d. The President of the Commission shall appoint the Head of the Chamber.
e. If a Member appointed as a member of a Chamber believes that there are reasons disqualifying him from participating in the enquiry,

he shall immediately impart them to the President, who may appoint another member.

Rule 24 – Custody of documents

All documents relating to an enquiry shall, as soon as possible, be handed over to the Head of the Chamber who shall be responsible for their registration and custody until the conclusion of the enquiry. They shall then be put in the custody of the Secretariat.

Rule 25 – Assistants

1. The Chamber may decide that it shall be assisted by one or more experts or interpreters.
2. All persons assisting the Chamber shall act on the instructions and under the authority of the Head of the Chamber.

Chapter III – Enquiry Procedure

Rule 26 – Instructions

The Commission may establish general or specific instructions or guidelines concerning the enquiry.

Rule 27 – Procedure

1. The Chamber shall invite the parties to the conflict to assist it and to present evidence within a fixed time period. It may also seek any other evidence it considers relevant and may carry out an enquiry in loco.
2. The Chamber shall determine the admissibility and the weight of the evidence presented by the parties to the conflict, and the conditions under which witnesses shall be heard.
3. The President shall remind the interested parties that, during an enquiry in loco, they must assure to the members of the Chamber and all persons accompanying them the privileges and immunities necessary for the discharge of their functions which shall not be less extensive than those accorded to the experts on mission under the 1946 Convention on Privileges and Immunities of the United Nations, as well as their adequate protection.
4. During an enquiry in loco, the members of the Chamber shall be issued a document stating their capacity, as well as a white badge displaying in clearly visible black letters the name of the Commission in the local language.

5. The members of the Chamber may separate in order to conduct simultaneous enquiries at different places. In particular, the Chamber may, at any time, detach two or more of its members for an urgent enquiry on the spot and, if necessary, to ensure the preservation of evidence.
6. The quorum of the Chamber shall be fixed by the Commission in its instructions to the Chamber.
7. The Chamber shall, as soon as possible, communicate the results of its enquiry to the Commission in accordance with the instructions given to it.
8. All the evidence shall be fully disclosed to the parties concerned who shall be informed of their right to comment on it to the Commission.
9. If necessary, the Commission may instruct the Chamber to undertake a complementary enquiry.

Chapter IV – Report and Obligation of Confidentiality

Rule 28 – Preparation of the Commission's Report

1. After each enquiry the Commission shall draw up, in the light of the Chamber's findings, a report to be transmitted to the parties concerned. In particular, the Commission shall consider, as appropriate, whether it should take steps to facilitate, through its good offices, the restoration of an attitude of respect for the Geneva Conventions and the Protocol.
2. The President shall transmit the report together with any recommendations the Commission considers appropriate to the parties concerned.
3. The President shall have the date on which the Commission's report was sent to the interested parties duly registered. The Secretariat shall keep in its archives copies of the communications of the Chambers and the reports of the Commission in its custody. These records are accessible only to Members while in office.

Rule 29 – Confidentiality

1. No personal data shall be published without the express consent of the person concerned.
2. Members of the Commission, *ad hoc* members of the Chambers, experts and other persons assisting the Commission or a Chamber are

under an obligation, during and after their terms of office, to keep secret the facts or information of which they have become aware during the discharge of their functions.
3. The experts and other persons hired to assist the Commission or a Chamber shall, as a condition of their engagement, be required to agree, as a rule in writing, to comply with paragraph 2.

PART IV – METHODS OF WORK

Chapter I – Conduct of Business

Rule 30 – Powers of the President

The President shall declare the opening and closing of each meeting of the Commission, direct the discussion, ensure observance of these Rules, accord the right to speak, put questions to the vote and announce decisions. The President, subject to these Rules, shall have control over the proceedings of the Commission and over the maintenance of order at its meetings. The President may, in the course of the discussion of an item, propose to the Commission the limitation of the time to be allowed to speakers, the limitation of the number of times each speaker may speak on any question and the closure of the list of speakers. He shall rule on points of order. He shall also have the power to propose adjournment or closure of the debate or adjournment or suspension of a meeting.

Rule 31 – Proposals

A proposal must be submitted in writing, if a Member so requests.

Rule 32 – Order of Voting on Proposals and Amendments

1. Where a number of proposals relate to the same subject, they shall be put to the vote in the order in which they were submitted. In case of doubt about priority, the President shall decide.
2. Where a proposal is the subject of an amendment, the amendment shall be put to the vote first. Where two or more amendments to the same proposal are presented, the Commission shall vote first on whichever departs furthest in substance from the original proposal, and so on until all the amendments have been put to the vote. However, where the acceptance of one amendment necessarily entails rejection of

another, the latter shall not be put to the vote. The final vote shall then be taken on the proposal as amended or not amended. In case of doubt as to the order of priority, the President shall decide.
3. A motion may be withdrawn by the Member who proposed it at any time before voting on it has commenced, provided that the motion has not been amended. A motion which has thus been withdrawn may be reintroduced by any Member.

Rule 33 – Order of Procedural Motions

Procedural motions shall take precedence over all other proposals.

Rule 34 – Voting

As a rule, the Commission decides by consensus. In the absence of consensus, the following provisions apply:

a. Subject to the provisions of Rules 6(4), 39 and 40, the decisions of the Commission shall be taken by a majority of the Members present.
b. In matters other than elections, a proposal shall be regarded as rejected if the majority referred to under letter (a) heretofore is not obtained.
c. Subject to Rules 5 (2)(d) and 6 (4), the Commission shall vote by show of hands, unless a Member requests a roll call vote.
d. After a vote has commenced, there shall be no interruption of the voting except on a point of order by a Member in connection with the actual conduct of the voting.

Chapter II – Working Modalities

Rule 35 – Reports of Meetings

1. The Secretariat shall prepare a draft report of the Commission's deliberations and decisions following each meeting. The draft report shall be circulated as soon as possible to the Members of the Commission, who will be given the opportunity to submit corrections within a prescribed time-limit.
2. If no corrections are submitted, the meeting report shall be deemed adopted. If corrections are submitted, they shall be consolidated in a single document and circulated to all Members. In this latter case, the adoption of the report of the meeting shall be taken up at the next meeting of the Commission.

Rule 36 – Working Groups

The Commission may set up *ad hoc* working groups comprising a limited number of its Members. The terms of reference of such working groups shall be defined by the Commission.

Rule 37 – Communications

1. The Secretariat shall register and bring to the Commission's attention communications received containing information which may be of interest to the Members.
2. Such communications received by a Member shall be forwarded to the Secretariat.
3. The Secretariat shall acknowledge receipt of the communications to their authors.

Rule 38 – Report of Activities

Subject to the obligation of confidentiality stated in Rule 29, the Commission shall issue, whenever it considers it useful, a general report on its activities to the governments of the High Contracting Parties to the Geneva Conventions. The Commission may also prepare such reports and make such public statements relating to its functions as it considers appropriate and in conformity with the provisions of the Protocol and these Rules concerning confidentiality.

PART V – AMENDMENTS AND SUSPENSION

Rule 39 – Amendments of the Rules

The present Rules may be amended by a decision taken by a majority of the Members, subject to the provisions of the Protocol.

Rule 40 – Suspension of a Provision of the Rules

Upon the proposal of a Member, the application of a provision of these Rules may be suspended by a decision taken by a majority of the Members, subject to the provisions of the Protocol. The suspension of a provision shall be limited in its operation to the particular purpose for which such suspension has been sought.

Guidelines for the Conduct of UN Inquiries into Allegations of Massacres (1995) – DPI/1710

Introduction

1. On 9 June 1993, the President of the Security Council made a statement on behalf of the Council, in which he, inter alia, condemned a massacre of civilians which had occurred on 6 June 1993 near Harbel, Liberia, and requested the Secretary-General to undertake a thorough and full investigation and to report to the Council as soon as possible. By a letter dated 4 August 1993, the Secretary-General informed the President of the Security Council that he had appointed a three-member panel of inquiry with the following mandate: (a) to establish the facts and circumstances relating to the incident at Harbel; (b) to examine allegations regarding responsibility for the massacre; and (c) to make appropriate recommendations.
2. The panel of inquiry submitted to the Secretary-General an executive summary of its report, dated 10 September 1993. Among its conclusions, the panel stated that "There was no procedure in place to systematically collect and preserve readily available information concerning the massacre which could have served as a basis for future investigations" (paragraph 108). Furthermore, the panel recommended, inter alia, that "The UN should develop practical guidelines and procedures for rapid, methodical collection and preservation of evidence and interviews of eyewitnesses, for use wherever such tragedies may occur" (paragraph 112).
3. The Secretary-General on 17 September 1993 informed the members of the Council of the findings of the Panel of Inquiry, and indicated that he would carefully study the recommendations contained in its report in order to determine what further actions would be appropriate on the part of the United Nations. In a letter dated 17 November 1993 to the President of the Security Council, the Secretary-General spelled out a number of recommendations and decisions, among which was that he had asked the Legal Counsel of the United Nations, in cooperation with other relevant departments of the United Nations, to undertake the preparation of guidelines and procedures for the conduct of inquiries by the United Nations into allegations of massacres.
4. The guidelines and procedures mentioned in the preceding paragraph are set out below.

5. Since massacres or other atrocities have been investigated in the past by the United Nations, through *ad hoc* missions or assignments, the guidelines set out below do not purport to replace or overlap with existing missions or assignments. They rather provide a frame of reference and guidance for *ad hoc* investigations for which there are no or few specific guidelines or rules already in place. However, certain provisions of the guidelines may not be appropriate in all cases. The guidelines must be tailored to the mandate of each particular inquiry, as well as to its object and purpose. It should also be noted that the Special Rapporteur of the Commission on Human Rights on Extrajudicial, Summary or Arbitrary Executions (hereafter "Special Rapporteur") has been entrusted by the Commission with a standing mandate to investigate allegations of massacres and other violations of the right to life. The present guidelines are without prejudice to the mandate of the Special Rapporteur, and to the possible participation of the Special Rapporteur in commissions of inquiry established under the present guidelines.

6. The term "massacre" is used to indicate the extrajudicial killing of a number of persons. While these guidelines do not indicate a precise number of victims to qualify the killings as a "massacre", it should be noted that, according to the Special Rapporteur, the term "massacre" should refer to the extrajudicial, summary or arbitrary killing of at least three persons.

7. Under international law, States are obliged to carry out impartial and exhaustive investigations into all allegations of massacres and other extrajudicial, summary or arbitrary killings, with a view to clarifying the circumstances, identifying those responsible, bringing them to justice, compensating the victims or their families and taking all necessary action to prevent the recurrence of similar acts in the future. The results of such investigations must be made public. An inquiry by a United Nations organ cannot absolve Governments from their obligation under international law to investigate violations of the right to life. The obligations of States in this respect have been spelled out, inter alia, in the "Principles on the Effective Prevention and Investigation of Extralegal, Arbitrary and Summary Executions" annexed to Economic and Social Council resolution 1989/65 (attached as Annex I). The task of the United Nations may consist in the gathering of the available evidence and a prima facie assessment of the evidence received as well as the situation surrounding the investigation, but it may also consist of a thorough in-depth investigation or in the monitoring and supervision

of investigations undertaken by the competent authorities. These guidelines should be applied by the United Nations in any such inquiry, irrespective of procedures provided for in the legislation in force in the area concerned.

I Mandate for the Conduct of an Inquiry

8. The guidelines are based on the assumption that an appropriate mandate has been given to the Secretary-General for the conduct of an inquiry by an intergovernmental organ of the United Nations. It is also assumed that the Government or the authorities exercising jurisdiction or control over the area, persons and information concerned, will cooperate with the United Nations and grant it full access to all places, persons and information deemed relevant for the investigation. The intergovernmental organ requesting or authorizing the Secretary-General to carry out the inquiry should call upon the State or States concerned, and any other authority in control of the area concerned, to fully cooperate with the United Nations in the discharge of its mandate.
9. The Secretary-General should establish terms of reference for any inquiry requested, subject to such terms as may be provided by the requesting or authorizing organ. The terms of reference of an inquiry should include the following:

(a) To determine whether a massacre has been committed;
(b) To collect evidence related to the massacre;
(c) To obtain statements and testimony concerning the massacre;
(d) To determine the cause, manner, location and time of the massacre;
(e) To identify, as far as possible, the victims;
(f) To identify the persons involved in committing the massacre;
(g) To make recommendations to the Secretary-General or to other appropriate United Nations organs or officials, and to the State or States concerned.

II Preliminary Assessment

10. On the basis of the appropriate mandate requesting or authorizing the Secretary-General to carry out an inquiry, and if circumstances so

require (e.g. if a commission of inquiry cannot be established promptly or travel to the area and there is a risk that evidence may be lost) the Secretary-General may request or invite personnel of UN offices or agencies present in the area or in the country concerned, to gain access to the place of the alleged event.

11. The Secretary-General shall seek the express consent of the relevant authorities to this course of action. If such consent is given, UN personnel should, together with the competent authorities, make a preliminary on-site assessment; establish a photographic record; establish what steps have been taken to investigate the facts and determine responsibilities; and verify what remedial action has been taken. The Secretariat of the United Nations should disseminate as widely as possible to UN bodies and agencies normally having a presence in the field (e.g. UNDP, UNICEF, UNHCR, WFP, peace-keeping operations, and specialized agencies) a form to facilitate and standardize this preliminary collection of information. Reference could be made for this purpose to the Database Incident Form developed by the Commission of Experts established by Security Council resolution 780 (1992), which is attached to these guidelines as Annex II.

12. UN personnel involved should also, if feasible, compile a list of witnesses or other persons who may provide relevant information. These persons should be fully identified, including their address and telephone number, with a view to contacting them in the future. They should be encouraged to inform the United Nations if they move to a different locality. Even at this stage, however, persons identified and contacted as possible witnesses should be encouraged to give written declarations, should it not be possible to contact them in the future and in order to assess what kind of security measures may be needed for their protection.

13. The competent authorities in the area must provide continuous surveillance and security of the scene of the massacre, in order to prevent and deter destruction of, or tampering with, material evidence. With the consent of the competent authorities, such security should be complemented by the presence of United Nations personnel.

14. UN personnel should report their preliminary findings as soon as possible to the Secretary-General, who in turn should submit a report on such findings to any commission of inquiry subsequently established (see below).

15. It should be noted that the Secretary-General may not need to request a preliminary assessment if, pursuant to the relevant mandate, a commission of inquiry can be appointed and travel to the area

promptly and if there is little risk that evidence might be tampered with or be lost.

III Commission of Inquiry

16. Having received a request or authorization from a competent intergovernmental organ to conduct an inquiry, the Secretary-General should appoint a commission of inquiry as soon as possible to assist him in conducting the inquiry, unless he concludes, on the basis of the preliminary assessment carried out, that there is no basis to continue the inquiry. Members of the commission should be selected on the basis of their impartiality, competence and independence. The commission should consist of at least three members and include individuals with expertise in medicine, forensic science, crime investigation, criminal law and other specialized fields, as appropriate. The Secretary-General may arrange assistance to the commission in carrying out its tasks *[1 If the Secretary-General retains the services of organizations or entities outside the United Nations system to assist the commission, an agreement should be concluded for this purpose. The agreement should indicate the requirements and conditions applicable, including in particular, a commitment by the organization to keep their findings strictly confidential and to transmit the results of its work solely to the Secretary-General].* United Nations personnel should in any case participate and assist in the investigation. The commission should travel to the area concerned as soon as possible.
17. Even in the variety of concrete situations that a commission of inquiry might face, it should monitor activities undertaken by Government or other authorities in control of the area in the following fields:

(a) Preliminary investigations, if necessary, to locate the burial site;
(b) Processing of the crime scene and on-site investigation, including exhumations;
(c) Autopsies and other laboratory analyses;
(d) Interviews and gathering of testimonies;
(e) Examination of governmental records and documents, and monitoring of governmental or judicial activities in connection with the alleged massacre.

18. If necessary and appropriate, the commission itself may undertake the above activities. If the mandate of the commission consists wholly or partly of the gathering of evidence for future prosecution, the

commission should bear in mind the rules and conditions for the admissibility of evidence by the authorities which will carry out the prosecution.
19. The commission shall utilize to the maximum extent feasible technical documents prepared by the United Nations to assist in investigations of extrajudicial killings, in particular the protocols contained in the Manual on the Effective Prevention and Investigation of Extralegal, Arbitrary and Summary Executions (hereafter "the Manual"). Particular attention should be paid to the Model Protocol for a Legal Investigation of Extralegal, Arbitrary and Summary Executions ("Minnesota Protocol"), attached to these guidelines as Annex III.

IV Right of Access and Cooperation of the Competent Authorities

20. The commission, on the basis of the authority provided for in its mandate, should receive assurances from the relevant authorities that its members and accompanying UN staff will enjoy the following:

- Freedom of movement and facilitation of transport.
- Freedom of inquiry, in particular (a) access to prisons, detention centres and places of interrogation; (b) contacts with central and local authorities through the establishment of clear lines of communication, including the appointment of one or more contact persons; (c) contacts with representatives of NGOs, other private institutions and the media; (d) contacts with witnesses and other persons considered necessary for the fulfilment of the mandate; (e) full access to all documentary material relevant to the mandate.
- Appropriate security arrangements, without restricting the freedom of movement and inquiry.
- The written material and records of the commission, including all written, audio and video records of interviews, as well as all other material evidence gathered by the commission during the inquiry, shall constitute property and archives of the United Nations and shall enjoy the treatment granted to such property and archives under Article II of the Convention on the Privileges and Immunities of the United Nations.

21. The conclusion of an agreement or arrangements on the privileges and immunities of the members and the secretariat of the commission

may be necessary. The agreement should, as a minimum, contain the provisions indicated in the previous paragraph.

V Collection and Preservation of Material Evidence

(a) Location of burial sites

22. If the location of a burial site is unclear, the commission shall conduct interviews (see section VI below), review documents and make on-site investigations to ascertain the location of the burial sites. The commission should interview survivors, witnesses to the event, people living in the locality of the possible burial site, individuals who may have information about the use of a certain area as a burial site. The commission should also try to gather antemortem records of the persons believed to be buried in a specific site, e.g. through interviews with relatives.

23. To locate the burial site within an approximate area, the commission should use the services of a forensic archaeologist. The commission should photograph and sketch the area before any excavation or other activity is commenced.

(b) On-site investigation and disinterment

24. The processing of the crime scene may entail different activities, according to whether the site has already been wholly or partly excavated or has been otherwise disturbed; whether the bodies have been removed; whether the area has already undergone a thorough analysis and search for possible remains and other evidence. In any case, the commission should have among its members or technical experts experienced crime investigators and forensic experts, possibly including archaeologists and anthropologists.

25. If the site has not been excavated, the commission should either undertake the excavation and disinterment, or should monitor and supervise a disinterment undertaken by the relevant authorities. In the latter case, if the authorities so request, the commission may give advice and guidance on the technical aspects of the disinterment. The dates, location, starting and finishing time of the disinterment, and the name of all workers should be recorded. During the disinterment process, the work area should be photographed from the same perspective before work begins and after it ends every day to document any extraneous disturbance.

26. Any material evidence gathered in the course of the disinterment should be recorded, photographed, numbered and packaged. Their custody, in the course of their analysis and processing, should be entrusted to the commission or to a clearly designated authority accessible by the commission.
27. The disinterment should be carried out following the archeological and anthropological criteria and procedures provided for in the Model Protocol for Disinterment and Analysis of Skeletal Remains, contained in Chapter V of the Manual. This should also be used, as relevant, in case the burial site has already been excavated and the bodies or skeletal remains removed. The Model Protocol is attached to these guidelines as Annex V.
28. It is possible, especially in the case of investigations taking place some time after the alleged massacre, that bodies have been removed from the place of the massacre. In such cases, the commission should also conduct onsite investigations, using as much as possible the criteria and procedures set out above, in order to collect any relevant evidence with a view to reconstructing the sequence of events concerning the massacre.

(c) Autopsy and laboratory analysis
29. Bodies and human remains should, if circumstances so warrant, be subject to laboratory analysis either by the commission of inquiry or by the competent authorities under the monitoring of the commission of inquiry. It is particularly important that appropriate laboratory analyses are performed when the cause, manner or time of death are disputed or difficult to ascertain. The commission of inquiry should request adequate facilities from the relevant authorities for the performance of the necessary analyses, including autopsy rooms, X-ray equipment and adequately trained personnel; the bodies to be subject to analysis should be put at the disposal of the commission for a minimum of 12 hours. Since investigations of cases of multiple killings frequently involve analysis of both soft and hard tissues, the commission should comprise, or use the services of, both a prosecutor and a forensic anthropologist.
30. A record should be established of which autopsy specimens have been saved. The specimens should be labeled with the name of the deceased, an autopsy number, the date of collection and the contents. The specimens should be left in the custody of a clearly identified authority with competence for such custody. Access to the specimens

should be limited to as few persons as possible. The chain of custody and the authority to order release should be clarified and fully disclosed to the commission; the specimens should be made promptly available to the commission upon request for possible further examination.
31. Autopsies carried out should follow the procedures and principles provided for in the Model Autopsy Protocol set out in Chapter IV of the Manual and attached to these guidelines as Annex IV.

(d) Analysis of skeletal remains
32. In the event of laboratory analysis of skeletal remains, the commission of inquiry should follow the procedures set out in the Model Protocol for Disinterment and analysis of Skeletal Remains, set out in Chapter V of the Manual and attached to these guidelines as Annex V. It is particularly important that skeletal remains which are retained for possible further analysis be placed in the custody of the competent authorities under the arrangements described in paragraph 32 above.

VI Interviews and Testimonies

(a) General
33. Gathering of evidence through interviews is an essential part of the inquiry. The kind of information to be sought, the persons to be interviewed and the objective of the interviews may differ according to the mandate of the commission (e.g. determine whether a massacre has taken place; ascertain the facts; determine responsibilities; assess the actions taken by the competent authorities; prepare evidence for possible prosecution; make recommendations for follow-up actions, etc., as well as any combination of the foregoing).
34. The persons to be interviewed would normally fall within one or more of the following categories: survivors; alleged perpetrators; officials or authorities involved at some stage in the event or with knowledge of it; friends and relatives of the victims; direct witnesses or persons with indirect knowledge of the event (e.g. by hearsay); persons with a specific knowledge of the event for particular reasons (e.g. staff of international organizations, members of the press, etc.). All information received by the commission of inquiry, especially if provided by political parties and other groups which might attempt to use the inquiry as an instrument for their own ends, should be evaluated with caution.

35. The commission should be flexible as to the manner of conducting its interviews and adapt it to the circumstances of the case and the individual interviewees, in order to gather an optimal amount of evidence from its interviews. At the same time, it should ensure consistency in its methodology and approach, so as to facilitate comparisons between interviews and any necessary follow-up.
36. Survivors, eyewitnesses and alleged perpetrators should be interviewed by persons with a specific background such as lawyers or trained military or police investigators. This is particularly important in case the information gathered by the commission could serve for future prosecution. In case of interviews with alleged perpetrators, the commission should advise them as to the possible consequences of their statements and that they may, should they so wish, be assisted by counsel. The commission of inquiry, however, is itself an investigative body, not a judicial organ, and this should be made clear to persons being interviewed. If the commission deems it desirable, in the light of the circumstances, that a formal interrogation or hearing be conducted by the competent authorities, the commission should be satisfied that the interviewees will have a right to their own counsel and enjoy other guarantees of a fair hearing.
37. The commission should protect, as appropriate, the identity of the interviewee and the confidentiality of the information provided by him or her. To this end, and to avoid intimidation, the commission should seek from the outset clear assurances as to its right to conduct interviews independently and in private. The commission should limit in principle participation of Government officials or other authorities in the interviews. This should only be allowed on a case by case basis and with the explicit consent of the interviewee.

(b) Conduct of interviews *[2 The following section is excerpted from the document Guidelines for the Gathering of Information and the Conduct of Interviews, prepared by the Secretariat of the Commission of Experts Established Pursuant to Security Council resolution 780 (1992).]*
38. Pre-interview. A background interview should be conducted before having the interviewees give their statement for the record. This will typically consist of several preliminary, but important, questions: name, address, date of birth, other personal information, and some informal questions to help the interviewee feel more at ease. The interviewer can use the background interview to identify any bias, motive, or inconsistencies in the interviewee's statement.

39. The interviewer must clearly identify the interviewee as a victim, witness or alleged perpetrator as this will determine the method and line of questioning.
40. The interviews must be freely and voluntarily provided. The interviewer should establish this as part of the record of the interview by asking specific questions as to whether the interviewee's statement is being given voluntarily. In the case of an alleged perpetrator, a photograph of the interviewee before the statement and another thereafter should be made part of the record to demonstrate that the interviewee was not physically abused during the statement.
41. There should always be at least two persons present during the interview, with the addition of a professional interpreter if necessary. One person prepares the interview and asks the questions, and the other takes notes and ensures that a complete record of the interview is made. Whenever possible a trained professional of the same sex as the interviewee should conduct the interview. A high level of sensitivity must be used in case of interviews with survivors and traumatized witnesses.
42. The interviews should preferably be conducted in a private room with only the interviewee, the interviewers and the interpreter present. In certain cases the person interviewed may wish or need someone else to be present for support or counsel. This person's role should be limited to support or counsel the interviewee in case of need.
43. Method of recording. The interview should be recorded if the person being interviewed consents.
(1) Video taping. If the interviewee does not wish to be identified, the interviewer should assure him or her that measures can be employed to conceal his or her identity (e.g. electronic alteration or obscuring facial features). The video recorder should be unobtrusive, run continuously throughout the interview and display the date and time of the interview. All videotaped interviews should be transcribed.
(2) Audio taping. The audio recorder should run continuously throughout the interview. Documents, photographs or other objects utilized or referred to in the statement should be described for the record. Physical gestures and indicators of demeanor should also be described. All audiotaped interviews should be transcribed.
(3) Written record. Comprehensive notes must be taken by the person assisting the interviewer. Documents, photographs or other objects utilized or referred to in the statement should be described for the

record. Physical gestures and indicators of demeanor should also be described.

44. Interpreters. Interpreters must understand that everything the interviewer and interviewee say must be interpreted. It is not sufficient to summarize. They cannot fill in missing information from their own knowledge, nor "improve" the words of the interviewees so that they sound more coherent, credible or educated. The interpreter must allow interviewer and interviewee to ask for clarification whenever necessary. Any names must be clearly spelled out. There must be clear agreement between the interpreter and the interviewer on the spelling of certain words in the language in which the interview is being conducted as well as the alphabet to be used.

45. Conducting the interview. Each interview should begin with the establishment, in writing or other means, for the record, of the conditions under which the interview was conducted. This should include:

(a) an introduction of all those present and an explanation of their role, to be repeated at the beginning of each new audio or video tape if the interview requires more than one;
(b) a statement from the interviewee that the interview is being given freely and voluntarily. In the case of an alleged perpetrator, the statement should also include a full reading of all applicable rights, including the right to counsel;
(c) the agreement from the interviewee on the method of recording;
(d) any confidentiality restriction;
(e) a full identification of the interviewee and how he or she can be contacted;
(f) a statement from the interviewee that he or she understands the interpreter and is satisfied with the interpretation.

46. The interviewer should guide the conversation to keep the interviewee from rambling and corroborate information collected from other sources. The interviewer should employ the following techniques: (a) ask one question at a time; (b) avoid leading questions; (c) keep the questions simple; (d) ask questions that encourage a narrative response and avoid questions that lead to "yes" and "no" answers; (e) frame questions in a positive manner.

47. Any documents, records, recording, statements or other items obtained during the interview should be handled as potential evidence.

These items should be kept under the custody of the commission. A record should be kept of all those who have access to this material so that a chain of custody can be established.
48. At the end of the interview, the interviewee should have the opportunity of adding further statements, orally or in writing, before any final initialing or signing of notes or statements.
49. Verifying statement. The interviewee should verify his or her statement. It is preferable to obtain the interviewee's statement in writing, to be initialed on every page and signed at the end by the interviewee, the interviewer and the interpreter. If a written statement cannot be obtained from the interviewee, it should be prepared for him or her, preferably under his or her dictation, and should be initialed and signed by him or her. If this cannot be obtained, the interviewee should read, initial and sign the notes taken by the person recording the interview. In the absence of any written record or notes, the interviewee should listen to or view, and confirm in writing, the audio-or videotaped recording of the interview. In case the interviewee is illiterate, his/her statement should be read out to him/her, if needed with the help of an interpreter. It should be mentioned at the end of the written statement that the interviewee has fully understood the statement and agrees with its contents; this clause should be certified by the interviewer and the interpreter through their signature, and by the interviewee with his/her fingerprint.

VIII Report of the Secretary-General

50. The inquiry conducted by the commission should lead to a detailed report of its findings. The contents and format of the report, however, will depend on the mandate and the terms of reference of the commission (e.g. determine whether a massacre has taken place; ascertain the facts; determine responsibilities; assess the actions taken by the competent authorities; prepare evidence for possible prosecution; make recommendations for follow-up actions, etc., as well as any combination of the foregoing), thus it is not possible to give exhaustive indications in these guidelines as to how a report should be structured and what it should contain.
51. The commission should decide at the outset of its inquiry whether, in case of a decision by majority vote, the minority commissioner(s) may file a dissenting opinion.

52. The final report of a commission of inquiry should contain as a minimum the following elements:

(a) The scope of inquiry and terms of reference, the composition of the commission and a chronological description of its activities;
(b) The background to the inquiry such as relevant social, political and economic conditions;
(c) Evaluation of the evidence, and description of the procedures and methods used in such evaluation;
(d) A list of all persons who have testified, except for those whose identities are withheld for protection, and a list of the exhibits received in evidence during the interviews;
(e) An analytical description of the on-site investigations, laboratory analysis and other activities carried out by the commission, together with a list of items gathered in this connection and an indication of the arrangements made for their custody;
(f) A description of the events as reconstructed by the commission and the evidence upon which such findings are based;
(g) If applicable, the law upon which the commission relied;
(h) The commission's conclusions based upon findings of fact and, if relevant, the applicable law;
(i) If in line with the mandate of the commission, recommendations based upon its findings.

53. The commission should prepare an executive summary of its report as well as a full version. The executive summary should be submitted as soon as possible to the Secretary-General after the conclusion of the inquiry, especially in case the preparation of the full report may take longer. The executive summary should contain the elements mentioned in the previous paragraph under (a), (b), (c), (f), (g), (h) and (i).
54. The commission shall not disclose the outcome of its investigations.
55. The Secretary-General shall include the report of the commission of inquiry in any report he submits to the intergovernmental organ which requested or authorized the inquiry. The Secretary-General should, in principle, make his report available to the Special Rapporteur as well as to the public, subject to any decisions taken by the intergovernmental organ concerned. However, the report, or parts thereof, shall not be made public in cases in which the Secretary-General concludes that disclosure would lead to the destruction of evidence, put persons involved in the investigation at risk, or place in jeopardy the success of any future prosecutions.

Methods of Work of the Special Rapporteur on Torture

Annex to E/CN.4/1997/7, approved by the Commission in resolution 2001/62 (E/CN.4/RES/2001)

1. The Special Rapporteur's methods of work are based on his mandate as stipulated originally in Commission on Human Rights resolution 1985/33 and as developed by the Commission in numerous further resolutions. The parameters of his work are set forth in the International Bill of Human Rights and other United Nations instruments containing provisions that guarantee the right not to be tortured or subjected to cruel, inhuman or degrading treatment or punishment.
2. The Special Rapporteur carries out the following main types of activity:

(a) Seeking and receiving credible and reliable information from Governments, the specialized agencies and intergovernmental and non-governmental organizations;
(b) Making urgent appeals to Governments to clarify the situation of individuals whose circumstances give grounds to fear that treatment falling within the Special Rapporteur's mandate might occur or be occurring;
(c) Transmitting to Governments information of the sort mentioned in (a) above indicating that acts falling within his mandate may have occurred or that legal or administrative measures are needed to prevent the occurrence of such acts;
(d) carrying out visits in situ with the consent of the Government concerned.

3. An urgent appeal is made on the basis of information received by the Special Rapporteur expressing concern about the fact that a person is at risk of being subjected to torture. Such concern may be based, inter alia, on accounts by witnesses of the person's physical condition while in detention, or on the fact that the person is kept incommunicado, a situation which may be conducive to torture. The Special Rapporteur, when making a determination as to whether there are reasonable grounds to believe that an identifiable risk of torture exists, takes into account a number of factors, any one of which may be sufficient, though generally more than one will be present. These factors include: (a) the previous reliability of the source of information; (b) the internal consistency of the information; (c) the consistency of

the information with information on other cases from the country in question that has come to the Special Rapporteur's attention; (d) the existence of authoritative reports of torture practices from national sources, such as official commissions of inquiry; (e) the findings of other international bodies, such as those established in the framework of the United Nations human rights machinery; (f) the existence of national legislation, such as that permitting prolonged incommunicado detention, that can have the effect of facilitating torture; and (g) the threat of extradition or deportation, directly or indirectly, to a State or territory where one or more of the above elements are present.

4. The urgent appeal procedure is not per se accusatory, but essentially preventive in nature and purpose. The Government concerned is merely requested to look into the matter and to take steps aimed at protecting the right to physical and mental integrity of the person concerned, in accordance with the international human rights standards.

5. In view of the fact that the urgent appeal contains information that is extremely time-sensitive, the appeal is addressed directly to the foreign affairs ministry or department of the country concerned.

6. The Special Rapporteur, where appropriate, sends urgent appeals jointly with other organs of the United Nations human rights machinery.

7. The Special Rapporteur transmits to Governments summaries of all credible and reliable information addressed to him alleging individual cases as well as practices of torture. At the same time he requests the Governments to look into those allegations and to provide him with relevant information on them. In addition, the Special Rapporteur urges Governments to take steps to investigate the allegations; to prosecute and impose appropriate sanctions on any persons guilty of torture regardless of any rank, office or position they may hold; to take effective measures to prevent the recurrence of such acts; and to compensate the victims or their relatives in accordance with the relevant international standards.

8. The Special Rapporteur analyses responses from Governments and transmits the contents to the sources of the allegations, as appropriate, for comment. If required, dialogue with the Government is then pursued further.

9. The Special Rapporteur does, where appropriate, acknowledge the existence of persistent acts of violence, including torture, committed by armed groups when these are brought to his attention.

However, in transmitting allegations of torture he deals exclusively with Governments, as the authorities bound by the regime for the international legal protection of human rights.

10. The Special Rapporteur maintains contact and, where appropriate, engages in consultation with related bodies and mechanisms of the United Nations human rights machinery, such as the Committee against Torture and other organs of the Commission on Human Rights, the Board of Trustees of the United Nations Voluntary Fund for Victims of Torture and the Commission on Crime Prevention and Criminal Justice.

11. The Special Rapporteur does not, as a rule, seek to visit a country in respect of which the United Nations has established a country-specific mechanism such as a special rapporteur on the country, unless a joint visit seems to both to be indicated. As regards countries where the mandates of other thematic mechanisms may also be affected, he seeks consultation with them with a view to exploring with the Government in question, either jointly or in parallel, the possibility of a joint visit. Similarly, where the Committee against Torture is considering the situation in a country under article 20 of the Convention against Torture and Other Cruel, Inhuman or Degrading Treatment or Punishment, especially if that consideration involves a visit or possible visit to the country in question, the Special Rapporteur does not seek a visit.

12. The Special Rapporteur carries out visits to countries on invitation, but also takes the initiative of approaching Governments with a view to carrying out visits to countries on which he has received information indicating the existence of a significant incidence of torture. Such visits allow the Special Rapporteur to gain more direct knowledge of cases and situations falling within his mandate, and are intended to enhance the dialogue between the Special Rapporteur and the authorities most directly concerned, as well as with the alleged victims, their families and their representatives and concerned non-governmental organizations. The visits also allow the Special Rapporteur to address detailed recommendations to Governments.

13. With regard to countries in which visits have been carried out, the Special Rapporteur periodically reminds Governments concerned of the observations and recommendations formulated in the respective reports, requesting information on the consideration given to them and the steps taken for their implementation, or the constraints which might have prevented their implementation.

14. The Special Rapporteur reports annually to the Commission on Human Rights on the activities which he has undertaken since the Commission's previous session. He may also make observations on specific situations, as well as conclusions and recommendations, where appropriate.

International Non-Governmental Organisations Accountability Charter December 20, 2005

International NGO Charter of Accountability Ltd. www.ingoaccountabilitycharter.org

Who We Are

We, international non-government organisations (INGOs) signatory to this Charter, are independent non-profit organisations that work globally to advance human rights, sustainable development, environmental protection, humanitarian response and other public goods.
Our organisations are proud and privileged to work across a wide range of countries and cultures, with a diverse range of peoples and in varied eco- and social and political systems.
Our right to act is based on universally-recognised freedoms of speech, assembly and association, on our contribution to democratic processes, and on the values we seek to promote.
Our legitimacy is also derived from the quality of our work, and the recognition and support of the people with and for whom we work and our members, our donors, the wider public, and governmental and other organisations around the world.
We seek to uphold our legitimacy by responding to inter-generational considerations, public and scientific concerns, and through accountability for our work and achievements.
By signing this Charter we seek to promote further the values of transparency and accountability that we stand for, and commit our INGO to respecting its provisions.

How We Work

NGOs can complement but not replace the over-arching role and primary responsibility of governments to promote equitable human development and wellbeing, to uphold human rights and to protect ecosystems.
We also seek to promote the role and responsibilities of the private sector to advance human rights and sustainable development, and protect the environment.
We can often address problems and issues that governments and others are unable or unwilling to address on their own. Through

constructive challenge, we seek to promote good governance and foster progress towards our goals.

We seek to advance our mission through research, advocacy and programmes. It is common for our work to be at the international, national, regional and local levels, either directly or with partners.

We work with other organisations where this is the best way to advance our individual missions.

The Charter's Purpose

This Charter outlines our common commitment to excellence, transparency and accountability. To demonstrate and build on these commitments, we seek to:

- Identify and define shared principles, policies and practices;
- Enhance transparency and accountability, both internally and externally;
- Encourage communication with stakeholders; and
- Improve our performance and effectiveness as organisations.

We recognise that transparency and accountability are essential to good governance, whether by governments, businesses or non-profit organisations.

Wherever we operate, we seek to ensure that the high standards which we demand of others are also respected in our own organisations.

The Charter complements and supplements existing laws. It is a voluntary charter, and draws on a range of existing codes, norms, standards and guidelines.

We agree to apply the Charter progressively to all our policies, activities and operations. The Charter does not replace existing codes or practices to which signatories may also be party, except as specified by them. Its adoption does not prevent signatories from supporting or using other tools to promote transparency and accountability.

We will refine the Charter through experience, taking into account future developments, particularly those that improve accountability and transparency.

Our Stakeholders

Our first responsibility is to achieve our stated mission effectively and transparently, consistent with our values. In this, we are accountable to our stakeholders.

Our stakeholders include:

- Peoples, including future generations, whose rights we seek to protect and advance;
- Ecosystems, which cannot speak for or defend themselves;
- Our members and supporters;
- Our staff and volunteers;
- Organisations and individuals that contribute finance, goods or services;
- Partner organisations, both governmental and non-governmental, with whom we work;
- Regulatory bodies whose agreement is required for our establishment and operations;
- Those whose policies, programmes or behaviour we wish to influence;
- The media; and
- The general public.

In balancing the different views of our stakeholders, we will be guided by our mission and the principles of this Charter.

Principles

Respect for Universal Principles

INGOs are founded on the rights to freedom of speech, assembly and association in the Universal Declaration of Human Rights. We seek to advance international and national laws that promote human rights, ecosystem protection, sustainable development and other public goods.
Where such laws do not exist, are not fully implemented, or abused, we will highlight these issues for public debate and advocate appropriate remedial action.
In so doing, we will respect the equal rights and dignity of all human beings.

Independence

We aim to be both politically and financially independent. Our governance, programmes and policies will be non-partisan, independent of specific governments, political parties and the business sector.

Responsible Advocacy

We will ensure that our advocacy is consistent with our mission, grounded in our work and advances defined public interests.
We will have clear processes for adopting public policy positions, (including for partners where appropriate,) explicit ethical policies that guide our choices of advocacy strategy, and ways of identifying and managing potential conflicts of interest among various stakeholders.

Effective Programmes

We seek to work in genuine partnership with local communities, NGOs and other organisations aiming at sustainable development responding to local needs.

Non-Discrimination

We value, respect and seek to encourage diversity, and seek to be impartial and nondiscriminatory in all our activities. To this end, each organisation will have policies that promote diversity, gender equity and balance, impartiality and non-discrimination in all our activities, both internal and external.

Transparency

We are committed to openness, transparency and honesty about our structures, mission, policies and activities. We will communicate actively to stakeholders about ourselves, and make information publicly available.

Reporting

We seek to comply with relevant governance, financial accounting and reporting requirements in the countries where we are based and operate.
We report at least once a year on our activities and achievements. Reports will describe each organisation's:

- Mission and values;
- Objectives and outcomes achieved in programme and advocacy;
- Environmental impact;
- Governance structure and processes, and main office bearers;
- Main sources of funding from corporations, foundations, governments, and individuals;

- Financial performance;
- Compliance with this Charter; and
- Contact details.

Audit

The annual financial report will conform to relevant laws and practices and be audited by a qualified independent public accountant whose statement will accompany the report.

Accuracy of information

We will adhere to generally-accepted standards of technical accuracy and honesty in presenting and interpreting data and research, using and referencing independent research.

Good Governance

We should be held responsible for our actions and achievements. We will do this by: having a clear mission, organisational structure and decision-making processes; by acting in accordance with stated values and agreed procedures; by ensuring that our programmes achieve outcomes that are consistent with our mission; and by reporting on these outcomes in an open and accurate manner.
The governance structure of each organisation will conform to relevant laws and be transparent. We seek to follow principles of best practice in governance. Each organization will have at least:

- A governing body which supervises and evaluates the chief executive, and oversee programme and budgetary matters. It will define overall strategy, consistent with the organisational mission, ensure that resources are used efficiently and appropriately, that performance is measured, that financial integrity is assured and that public trust is maintained;
- Written procedures covering the appointment, responsibilities and terms of members of the governing body, and preventing and managing conflicts of interest;
- A regular general meeting with authority to appoint and replace members of the governing body.

We will listen to stakeholders' suggestions on how we can improve our work and will encourage inputs by people whose interests may be directly affected. We will also make it easy for the public to comment on our programmes and policies.

Ethical Fundraising

Donors

We respect the rights of donors: to be informed about causes for which we are fundraising; to be informed about how their donation is being used; to have their names deleted from mailing lists; to be informed of the status and authority of fundraisers; and to anonymity except in cases where the size of their donation is such that it might be relevant to our independence.

Use of Donations

In raising funds, we will accurately describe our activities and needs. Our policies and practices will ensure that donations further our organisation's mission. Where donations are made for a specific purpose, the donor's request is honoured. If we invite the general public to donate to a specific cause, each organisation will have a plan for handling any shortfall or excess, and will make this known as part of its appeal.

Gifts in Kind

Some donations may be given as goods or services. To retain our effectiveness and independence, we will: record and publish details of all major institutional gifts and gifts-inkind; clearly describe the valuation and auditing methods used; and ensure that these gifts contribute towards our mission.

Agents

We seek to ensure that donations sought indirectly, such as through third parties, are solicited and received in full conformity with our own practices. This will normally be the subject of written agreement between the parties.

Professional Management

We manage our organisations in a professional and effective manner. Our policies and procedures seek to promote excellence in all respects.

Financial Controls

Internal financial control procedures will ensure that all funds are effectively used and minimise the risk of funds being misused. We will follow principles of best practice in financial management.

Evaluation

We seek continuously to improve our effectiveness. We will have defined evaluation procedures for our boards, staff, programmes and projects on the basis of mutual accountability.

Public Criticism

We will be responsible in our public criticisms of individuals and organisations, ensuring such criticism amounts to fair public comment.

Partners

We recognise our that organisational integrity extends to ensuring that our partners also meet the highest standards of probity and accountability, and will take all possible steps to ensure that there are no links with organisations, or persons involved in illegal or unethical practices.

Human Resources

We recognise that our performance and success reflect the quality of our staff and volunteers and management practices, and are committed to investing in human resource development.
Remuneration and benefits should strike a balance between public expectations of voluntary based, not-for-profit organisations and the need to attract and retain the staff we need to fulfil our mission. Our human resources policies seek to conform fully with relevant international and national labour regulations and apply the best voluntary sector practices in terms of employee and volunteer rights and health and safety at work. Human resources policies will include procedures for evaluating the performance of all staff on a regular basis.

Bribery and Corruption

Human resources policies will specifically prohibit acts of bribery or corruption by staff or other persons working for, or on behalf of, the organisation.

Respect for Sexual Integrity

We condemn sexual exploitation, abuse and discrimination in all its forms. Our policies will respect sexual integrity in all our programmes and activities, and prohibit gender harassment, sexual exploitation and discrimination.

Whistle-Blowers

Staff will be enabled and encouraged to draw management's attention to activities that may not comply with the law or our mission and commitments, including the provisions in this Code.

Code of Conduct for Special Procedures Mandate-Holders of the Human Rights Council

Human Rights Council Res. 5/2, Annex, U.N. Doc. A/HRC/5/21, at 40 (Aug. 7, 2007)

5/2. Code of Conduct for Special Procedures Mandate-Holders of the Human Rights Council

The Human Rights Council,

Guided by the aims and principles of the Charter of the United Nations and the Universal Declaration of Human Rights and recognizing the ensuing obligations inter alia of States to cooperate in promoting universal respect for human rights as enshrined therein,

Recalling the Vienna Declaration and Programme of Action adopted on 25 June 1993 by the World Conference on Human Rights,

Recalling also that in resolution 60/251 of 15 March 2006, entitled "Human Rights Council", the General Assembly:

(a) Reaffirmed that all human rights are universal, indivisible, interrelated, interdependent and mutually reinforcing and that all human rights must be treated in a fair and equal manner on the same footing and with the same emphasis;

(b) Acknowledged that peace and security, development and human rights are the pillars of the United Nations system and that they are interlinked and mutually reinforcing;

(c) Decided that members elected to the Council shall uphold the highest standards in the promotion and protection of human rights and shall fully cooperate with the Council;

(d) Stressed the importance of "ensuring universality, objectivity and non-selectivity in the consideration of human rights issues, and the elimination of double standards and politicization";

(e) Further recognized that the promotion and protection of human rights "should be based on the principles of cooperation and genuine dialogue and aimed at strengthening the capacity of Member States to comply with their human rights obligations for the benefit of all human beings";

(f) Decided that "the work of the Council shall be guided by the principles of universality, impartiality, objectivity, and non-selectivity, constructive international dialogue and cooperation, with a view to enhancing the promotion and protection of all human rights, civil, political, economic, social and cultural rights, including the right to development";

(g) Also decided that "the methods of work of the Council shall be transparent, fair and impartial and shall enable genuine dialogue, be results-oriented, allow for subsequent follow-up discussions to recommendations and their implementation and also allow for substantive interaction with special procedures and mechanisms";

Underlining the centrality of the notions of impartiality and objectivity, as well as the expertise of mandate-holders, within the context of special procedures, along with the need to give the required degree of attention to all human rights violations, wherever they may be taking place,

Bearing in mind that the efficiency of the system of special procedures should be reinforced through the consolidation of the status of mandate-holders and the adoption of principles and regulations taking the specificities of their mandate into consideration,

Considering that it is necessary to assist all stakeholders, including States, national human rights institutions, non-governmental organizations and individuals, to better understand and support the activities of mandate-holders,

Recalling articles 100, 104, 105 of the Charter of the United Nations, section 22 of article VI of the Convention on the Privileges and Immunities of the United Nations of 13 February 1946 and paragraph 6 of General Assembly resolution 60/251,

Noting decision 1/102 of 30 June 2006, in which the Council decided to extend exceptionally for one year the mandates and mandate-holders of the special procedures of the Commission on Human Rights, of the Sub-Commission for the Promotion and Protection of Human Rights as well as the procedure established pursuant to Economic and Social Council resolution 1503 (XLVIII) of 27 May 1970,

Noting also decision 1/104 of 30 June 2006, in which the Council established the Open-ended Intergovernmental Working Group entrusted with the task of formulating recommendations on the issue of the review and possibly the enhancement and rationalization of all mandates, mechanisms, functions and responsibilities of the Commission on Human Rights, in order to maintain a regime of special procedures in accordance with paragraph 6 of General Assembly resolution 60/251,

Noting further resolution 2/1 of 27 November 2006, in which the Council requested the Open-ended Intergovernmental Working Group to "draft a code of conduct regulating the work of the special procedures",

Considering that this code of conduct is an integral part of the review, improvement and rationalization called for in General Assembly resolution 60/251 that, inter alia, seeks to enhance the cooperation between Governments and mandate-holders which is essential for the effective functioning of the system,

Considering also that such a code of conduct will strengthen the capacity of mandate-holders to exercise their functions whilst enhancing their moral authority and credibility and will require supportive action by other stakeholders, and in particular by States,

Considering further that one should distinguish between, on the one hand, the independence of mandate-holders, which is absolute in nature, and, on the other hand, their prerogatives, as circumscribed by their mandate, the mandate of the Human Rights Council, and the provisions of the Charter of the United Nations,

Mindful of the fact that it is desirable to spell out, complete and increase the visibility of the rules and principles governing the behaviour of mandate-holders,

Noting the Regulations Governing the Status, Basic Rights and Duties of Officials other than Secretariat Officials, and Experts on Mission that was adopted by the General Assembly in resolution 56/280 of 27 March 2002,

Noting also the draft Manual of the United Nations Human Rights Special Procedures adopted in 1999 by the sixth annual meeting of mandate-holders, as revised,

Taking note of the deliberations and proposals of the Open-ended Intergovernmental Working Group on Review of Mandates,

1. Urges all States to cooperate with, and assist, the special procedures in the performance of their tasks and to provide all information in a timely manner, as well as respond to communications transmitted to them by the special procedures without undue delay;

2. Adopts the Code of Conduct for Special Procedures Mandate-Holders of the Human Rights Council, the text of which is annexed to the present resolution and whose provisions should be disseminated by the Office of the United Nations High Commissioner for Human Rights, to the mandate-holders, to the Member States of the United Nations and to other concerned parties.

Annex

DRAFT CODE OF CONDUCT FOR SPECIAL PROCEDURES MANDATE-HOLDERS OF THE HUMAN RIGHTS COUNCIL

Article 1 - Purpose of the Code of Conduct

The purpose of the present Code of Conduct is to enhance the effectiveness of the system of special procedures by defining the standards of ethical behaviour and professional conduct that special procedures mandate-holders of the Human Rights Council (hereinafter referred to as "mandate-holders") shall observe whilst discharging their mandates.

Article 2 - Status of the Code of Conduct

1. The provisions of the present Code complement those of the Regulations Governing the Status, Basic Rights and Duties of Officials other than Secretariat Officials, and Experts on Mission (ST/SGB/2002/9) (hereinafter referred to as "the Regulations");

2. The provisions of the draft manual of United Nations Human Rights Special Procedures should be in consonance with those of the present Code;

3. Mandate-holders shall be provided by the United Nations High Commissioner for Human Rights, along with the documentation pertaining to their mission, with a copy of the present Code of which they must acknowledge receipt.

Article 3 - General Principles of Conduct

Mandate-holders are independent United Nations experts. While discharging their mandate, they shall:

(a) Act in an independent capacity, and exercise their functions in accordance with their mandate, through a professional, impartial assessment of facts based on internationally recognized human rights standards, and free from any kind of extraneous influence, incitement, pressure, threat or interference, either direct or indirect, on the part of any party, whether stakeholder or not, for any reason whatsoever, the notion of independence being linked to the status of mandate-holders, and to their freedom to assess the human rights questions that they are called upon to examine under their mandate;
(b) Keep in mind the mandate of the Council which is responsible for promoting universal respect for the protection of all human rights and fundamental freedoms for all, through dialogue and cooperation as specified in General Assembly resolution 60/251 of 15 March 2006;
(c) Exercise their functions in accordance with their mandate and in compliance with the Regulations, as well as with the present Code;
(d) Focus exclusively on the implementation of their mandate, constantly keeping in mind the fundamental obligations of truthfulness, loyalty and independence pertaining to their mandate;

(e) Uphold the highest standards of efficiency, competence and integrity, meaning, in particular, though not exclusively, probity, impartiality, equity, honesty and good faith;
(f) Neither seek nor accept instructions from any Government, individual, governmental or non-governmental organization or pressure group whatsoever;
(g) Adopt a conduct that is consistent with their status at all times;
(h) Be aware of the importance of their duties and responsibilities, taking the particular nature of their mandate into consideration and behaving in such a way as to maintain and reinforce the trust they enjoy of all stakeholders;
(i) Refrain from using their office or knowledge gained from their functions for private gain, financial or otherwise, or for the gain and/or detriment of any family member, close associate, or third party;
(j) Not accept any honour, decoration, favour, gift or remuneration from any governmental or non-governmental source for activities carried out in pursuit of his/her mandate.

Article 4 - Status of Mandate-Holders

1. Mandate-holders exercise their functions on a personal basis, their responsibilities not being national but exclusively international.

2. When exercising their functions, the mandate-holders are entitled to privileges and immunities as provided for under relevant international instruments, including section 22 of article VI of the Convention on the Privileges and Immunities of the United Nations.

3. Without prejudice to these privileges and immunities, the mandate-holders shall carry out their mandate while fully respecting the national legislation and regulations of the country wherein they are exercising their mission. Where an issue arises in this regard, mandate-holders shall adhere strictly to the provisions of Regulation 1 (e) of the Regulations.

Article 5 - Solemn Declaration

Prior to assuming their functions, mandate-holders shall make the following solemn declaration in writing:

"I solemnly declare that I shall perform my duties and exercise my functions from a completely impartial, loyal and conscientious standpoint, and truthfully, and that I shall discharge these functions and regulate my conduct in a manner totally in keeping with the terms of my mandate, the Charter of the United Nations, the interests of the United Nations, and with the objective of promoting and protecting human rights, without seeking or accepting any instruction from any other party whatsoever."

Article 6 - Prerogatives

Without prejudice to prerogatives for which provision is made as part of their mandate, the mandate-holders shall:

(a) Always seek to establish the facts, based on objective, reliable information emanating from relevant credible sources, that they have duly cross-checked to the best extent possible;

(b) Take into account in a comprehensive and timely manner, in particular information provided by the State concerned on situations relevant to their mandate;

(c) Evaluate all information in the light of internationally recognized human rights standards relevant to their mandate, and of international conventions to which the State concerned is a party;

(d) Be entitled to bring to the attention of the Council any suggestion likely to enhance the capacity of special procedures to fulfill their mandate.

Article 7 - Observance of the Terms of the Mandate

It is incumbent on the mandate-holders to exercise their functions in strict observance of their mandate and in particular to ensure that their recommendations do not exceed their mandate or the mandate of the Council itself.

Article 8 - Sources of Information

In their information-gathering activities the mandate-holders shall:

(a) Be guided by the principles of discretion, transparency, impartiality, and even-handedness;

(b) Preserve the confidentiality of sources of testimonies if their divulgation could cause harm to individuals involved;

(c) Rely on objective and dependable facts based on evidentiary standards that are appropriate to the non-judicial character of the reports and conclusions they are called upon to draw up;

(d) Give representatives of the concerned State the opportunity of commenting on mandate-holders' assessment and of responding to the allegations made against this State, and annex the State's written summary responses to their reports.

Article 9 - Letters of Allegation

With a view to achieving effectiveness and harmonization in the handling of letters of allegation by special procedures, mandate-holders shall assess their conformity with reference to the following criteria:

(a) The communication should not be manifestly unfounded or politically motivated;

(b) The communication should contain a factual description of the alleged violations of human rights;

(c) The language in the communication should not be abusive;

(d) The communication should be submitted by a person or a group of persons claiming to be victim of violations or by any person or group of persons, including non-governmental organizations, acting in good faith in accordance with principles of human rights, and free from politically motivated stands or contrary to, the provisions of the Charter of the United Nations, and claiming to have direct or reliable knowledge of those violations substantiated by clear information;

(e) The communication should not be exclusively based on reports disseminated by mass media.

Article 10 - Urgent Appeals

Mandate-holders may resort to urgent appeals in cases where the alleged violations are time-sensitive in terms of involving loss of life, life-threatening situations or either imminent or ongoing damage of a very grave nature to victims that cannot be addressed in a timely manner by the procedure under article 9 of the present Code.

Article 11 - Field Visits

Mandate-holders shall:

(a) Ensure that their visit is conducted in compliance with the terms of reference of their mandate;

(b) Ensure that their visit is conducted with the consent, or at the invitation, of the State concerned;

(c) Prepare their visit in close collaboration with the Permanent Mission of the concerned State accredited to the United Nations Office at Geneva except if another authority is designated for this purpose by the concerned State;

(d) Finalize the official programme of their visits directly with the host country officials with administrative and logistical back-up from the local United Nations Agency and/or Representative of the High Commissioner for Human Rights who may also assist in arranging private meetings;

(e) Seek to establish a dialogue with the relevant government authorities and with all other stakeholders, the promotion of dialogue and cooperation to ensure the full effectiveness of special procedures being a shared obligation of the mandate-holders, the concerned State and the said stakeholders;

(f) Have access upon their own request, in consultation with the Office of the High Commissioner for Human Rights and after a common understanding between the host Government and the mandate-holder, to official security protection during their visit, without prejudice to the privacy and confidentiality that mandate-holders require to fulfill their mandate.

Article 12 - Private Opinions and the Public Nature of the Mandate

Mandate-holders shall:

(a) Bear in mind the need to ensure that their personal political opinions are without prejudice to the execution of their mission, and base their conclusions and recommendations on objective assessments of human rights situations;

(b) In implementing their mandate, therefore, show restraint, moderation and discretion so as not to undermine the recognition of the independent nature of their mandate or the environment necessary to properly discharge the said mandate.

Article 13 - Recommendations and Conclusions

Mandate-holders shall:

(a) While expressing their considered views, particularly in their public statements concerning allegations of human rights violations, also indicate fairly what responses were given by the concerned State;

(b) While reporting on a concerned State, ensure that their declarations on the human rights situation in the country are at all times compatible with their mandate and the integrity, independence and impartiality which their status requires, and which is likely to promote a constructive dialogue among stakeholders, as well as cooperation for the promotion and protection of human rights;

(c) Ensure that the concerned government authorities are the first recipients of their conclusions and recommendations concerning this State and are given adequate time to respond, and that likewise the Council is the first recipient of conclusions and recommendations addressed to this body.

Article 14 - Communication with Governments

Mandate-holders shall address all their communications to concerned Governments through diplomatic channels unless agreed otherwise between individual Governments and the Office of the High Commissioner for Human Rights.

Article 15 - Accountability to the Council

In the fulfillment of their mandate, mandate-holders are accountable to the Council.

Guidelines on International Human Rights Fact-Finding Visits and Reports

(The Lund-London Guidelines)

Raoul Wallenberg Institute of Human Rights and Humanitarian Law, Lund University & International Bar Association

Preamble

Human rights are the concern of all members of the international community. We all hold a right and an obligation to promote and encourage respect for human rights, as pronounced in the 1998 United Nations Declaration on the Right and Responsibility of Individuals, Groups and Organs of Society to Promote and Protect Universally Recognised Human Rights and Fundamental Freedoms.

These guidelines have been developed by the International Bar Association and the Raoul Wallenberg Institute following wide consultation and extensive analysis of human rights fact-finding reports in order to contribute to good practice in the conduct of fact-finding visits and in the compilation of reports.

Fact finding and report writing are essential to human rights monitoring. Although primarily intended for the use of non-governmental organisations (NGOs), the present guidelines can provide direction to all those engaged in this exercise with a view to improving accuracy, objectivity, transparency and credibility in human rights fact finding.

The independence and integrity of NGOs must be respected, but fact-finding missions must nevertheless be, and be seen to be, conducted in a bona fide manner. Reports must be clearly objective and properly sourced, and the conclusions in them reached in a transparent manner.

If a report has been compiled in accordance with these guidelines it indicates that the allegations, observations and conclusions in it can be reasonably relied upon, thus enhancing the efficacy and credibility of the report. This will enhance fact-finding as a step in a constructive process to improve the general climate of human rights compliance and to protect the victims of human rights violations.

Definition of Fact-Finding

1 For the purpose of these guidelines, fact-finding means a mission or visit mandated by an NGO to ascertain the relevant facts relating to

and elucidating a situation of human rights concern, whether allegedly committed by state or non-state actors. In many instances this activity will result in a report. These guidelines do not prejudice the use of other methods of collecting information, other ventures or the use of fact finding in other contexts.

Instigation of a Fact-Finding Mission

2 Where a situation of concern is identified, a fact-finding mission should be considered in the light of the mandate, priorities, resources and procedures of the NGO. The NGO should consider the possible negative consequences of undertaking a mission.

3 The NGO should take into account the work that other relevant organisations have done or are doing on the same situation and of the effect any previous missions or public statements relating to the situation have had. In order to strengthen efforts and maximise the effective use of resources, cooperation with those other organisations should be considered.

Terms of Reference for the Mission

4 The terms of reference must be determined prior to the mission. These should relate to the specific situations under investigation bearing in mind the NGO's mandate.

5 The terms of reference must not reflect any predetermined conclusions about the situation under investigation.

6 The terms of reference should be clear, concise and relevant. However, they should be sufficiently flexible to permit the investigation of and reporting on any other related relevant circumstances.

7 If unforeseen situations arise which are outside of the mission's terms of reference the delegation should report those to the relevant NGO contact person as soon as possible. If the new situation falls within the mandate and expertise of the NGO, it may decide to extend the terms of reference or create a second mission. If the former, the NGO should be confident that the delegation has the competence and expertise to deal with the new situation. If the new situation falls outside the mandate and expertise of the NGO, it should refer the matter to another organisation which can take action.

Composition of the Delegation

8 The mission's delegation should comprise individuals who are and are seen to be unbiased. The NGO should be confident that the

delegation members have the competence, experience and expertise relevant to the matters pertaining to the terms of reference.

9 The NGO should ensure that delegation members have sufficient time for pre-mission briefings and/or training for implementation of the mission and any proposed follow-up work, including contributing to the report.

10 The NGO should ensure that all members of the delegation are aware that they must, at all times, act in an independent, unbiased, objective, lawful and ethical manner.

11 The NGO should ensure appropriate gender balance in the composition of the delegation. Where relevant, the NGO may wish to consider such issues as geographic, racial, ethnic or other types of balance and diversity when selecting the delegation members. The NGO may also wish to consider the importance of linguistic expertise and/or in-country knowledge.

12 The NGO should identify a leader of the delegation and/or a rapporteur.

13 As and where appropriate, delegations should be comprised of people with relevant expertise and skills in interviewing members of specific victim groups, especially when these are children, women, victims of torture or other vulnerable groups and internally displaced persons. See also paragraph 45.

14 When appointing a member of a delegation, the NGO should take into account any potential risk in appointing people of specific nationalities or members of particular religious groups, and any other reasons which might make it too dangerous for an individual to participate in the mission, or create danger for that person's family or others. This possibility should always be kept under review by the delegation and the NGO both before and during the visit.

Interpreters and Other Persons Associated with the Mission and/or Report

15 The NGO should ensure that all persons associated with a mission and/or a report are aware that they must, at all times, act in an independent, unbiased, objective, lawful and ethical manner.

16 The NGO should ensure that the delegation and other persons associated with the mission in the field develop inclusive operational methods that encourage the development of a participatory and unified team spirit.

17 The delegation should maintain as a principal consideration the safety of all persons associated with a mission and/or report, keeping personal details confidential. If there is a risk to any such person during the mission or afterwards, the NGO should seek assurances from the government that they will not be persecuted, victimised or otherwise put in a worse position for having worked with the delegation.
18 Where necessary, interpreters should be used during the course of the mission. Every care must be taken in selection to ensure that interpreters are expert in the required languages and relevant technical concepts, as well as independent and professional.
19 If the interpretation is not satisfactory, if the interpreters are not independent, or if they pose a risk to the safety of the delegation or those being interviewed, the delegation must desist from using the interpreters and where possible make alternative arrangements.

Pre-Visit

20 The NGO should provide a pre-visit briefing for members of the delegation, which includes balanced material relating to the reason for the visit and any relevant cultural, economic, political, historical and legal information. Where necessary, any relevant material should be translated.
21 The NGO should also provide a briefing on local logistical issues, operating procedures, medical issues (including preparation for travel), appropriate conduct in-country and other relevant matters. All members of the delegation should be provided with a copy of these guidelines.
22 The NGO should ensure that the members of the delegation are confident that they have been adequately briefed and understand the terms of reference, the initial reason for the visit and the mandate of the NGO. If any member of the delegation is not sufficiently confident that their briefing has been adequate, the NGO should be informed and it should then provide additional briefing.
23 The NGO should ensure that the members of the delegation understand the need to be unbiased and not pre-judge any issues during the mission. The NGO must also ensure that the delegation understands the need to act in an ethical manner and in accordance with the laws of the country and internationally accepted human rights standards. Awareness training, including gender sensitivity, should be provided where necessary.

24 The NGO should ensure that members of the delegation and persons associated with the mission receive clear and consistent messages about the mission, specifically its objectives and limitations, to ensure that the mission can be clearly explained to the people with whom they meet, so as to manage expectations and avoid miscommunication.
25 Where necessary, the NGO should ensure that all members of the delegation are fully briefed on recognising and managing stress and psychosocial trauma to prepare them properly for the realities of the situation and to promote the well-being of persons they interview, persons otherwise associated with the mission, and themselves.
26 The NGO is responsible for organising the visit, including the security, health and safety of the delegation. The NGO should ensure that appropriate emergency procedures are in place and that the delegation is fully briefed. It is the responsibility of the members of the delegation to act in accordance with any risk assessment made by the NGO and any formal requirements such as visa conditions as required by the laws of the country.
27 The NGO should as appropriate inform the government of the state in which the mission is to take place or any other relevant authorities that the mission will take place.
28 The NGO should consider what, if any, media strategy is appropriate for the delegation and for the mission overall. The NGO should ensure that all members of the mission are familiar with any strategy adopted.

Working Methods

General

29 The NGO has overall responsibility for the delegation and the mission.
30 The members of the delegation must conduct themselves with integrity, professionalism and in accordance with international human rights law standards at all times during the mission.
31 If a member of the delegation, or any other person associated with the mission, conducts him- or herself in a way which jeopardises the mission, the safety of others or the confidentiality of sources, or in any other way acts without sufficient professionalism or integrity, that person should be required to leave the mission. In such situations it will be for the NGO, in consultation with the leader of the delegation, to determine whether to abandon the mission or replace that person.

If the team leader is implicated, or is otherwise unavailable, any other member of the delegation may draw the matter to the attention of the NGO.

32 If it transpires during the course of the mission that there is a conflict of interest or other circumstances involving any member of the delegation which might jeopardise their independence and impartiality, or which might give the appearance that their independence and integrity is compromised, the leader of the delegation should inform the NGO and that member should desist from participating in a particular meeting, or where necessary from the remainder of the mission. If the team leader is implicated, or is otherwise unavailable, any other members of the delegation may draw the matter to the attention of the NGO.

33 Any threats to, or intimidation of, the delegation must be reported immediately to the NGO.

Where appropriate, the NGO will need to seek assurances from the government as to the safety of the delegation and should initiate emergency procedures should they be required.

Agenda

34 The NGO, in collaboration with the delegation, should determine criteria for selecting the people and locations it wishes to visit, make the necessary arrangements and draw up a schedule for the visit, as far as possible. In so doing, the NGO should take into account the safety and security of potential interviewees and persons associated with them. It may be necessary to amend the schedule as the mission progresses.

35 Wherever possible the delegation should interview all parties relevant to the situation under consideration in order to achieve a balanced, comprehensive picture. This might include members of the government, judiciary, parliamentarians, opposition party members, journalists, NGO personnel, academics, staff of intergovernmental organisations, or any other person who could reliably shed light on the situation under review.

36 The delegation is under no obligation to advise the government of the people it intends to meet.

If the government or any other party finds out this information and there are concerns as to the safety of an interviewee, then the NGO may wish to cancel the interview or to abandon the mission and should seek a guarantee from the government that the interviewee or prospective interviewee will not be persecuted, victimised or otherwise put in a worse position for having been willing to cooperate with the delegation. The same principle applies if the interviewee is threatened as a result of identification by other people.

37 The delegation may wish to operate as a whole group, or may wish to separate into smaller groups for specific assignments.

Interviews

38 The delegation must take into account the safety and security of the interviewees.

39 The delegation should be mindful that the venues for interviews will ensure the protection and confidentiality of all involved and are culturally appropriate.

40 Interviews should be scheduled with sufficient time for the ascertainment of all the relevant facts and to give the interviewee an opportunity to express their opinion.

41 The delegation should inform interviewees of the terms of reference, as well as giving reasons for the visit, prior to or at the meeting, in a language they understand.

42 The delegation should take a careful note of whether an interviewee provides informed consent to be interviewed and identified or quoted and of future possible uses of their statements. If they do not consent, their wishes must be respected.

43 Where appropriate, interviews should be conducted by at least two members of the delegation. It should be clarified in all cases whether interviewees wish to have a supporting person present, or wish for some person to absent themselves during the interview.

44 Interviews should be consistent and thorough and be conducted in a professional manner.

45 Members of the mission should be especially aware of the vulnerabilities of particular categories of potential interviewees and such interviewees should be approached with the utmost care. Interviews of vulnerable groups must only be undertaken by those with the relevant expertise and skill (see paragraph 13). Particular methodological techniques should be considered in certain cases: for example, female victims of sexual abuse should be offered the choice of being interviewed by a female member of the delegation and a clear explanation given of the possible future need for testimony in criminal or other proceedings.

46 Members of the delegation should be alert to the possibility of stress or trauma experienced by interviewees and be ready to terminate the interview if necessary. Wherever possible, the delegation

members should ensure that interviewees are referred to appropriate victim support services.

47 Members of the delegation should be alert to the humanitarian needs of interviewees and, wherever possible, should ensure that interviewees are referred to appropriate humanitarian or other organisations which might be able to meet those needs.

Information Gathering

48 It is essential that the delegation make use of all data collection techniques available. In addition to interviews, these may include site visits, collation of documents, or assessment of local laws and practices. Where the delegation relies upon information gathered by a third party, the delegation should take all reasonable measures to verify the objectivity of that information gathering process in order to rely on the evidence collected. See also paragraph 60 (ix).

49 The delegation should take full and fair notes or, where necessary, ensure that these are being taken on the delegation's behalf.

50 The delegation should endeavour to obtain and review all relevant written materials and documents.

51 The delegation must ensure that all materials and information are collated for the drafter of the report.

52 All notes, transcripts and documents, including electronic date, together with other materials from the visit, should be kept secure at all times. If confidentiality cannot be secured, the interviewee should be informed in accordance with paragraph 42.

53 The delegation should document any relevant obstacles it has met during its visit and in relation to the collection of information.

54 In making their findings the delegation should try to verify alleged facts with an independent third party or otherwise. Where this is not possible, it should be noted.

55 In making their findings the delegation should work independently having regard to the terms of reference, the situation giving rise to the visit, and the mandate of any reasonable directions from the NGO.

56 The delegation should assess all the information gathered and reach conclusions to its reasonable satisfaction based on this assessment.

Fact-Finding Report

57 If not already decided, the delegation and the NGO should identify the person or persons with responsibility for drafting the report. Unless

there are exceptional circumstances, this should be a person or persons who was a delegate or who participated in the mission.

58 The delegation as a whole should reach its conclusions and make recommendations where required by the terms of reference. Where possible, recommendations should attempt to outline possible practical solutions. Every effort should be made to reach a consensus on conclusions and recommendations. If there is a dissenting viewpoint, the NGO should consider publishing it.

59 In order to enhance the overall quality and credibility of the report, it must be accurate, clear and drafted objectively so that the processes of the mission are transparent. It should fairly reflect all the information gathered and must refrain from bias. It is good practice to identify the standards against which the delegation members weigh the information obtained.

60 As good practice, reports should include:

i) an executive summary;
ii) the mandate of the sending NGO;
iii) the reason for the visit and terms of reference of the mission;
iv) the names of the delegation members, including brief particulars as to their relevant expertise and experience, to assure transparency;
v) the dates of the visit;
vi) sufficient background information to enable readers to contextualise the evidence;
vii) the methodology used during the visit, especially regarding interviews;
viii) as appropriate and where safety and confidentiality would not be compromised, a list of the sites visited and organisations and categories of people interviewed;
ix) identification of any other sources of information relied upon, including disclosure of unverified third party evidence (see paragraph 48);
x) disclosure of the source of funding for the mission;
xi) the applicable law;
xii) where applicable, complementary secondary sources should be identified as such;
xiii) identification of any circumstances relevant to the mission, including anything that impeded it;
xiv) the findings of the report;
xv) an acknowledgment of any contributions by people or organisations who rendered assistance to the delegation or NGO, where it would not compromise their safety;

xvi) conclusions and recommendations, indicating to whom the latter are addressed;
xvii) details of any significant developments occurring after the conclusion of the mission.

61 Where it is the practice for the NGO to submit the report to the government for its response in advance of publication, any comments received should be included if the government consents.
Any failure of the government to respond should be noted in the report.
62 The report should be written and published within a reasonable time following the conclusion of the mission.

Translation

63 The report should be made available in the languages of the NGO and of the country being investigated, or in a language of common use in that country.
64 Every effort should be made to ensure the translation is of the highest quality.

Publication

65 The NGO has overall responsibility for decisions about the publication and dissemination of the report.
66 The NGO should, wherever possible, widely publicise and disseminate the report, particularly in the locality of the visit, including to relevant governments, individuals or organisations.
67 The NGO should consider what, if any, media strategy is appropriate for disseminating the report.

Follow-up

68 The safety of those interviewed or engaged by a fact-finding delegation should continue to be monitored by the NGO, particularly where safety concerns were already present. Any post-mission threats or hostile acts should be acted upon immediately by the NGO including, where necessary, notifying the government, assisting with protective measures and alerting the wider international community.
69 The NGO should offer post-mission debriefing to members of the delegation and persons associated with the mission where necessary to deal with stress and psychosocial trauma that may be experienced after a mission.

70 The NGO should consider any opportunities to cooperate with other NGOs, international organisations and relevant governments working on the same situation, subject area or country so as to maximise the effectiveness of the report.

71 The NGO should consider the best means by which to encourage governments and other relevant entities to be receptive of its report and to act upon its recommendations.

72 The NGO may wish to monitor any relevant developments in the country which is the subject of the report, occurring after the report has been published. In such a case a follow-up mission and/or report may be considered.

73 The NGO should review all aspects of the mission, including the delegation's performance and the adequacy of the NGO's procedures. The NGO should endeavour to disseminate the lessons learned within the NGO and to others, in order to promote the development of good practice and the implementation of these guidelines.

NGOs working in the field of human rights recognise that fact-finding is not an end in itself. It is a crucial vehicle for the implementation of human rights in all countries or situations under examination.

Human Rights Fact-Finding: Some Legal and Ethical Dilemmas[1]

Geoffrey Robertson QC
(International Bar Associate Human Rights Institute)

This paper was originally delivered as the Keynote Address at the conference on Human Rights Fact-Finding Missions, held at the British Institute of International and Comparative Law, London, on 1-2 June 2009.

Human rights fact-finding missions are of increasing importance, especially to the array of war crimes courts that have been established in the last decade. Their prosecutors draw on the reports of such missions as a basis for initiating investigations, and often seek to call evidence from the fact-finders as part of the prosecution case. A prosecution summons to go into the witness box can cause serious problems for human rights monitors, who must protect their sources and avoid being perceived as partisan. And because the reports of fact-finding missions can now lead to the prosecution of political and military leaders (or at least affect their post retirement travel plans) some leaders have devised new ways of attacking such reports, by threatening legal actions, usually in England, for libel or breach of confidence.

Academics have generally overlooked the importance of this subject—the most impressive exception being a study by Diane Orentlicher[2] back in 1990. It is time to take a more contemporary look at the ethical and legal dimensions of human rights fact-finding, and to applaud the launch of the Guidelines for International Human

---

[1] Reprinted with permission from the International Bar Association's Human Rights Institute. Originally published in the Human Rights Institute Thematic Papers No. 1, May 2010. Mr. Robertson has conducted many human rights fact-finding missions for Amnesty International, the Bar Council and other organisations. He served as the first President of the UN War Crimes Court in Sierra Leone and is currently a distinguished jurist member of the Internal Justice Council of the United Nations. He is the author of *Crimes Against Humanity: The Struggle for Global Justice* (3rd ed. Penguin and New Press). This is an edited version of his keynote address at the conference which inaugurated the *Lund-London Guidelines on International Human Rights Fact-Finding Visits and Reports*, prepared by the Raoul Wallenberg Institute.

[2] Diane F Orentlicher, 'Bearing Witness: the art and science of human rights fact finding', Harvard Human Rights Journal, Vol 3 1990 (p. 83).

Rights Fact-Finding Visits and Reports prepared by the International Bar Association and the Raoul Wallenberg Institute.[3]

There are different kinds of fact-finding exercises. At one level there is the Commission of Inquiry, with statutory powers to summon witnesses and obtain documents. It usually has a counsel to assist, and interested parties are entitled to be represented. Corruption Commissions in the Caribbean, conducted by Sir Louis Blom-Cooper and Sir Robin Auld, are good examples, whilst the current 'Bloody Sunday' inquiry into deaths caused by a demonstration in Belfast in 1971 by British paratroopers, which has already taken eight years and cost many millions, provides a particularly dreadful example. Statutory inquiries into human rights abuses are rare, if only because it usually takes international pressure for a government to set up a commission with the power to examine the misconduct of its own members. The Blom-Cooper Inquiry into the trafficking of arms to the Medallin Cartel, for example, was set up as the result of an international outcry, after guns imported from Israel by an Antiguan government minister on behalf of the Medallin cocaine cartel were used to assassinate a presidential candidate in Columbia.[4]

A more common form is an official inquiry by a distinguished personage who lacks legal power, but will obtain some co-operation from the state under scrutiny because of his or her standing. A UN rapporteur falls into this category—for example, Philip Alston's inquiry into the riots in Kenya and Richard Goldstone's inquiry for the Human Rights Council into the Israeli incursion in Gaza. These missions come with the moral force of the United Nations, although that does not always make them welcome: the Israeli government refused to co-operate with the Goldstone inquiry and the Kenyan government condemned the report of the Alston inquiry.

A third kind of inquiry is one set up by an NGO, conducted by an independent person (usually a jurist), who is invited to investigate and then write a report for publication. The IBA tends to send a number of prominent lawyers—most recently to Fiji. Sometimes they are not allowed in, and have to conduct witness interviews outside the country. Even though they can be handicapped by lack of investigative power, the legal conclusions of such an inquiry about facts that are in

---

[3] *Guidelines on International Human Rights Fact-Finding Visits and Reports: The Lund-London Guidelines,* Inaugurated 1 June 2009 www.factfindingguidelines.org.

[4] See Louis Blom-Cooper, *Guns to Antigua* (Duckworths 1990).

the public domain can be of great significance—especially if the conclusion is that such facts give rise to a prima facie case of genocide or a crime against humanity.

Another kind of inquiry is an independent expert mission which conducts confidential fact finding for an NGO which will not publish any report directly but will filter its findings into their campaigns and country assessments. Amnesty International missions provide examples. The Commonwealth Secretariat, too, holds inquiries of these kinds. Their advantage is that the fact-finder may obtain important information, and valuable perspective, by speaking confidentially to important government figures—to judges, prosecutors and prison officers who would not be prepared to speak openly. The disadvantage, of course, is that these reports cannot be published and the fact-finder enters into an obligation of confidentiality towards officials who may later become the subject of prosecution. In the case of the Red Cross, confidentiality is absolute and may be enforced under international law.

A fifth kind of human rights fact finding goes on all the time as a result of the work of human rights monitors (I would prefer to call them human rights reporters) working in country, gathering information from local sources. Human Rights Watch calls them 'country representatives' and often gives them awards or asks them to make presentations, and certainly makes no secret of their presence within a troubled state.

Other NGOs require their reporters to be more low profile. These 'monitors' are on a permanent fact-finding mission and their organisation will from time to time issue reports based on their work. There is a thin line dividing human rights reporters from newspaper reporters and there is no obvious reason, as a matter of law, why they should not have the same legal protection.

There are other models of human rights fact finding but all present similar problems of ensuring accuracy and impartiality, protecting sources, and avoiding being sued for libel—especially in London, the libel capital of the world—if the report makes accusations against identifiable persons. Although a statutory inquiry will generally have absolute privilege from libel action, reports of other inquiries will not have this protection, and this vulnerability is worrying for cash-strapped NGOs. Even UN rapporteurs have been sued, although the International Court of Justice in its Advisory Opinion on the immunity of UN Special Rapporteur Cumaraswamy has now ruled that rapporteurs have UN immunity. This was a case where the UN's rapporteur on the judiciary made some remarks about judicial corruption in his own country, Malaysia, and was sued by the lawyer widely accused of corrupting the judges. The Malaysian courts refused to acknowledge his UN immunity, until the ICJ ruled that he was entitled to it.[5]

The cause of human rights has progressed a long way in a very short time. I remember joining Amnesty at university in the early 1970s, when my first task was to compose grovelling letters to General Pinochet, requesting him to abandon the torture of political prisoners. A mere quarter of a century later, I had the pleasure of acting for Human Rights Watch in the House of Lords case that approved his extradition on torture charges. In the intervening period, before international criminal law delivered on the legacy of Nuremberg and before the internet revolution and satellite television, human rights fact-finding missions were the only way to prise information out of repressive regimes. Today there is more information available, but separating it from rumour, propaganda and blogging fantasies and analysing its legal significance is more important than ever.

Trial observation by international monitors is an important aspect of human rights fact finding. It is usually conducted by lawyers of some distinction who sit in court for as long as they or their supporting NGO can afford. They speak to the judge and the prosecutors as well as to the defence counsel, and provide their organisation with some insight into the fairness of the trial. In the case of Amnesty, which conducted many such observations from its inception in the 1960s, the interviewees would be offered a letter from its Secretary-General assuring them that their comments would be treated in utter confidence. The information provided would be factored into the observer's confidential report, which would never see the light of day; it would be considered along with information from other sources by office researchers and editors and find its filtered way into the next Amnesty annual report. The report itself would often be disputed by the government, but Amnesty reports in this period were recognised as fairly accurate and the organisation had a much higher reputation for getting at the truth than the government in question. This was largely as a result of the ability of its observers to speak confidentially to officials

[5] *Differences Relating to Immunity from Legal Process of a Special Rapporteur of the Commission on Human Rights, Advisory Opinion*, ICJ Reports 1999, p. 62.

of that government. There was no doubt that a binding offer of confidentiality was essential to the success of these trial observations.

Ethical problems were apt to arise. I remember conducting a mission for Amnesty to South Africa in relation to the 'Sharpeville Six' appeal—a half dozen protestors sentenced to death under a vague 'common purpose' doctrine for participating in a demonstration, in the course of which a 'necklacing' had occurred. I thought it would be useful to meet the trial judge who had convicted them (there was no jury) and sentenced them to death—a judge somewhat inappropriately named Human. I showed him the Secretary-General's letter and promised him confidentiality, and he took me to his club—the Pretoria Club—which he boasted was very progressive, having recently agreed to admit Jews (although it still banned black people and women). He was a lonely old racist, dying of alcohol poisoning, and after a few drinks made a number of admissions to me that might have founded a further appeal. If the men had not been reprieved, would I have broken my undertaking of confidentiality in order to save their necks? I would obviously have had to discuss this course with Amnesty, but ultimately my conscience would probably have made me speak out: after all, as every equity lawyer knows, there can be no confidence in iniquity.

History

Early twentieth-century fact finding on subjects we would now associate with 'human rights'[6] often had a propagandistic purpose, especially if appointed or backed by governments. At the outset of the First World War, the British Government supported 'fact finding' about the German invasion of Belgium; Wellington House produced stories from unidentified witnesses about German soldiers bayoneting pregnant women and cold-bloodedly murdering children that were later exposed as fraudulent. Lord James Bryce, formerly Oxford Regius Professor of Civil Law, oversaw this blatant propaganda exercise; its subsequent exposure has tainted the excellent work done by Arnold Toynbee on the Armenian Massacre (*The Blue Book*) to which Bryce wrote the introduction.[7] The most satisfactory human rights fact-finding mission in this period was that of Major General Harbord,

[6] The term was not much used until 1939: see Robertson, *Crimes Against Humanity* (Penguin 2006, Chapter I 'The Human Rights Story').

[7] See Phillip Knightly, *The First Casualty* (Andre Deutsch, 1975) p. 83–84.

conducted for the US Government in Turkey in September/October 1919. Its work was fast and efficient and its report eloquently described the horrors of what would later, and rightly, be termed 'genocide'.[8]

Fact-finding missions loomed large in the history of the League of Nations. In fact, it was the very failure of its fact-finding missions which contributed to bringing down the League, an organization based on the notion of 'collective security'—the principle that if one member state was attacked the others would declare war on the attacker. This illusion sustained the League's supporters throughout the 1920s. But in September 1931, Japan (a leading member of the League), invaded Manchuria after an incident in which it claimed that its railway there had been sabotaged by Chinese soldiers. China denied playing any part in this provocation and complained to the League about Japanese aggression. What was the League to do? A fact-finding mission was its first response and it sent Lord Lytton, an English notable who apparently disliked air or train travel, as he went by sea. It took him several months to get to Manchuria and several months to sail back and produce his report in September 1932—a full year since the incident. By this time Japan had already appointed 'the last Emperor' to be puppet governor of Manchukuo, its new name for the conquered territory. Lord Lytton's report—to the effect that the incident did not constitute provocation and Japan had acted unlawfully and should return the province to China—was too late to have any effect other than to undermine the League's credibility. By this time, aggression was a *fait accompli*.

Did the League learn the lesson that fact-finding missions upon which collective security might depend should find their facts quickly? Not at all. In December 1934 Mussolini contrived an incident at Wal-Wal oasis in Abyssinia, as a pretext for his invasion of that country. Emperor Haile Selassie was highly outraged, and complained to the League, which sent a fact-finding committee to investigate. But it still took them nine months to report that the Abyssinians were blameless. By this time, Mussolini had his canisters of poison gas in place on the border and had secured the silence of Britain and France (who wanted to appease Mussolini—so he would not strike up an alliance with

[8] Major General James G Harbord, *Conditions in the Near East. Report of the American Military Mission to Armenia*. 66th Congress, 2nd Session, Dec No 266, 13 April 1920. See Peter Balakian, *The Burning Tigris* (Heinemann 2003).

Hitler!) Once again, delay was fatal to the League's pretentions about collective security: Haile Selassie was highly deserted.

This early history emphasises that fact-finding investigations of recent human rights disasters must report as soon as possible after they have been set up; the more they delay, the less their impact. This can also apply to inquiries into events long past: judicial fact finding in the UK has been severely damaged by the incredible delays in the Saville Inquiry into 'Bloody Sunday'—it has taken eight years, and will probably end up taking ten, to investigate the events of one day in the life of Belfast, and the cost has already mounted to over $150 million for what has turned out to be a lawyer's banquet. In 2009 an Iraq War Inquiry was set up by the UK Government, run by civil servants and not by judges—a mistaken decision which it justified by reference to the disastrous 'Bloody Sunday' inquiry.

Funding

NGO fact finding began in earnest with the launch of Amnesty International in 1959. Early factfinding missions to Africa, notably conducted by Louis Blom-Cooper QC, were impressive. However, one such mission to Rhodesia was discredited when it leaked out that the money to fund the inquiry had come in secret from the UK Foreign and Commonwealth Office. This taught Amnesty's founder, Peter Benenson, the lesson that he should never again take money from governments, a rule that has been adopted by Human Rights Watch. I am not sure that this need be a universal rule, but there is one fundamental principle here for NGOs and foundations, namely that the funding for factfinding missions must always be disclosed. The general belief that 'he who pays the piper calls the tune' makes it all too easy to discredit mission reports, even if none of the participants is personally remunerated, if the costs of the hearings or of travel or of printing the report have been secretly paid by an interested party or a government. Fact-finding missions should be entirely transparent about their funding.

Composition of delegation

The Lund-London Guidelines correctly state:

> The mission's delegation must comprise individuals who are and are seen to be unbiased. The NGO should be confident that the delegation

> members have the competence, experience and expertise relevant to the matters pertaining to the terms of reference.[9]

Compliance with this principle will be crucial to the success of the mission. When the stakes are high, governments and their unscrupulous propagandists will not hesitate to defame the authors of critical reports and the NGOs which have tasked them. Pro-Israeli sources have recently attempted to discredit a Human Rights Watch fact-finder, who is an historian of Nazi (and American) war time medals and uniforms. They have even accused Richard Goldstone of bias, after his investigation for the Human Rights Council concluded that Israeli commanders committed war crimes in their attack on Gaza. Although the Council itself has displayed prejudice against Israel, its choice of Goldstone as a fact-finder meant that his report could not sensibly be assailed for partisanship. There have been outrageous cases in the past where trial observers have masqueraded as impartial—most notably the fellow travelling English barristers who white-washed Stalin's show trials (with dishonest reports entitled 'The Moscow Trials Were Fair').[10]

Expertise in the subject matter of the mission should be carefully evaluated, because some undoubted experts will already have committed themselves to an opinion, and could therefore be criticised for pre-judgment. Very often it will be most appropriate to choose individuals who have no connection at all with the country or the persons involved in the mission, but who have a reputation for independence and for good judgment. For trial observers, some familiarity with the system of law under which trial is held will avoid the ignorance sometimes displayed by continental observers of adversary trials and by Anglo-American observers of inquisitorial proceedings. The UN Secretary General appointed, as one of five *Lockerbie* trial observers, an obscure Austrian philosopher who has been condemning the verdict and everyone associated with it ever since, in a way that appears to reveal a lack of understanding of adversary trial procedure and evidence, and a propensity to impugn the integrity of defence lawyers, prosecutors and judges. The case for re-opening a trial verdict is not helped by unsupported allegations of this kind.[11]

---

[9] See Lund-London Guidelines on International Human Rights Fact-Finding Visits and Reports, paragraph 8.

[10] See Joseph Redman, 'The British Stalinists and the Moscow Trials' *Labour Review* Vol. 3 No. 2, March-April 1958 pp. 44–53.

[11] See *The Independent*, 21 August 2009, Hans Kochler, 'I Saw The Trial – And the Verdict Made No Sense'. This, according to Kochler, was because it was 'based on

Even-handedness

American NGOs have learnt to look at life from both sides now. America's Watch and the Lawyer's Committee were precursors of Human Rights Watch: they grew out of the civil disobedience movement of the 1960s and produced tough legal journalists like Michael Posner, Ray Bonner and Reed Brody. They exposed the US Government's behaviour in places like El Salvador (where the CIA was secretly supporting army death squads) and Nicaragua (where the CIA was secretly supporting the Contras). The Reagan Administration, most notably through the work of Elliot Abrams, an Assistant Secretary of State (ironically for Humanitarian Affairs), went for the jugular and tried to discredit Ray Bonner over his exposure of the El Mazote massacre and Reed Brody over his report about Contra funding, which Reagan personally condemned as 'bought and paid for by the Sandinistas'. The White House, in McCarthyite mode, enlisted all its tamed media connections: the *New York Times* dispensed with Bonner's services, and *Time* magazine attacked Brody. To their credit, calumny did not stop them and both were in time vindicated—Brody's reports proved accurate and, years later, Bonner's claim about the existence of a mass grave, derided by the Reagan Administration, was proved true when the grave, with the bodies of hundreds of women and children, was discovered.

Nonetheless, the criticism served to teach the lesson that human rights reports should be evenhanded, should examine and, if appropriate, should criticise both sides. Many fact-finding missions will focus upon the government over its oppression of insurgent groups, but the behaviour of these groups should be judged as severely and by the same criteria as government conduct. This has become a counsel not only of fairness but of prudence; it was much in evidence in those commentaries in 2009 on the Sri Lankan army's butchery of Tamils, balanced by references to the terrorist behaviour of the 'Tamil Tigers'.

---

circumstantial evidence' (which lawyers know is often the best evidence); because the co-defendant was acquitted (an indication of the fairness of the court); because one witness had been taken fishing by the Scottish police (what else is there to do in Scotland?), because information about a break-in at Heathrow was withheld (it was fully available to the Appeal Court, where the five judges analysed it carefully and concluded that it gave no possible support to the defence); and because only one person was convicted (which does not mean that the person they did convict was innocent!).

Amnesty, taking a purist position, has pointed out that its remit is to investigate the conduct of the state rather than the conduct of those opposed to the state. Thus it made no criticism of ANC guerilla actions when condemning the apartheid policies of the South African Government. However, the legitimacy of state counter-insurgency policies may depend upon the reasonableness of response to the conduct of insurgents. So it was right to condemn the Tamil Tigers for using their own people as human shields and virtual hostages, whilst criticising the conduct of the Sri Lankan army in putting civilians at risk during the final stages of the war.

One important example of the need for fact-finding missions to assess the behaviour of insurgents as well as governments is provided by Richard Goldstone's investigation into the Israeli-Palestinian conflict in Gaza. He had to lobby hard in order to obtain the Human Rights Council's approval to investigate the behaviour of Hamas as well as that of Israel. In such tit-for-tat conflicts, passing judgment on the conduct of both sides is inevitable: the whole question of proportionality justification for Israeli conduct is bound up with the degree of provocation constituted by Hamas rocket attacks on Israel. Despite Goldstone's attempt to avoid becoming one-eyed in Gaza, it is regrettable that the Israeli Government refused to co-operate with his mission and condemned his report as soon as it was published. His insistence on investigating Hamas underlines the principle of even-handedness; examine the conduct of insurgents as well as the response to that conduct by the government.

Obeying local laws

Another issue that can bedevil fact-finding missions is the question of whether they should obey the law in countries where nobody else seems to do so. This can be difficult in repressive regimes, where the official exchange rate, for example, bears no relationship to reality and the 'Black Market' rate is that at which money in almost all circumstances changes hands. I'm afraid that fact-finding mission members must remain in the minority, and scrupulously obey the local law. The importance of this principle was brought home to me on a pre-velvet revolution mission to Stalinist Czechoslovakia, when I invited Vaclav Havel to lunch. He was understandably nervous, because he was on bail and the authorities could return him to prison at any moment. When I did not have sufficient local currency to pay for our meal,

I assumed I could pay the rest in US dollars, accepted with alacrity everywhere in the city. But Havel was horrified, and explained that he would immediately be arrested by the secret police watching us from the far table, as an accomplice in 'black-marketeering'. 'This is the first rule of being a dissident' said Kafka's successor: 'you must scrupulously obey the law'.

Sometimes it is difficult to obey the local law, for practical reasons. When I was observing trials for Amnesty in the puppet homeland of Venda, I would arrive at Johannesburg airport from London at about 5am, hire a car and drive up an almost continually straight road for several hours before turning off to the court room. Inevitably, on one occasion I fell into a speed trap where an apologetic policeman issued me a ticket which I duly paid. When I mentioned this to Amnesty, they took it very seriously and a top-level meeting was convened on the question of whether they should repay my speeding ticket. They decided to do so – but I would not rely upon the case as a precedent.

Suppose, however, that you are the victim of breaches of the law. There is not much point in complaining if the perpetrator is the President. I recall one mission, which I led on behalf of the British Bar Council and Law Society, to Hasting Banda's Malawi, to investigate cases where he had ordered opponents to be killed without compunction. We obtained a meeting with the President for Life, who expressed himself as delighted that one of our number was female—she was a north London solicitor renowned for bringing cases of sexual harassment—'Ah, you have bought with you a Mbumba!' (a woman, in the Chichewa language), he chortled as he greeted our delegation. 'I am so pleased you have brought Mbumba. I am a powerful man and I like Mbumba! All Mbumba's in Malawi love me and I love them. They sing and dance for me!' At this point he began to paw our solicitor delegate, in a manner which would have him arrested for indecent assault in Britain but would have us all arrested for an attack on the President if our delegate reacted as she would doubtless have done in North London. We would then have had an unrivalled opportunity to find facts about Malawi's prison system, from the inside.

Surveillance

A more common problem for members of fact-finding missions is to find themselves followed by secret (and not so secret) police. Here, in such cases, it is important not to lead them to witnesses, and interviews should be cancelled rather than reliance placed upon 'giving them the slip' which may be more difficult than it seems in an unknown or hostile city. In Prague in Stalinist times, I was always followed rather clumsily by ill-paid surveillance operatives; I would head to the city's Jewish cemetery, with its towering forests of tall tombs, and try to lose them. If I failed I would take them behind me to the Terezin Museum, requiring them to pretend an interest in pictures painted by children of the ghetto en route to Auschwitz. But I would always avoid leading them to my contacts, unless they were well known dissidents whose meetings were monitored in any event.

Interviewing

The same principle of prudence should apply when interviewing people in prison or in any monitored space where guards are nearby or hidden microphones are possibly present. It is not fair to the prisoner, who either will not tell the truth if aware that his custodians are listening or will be punished if he does tell it. On an Amnesty mission to Vietnamese prisoners in re-education camps, it was very tempting to ask questions of prisoners during an organised visit, but we decided to avoid questioning because guards were invariably within earshot. The prisoners, of course, could volunteer whatever comments they wished, but their opinions were tempered by their fear of reprisals.

Refugees

Special problems are encountered in refugee camps. There is always a power structure within such camps—they are usually run by a political faction, whose representatives insist on escorting and introducing you to refugees who tend to say the same thing about the conditions from which they have escaped and about their treatment in the camp. The ideal on such missions is to interview new arrivals as they arrive or are being registered and before they come under the sway of local camp leaders who will indoctrinate them with the approved 'line' about political events back home, and will in certain cases coach them as to what to say. It may or may not be the truth—but because it is designed, for example, to support the political line of the faction, or to support a case for asylum rather than economic migration, such coached stories must be discounted.

Victims

Ideally, prisoners and refugees and all persons who may be subject to pressure from custodians or others should be interviewed alone. This is a counsel of perfection, because investigators will often need a translator present and the choice may be problematic, especially if there is no choice and the translator is officially imposed. Interviewing prisoners alone does insulate their testimony from influence, although it is important to remember that some victims—especially of sexual crime—are inhibited by the subject matter and do need support before they can bring themselves to speak freely.

Many traumatised victims of rape or torture simply will not divulge their excruciating experience to a stranger. In these circumstances, there can be no hard and fast rules about interviewing witnesses without anyone else present: a friend or counsellor may be a necessary companion.

Conduct of interviews

As with other interviews which can have serious consequences, the interviewer has a duty to conduct the discussion as fairly as possible. Leading questions must not put words into the interviewee's mouth. The questions asked must not suggest the answer that is sought or that others have given. (A good reality check in the event of an important allegation is the question 'how do you know?') The way to conduct an interview is to ask 'what happened then?' and not to say, for example, 'that is when they pulled your fingernails out, didn't they?' Always look for corroboration of serious allegations—ask if there is another prisoner who saw the victim immediately before and after; whether there is an autopsy report that confirms an eye witness account of a lethal beating; check whether there are newspaper reports that confirm dates and events. Wherever a 'story' is told there will usually be elements that can be checked with others or with public records.

There is much at stake in how witnesses can be brainwashed, or persuaded (often by money or by threats to relatives) to give false evidence. Human rights fact-finders must develop a degree of cynicism and street wisdom in relation to those who voluntarily testify to them, and be conscious of governments (who may lose aid donors in the event of adverse NGO reports). The more distinguished the fact-finding mission, the more vested interests will try to pull wool over the eyes of its members. Every fact-finder should have well in mind the saga of 'witness L' in the ICTY. He was a witness who was very credible and utterly believed by the prosecutors in the *Tadic* case and he certainly told them what they wanted to hear. He said that he had been an eye witness at Omarska camp, and had seen Tadic kill no less than 30 prisoners including Witness L's own father. I suppose it's a wise witness who knows his own father and 'L' was confounded when confronted by his, produced in the courtroom by the defence, alive and well. The trial was halted and the court abandoned all its previous efforts at keeping 'L's' identity a secret. He had been coached, and probably paid, by authorities in Bosnia Herzegovina in order to dishonestly demonise the Serbian defendant.[12]

It is important for NGO fact-finders, and for prosecutors who rely on the facts, to keep in mind the debacle that occurred in the very first trial at the ICC, with its very first witness.[13] This child witness not only recanted his testimony, but accused an NGO of fabricating it. It later turned out that he was too terrified by the sight of the defendant to testify against him in his presence (he should have been screened) but the incident showed how vulnerable NGOs are to this sort of allegation. Where witness' evidence is likely to go further—especially to court—the record should be signed, and preferably tape or video recorded.

The fact-finder must be astute to detect any personal or political motivations for lying or exaggerating or for blind partisanship. Many witnesses will have an axe to grind: they have undoubtedly suffered and will be anxious to emphasise the guilt of those they believe (or have been made to believe) are to blame. Fact-finders must also factor in the motive that many witnesses have to exaggerate or to emphasise their own innocence: when claiming refugee status, or hoping to claim such status, they will have a motive to exaggerate the extent of their persecution, especially if they think the factfinders' report may subsequently assist their asylum claim. Always ask: *cui bono?* (who benefits?).

---

[12] See Mark Zaid, 'Trial of the Century? Assessing the Case of Dusko Tadic before the International Criminal Tribunal for the Former Yugoslavia' 3 *ILSA J Int & Comp Law* 589.

[13] See http://newx.bbc.co.uk/1/hi/world/7857230.stm.

Admissions against interest

In law as in life, an admission by a state can be held against it, and it will be important to examine closely any justification or excuses offered by the regime for attacking its own citizens. One example derives from Singapore in 1988, where Catholics, lawyers and playwrights concerned with the problems of the poor were rounded up and tortured. The government, of course, denied torture, but its relevant minister (and now Prime Minister) Lee Hsien Loong admitted that the secret police used 'psychological pressure'.[14] This was an 'admission against interest' that is, the interest of maintaining the pretence that no pressure at all was used. (The 'psychological pressure' consisted of blasting sub-zero temperature air conditioning at naked detainees in order to force them to confess—without laying a mark upon them.)

Should fact-finders have prior knowledge?

Amnesty International has a rule that no national of a state under investigation can be part of a fact-finding mission to that state. This is appropriate, since those connected with a nation may have strong feelings for or against its government. But sometimes the alternative of parachuting in an investigator or members of a group who have no experience of a country can be made the butt of state criticism. This was suffered recently by the UN rapporteur who condemned Kenya after spending ten days in the country. The government asked how anyone who has been in Kenya for just over a week could begin to understand its complex society. This argument sounds impressive, although there is no reason why an objective and expert observer like Philip Alston could not decide issues relating to public order and policing by extensive reading of source materials and then visiting Kenya and hearing testimony as to how the authorities had behaved. Human rights fact finding does not require intimate knowledge of local society.

Nonetheless, it does help if fact-finders have experienced guides to the country under investigation. There are some countries where things are seldom what they seem. On my first mission to communist

---

[14] See www.opendemocracy.net/globalization-institutions_government/torture_3429.jsp.

Czechoslovakia, I attended trials of executives of the jazz society. After its leaders were sentenced to prison, I stood on the steps of the court house with Vaclav Havel while a group of young people in the square in front of us began singing 'we shall overcome'. I was heartened by the size of the chorus, until Havel turned to me and said 'on these occasions you can always tell who are the secret police. They are the ones who know all the words'. I conducted a number of human rights missions to apartheid-era South Africa, but I never knew that beneath the polite veneer of the trials I was observing, there was a sinister subculture of state assassination without trial. A friend who was one of the founders of the Black Sash movement was killed in what seemed to be a typical life-wasting South African car accident and it was only many years later, when the evidence emerged at a Truth and Reconciliation Commission hearing, that I discovered that the brakes of her car had been tampered with in a secret police operation.

Should human rights monitors be obliged to testify in international courts?

It is important to distinguish between three separate issues:

- the **competence** (or capacity) of a human rights reporter to be a witness;
- the **compellability** of human rights monitors—i.e. whether the court has power to order them
- to give evidence; and
- their **right to protect sources** once in the witness box.

Competence

All human rights monitors are competent to give evidence, except employees or former employees of the Red Cross. They have a special position under the Geneva Convention and the ICTY has held, albeit by a majority, that their duty of confidentiality is absolute and that they cannot give evidence, even if they want to and even if they have long left the organisation. An ICTY trial chamber decided in *Simic* that the ICRC was entitled in customary international law to an absolute privilege, which could be exerted to prevent employees from giving evidence of observations made whilst on Red Cross work.[15]

[15] International Criminal Tribunal for the Former Yugoslavia, Case No. IT-95-9-T, 17/10/2003.

This was a ruling that, in the eyes of the law, Red Cross employees and ex-employees lacked the capacity to testify.

Justice Hunt, who dissented, found no warrant in customary international law for such a sweeping and absolute exemption from those dictates of conscience and humanity which will sometimes impel witnesses of crimes against humanity to offer court testimony, irrespective of confidentiality obligations. Of course the ICRC has a duty to remain neutral, but that does not mean that customary international law should treat its ex-employees as incompetent to testify, certainly if their evidence is indispensible to the determination of guilt or innocence.

A preferable rule would be that the evidence should be excluded unless it is indispensible to prove or disprove a crime of the upmost gravity.[16] The Red Cross has long been criticised for choosing to say nothing about the Holocaust, in order that its work in prisoner of war camps in Nazi Germany might not suffer.[17] Should an ex-employee offer eye-witness evidence that a defendant ordered torture or (even more pointedly) offer conclusive evidence that a defendant was *not* involved in the acts of torture with which he is charged, the majority decision in *Simic* should not be followed so as to debar the court from hearing such crucial evidence. The approach of Justice Hunt (the minority judge in *Simic*) was to balance the competing interests. His test was 'whether the harm which would be done by the allowance of the evidence outweighs the harm done by the frustration or impairment to justice if the evidence is not available'.[18] While it would only be in a rare case that a Red Cross employee would be ordered to testify, he identified two such situations: 'where the evidence of an official or an employee of the ICRC is vital to establish the innocence of the accused person' and 'where the evidence of an official or an employee of the ICRC is vital to establish the guilt of the particular accused in a trial of transcendental importance'.[19] He concluded that:

> The correct test is whether the evidence to be given by the witness in breach of the obligations of confidentiality owed by the ICRC is so

[16] This was the ICRC fallback position in argument in *Simic*. See *Prosecutor v Simic et al.* Case number IT-95-9, *ex parte confidential decisions on the prosecution motion under rule 73 for a ruling concerning the testimony of the witness*, 27 July 1999, para 19.

[17] See David Rieff, *A Bed For A Night: Humanitarianism in Crisis* (Vintage 2002) pp 76–7, 148.

[18] Separate opinion of Judge David Hunt, 27 July 1999, para 27.

[19] Ibid, paras 29–31.

> essential to the case of the relevant party (here the prosecution) as to outweigh the risk of serious consequence of the breach of confidence in the particular case. Both the gravity of the charges and the availability of means to avoid disclosure of the fact that the evidence has been given would be relevant to that determination.[20]

Another court may prefer Judge Hunt's dissent—I certainly do. Red Cross confidentiality can be a Faustian bargain: the organisation kept silent about the torture at Abu Ghraib, for example, and the truth only emerged when a copy of one of its confidential reports, which had gathered dust on the desks of US generals and British bureaucrats, was leaked to the *Wall Street Journal*. And it was infuriating to watch Donald Rumsfeld at press conferences rejecting as ludicrous the idea that torture techniques were being used at Guantanamo: 'we have the Red Cross here every day: if there was any torture, they would be the first to complain.' But of course they could not complain publicly, by virtue of their vow of confidentiality. They are in danger of becoming complicit in the torture and ill-treatment that they observe if they can never divulge it to the public. The Red Cross justifies its privilege by pointing out that states would not permit its observers to enter prisoner of war camps if they were able to make their findings public. In the recent conflict in Sri Lanka, for example, all NGOs except the Red Cross were prevented from witnessing the army operation, the Sri Lankan military thinking, undoubtedly, was that they would be safe with the Red Cross as its employees could never testify.

One way forward would be for the UK or the US to take the lead in disclaiming any right of confidentiality in Red Cross reports, and to promise to disclose them six or nine months after they have been received. This waiver arrangement would ensure that the right to have Red Cross visits would become a meaningful safeguard against torture and abuse in prisoner of war camps run by states that were prepared for this degree of transparency.

Compellability of human rights monitors

Some human rights reporters are only too pleased to give evidence to international courts. But others, especially those still in the field, are horrified at the prospect of losing their perceived neutrality by

---

[20] Ibid, para 35.

appearing to endorse the prosecution (if the prosecution asks them to give evidence) or else by appearing to support the defence. Neutrality is vital to war correspondents and to human rights reporters working in war zones, and their own and their colleague's safety may be put at risk if they are perceived to be spies for the prosecutor of an international criminal court.

This was the dilemma that faced Jonathan Randall, a *Washington Post* correspondent who had interviewed a local Serb official named Brdanin, subsequently charged in the ICTY with complicity in war crimes. Randall was still actively engaged in reporting on terrorism, and did not want to be perceived by potential sources as a journalist who co-operated with prosecutors. He and his newspaper believed that his neutrality would be compromised. The ICTY Trial Chamber insisted that he had no testamentary privilege and had to give evidence against Brdanin, even though the quotations in his article had been obtained through the services of a translator. The ICTY Appeals Chamber decided, however, that war correspondents could not be compelled to testify in war crimes courts unless the party which subpoenaed them could establish that their evidence would be 'really significant'; that is, of direct and important value in determining a core issue in the case, and that in any event the evidence could not reasonably be obtained elsewhere.

It said:

> In war zones, accurate information is often difficult to obtain and may be difficult to distribute or disseminate as well. The transmission of that information is essential to keeping the international public informed about matters of life and death... there is the public interest in the work of war correspondents, which requires that the news gathering function be performed without unnecessary constraints so that the international community can receive adequate information on issues of public concern.[21]

The Court concluded that compelling war correspondents to testify on a routine basis 'may have a significant impact upon their ability to obtain information and thus their ability to inform the public on issues of general concern.'[22] In this context there can be no meaningful

---

[21] *Prosecutor v Drdanin* and *Tadic* Case number IT-99-36-AR73.9, Decision on Interlocutory Appeal, 11 December 2002, paras 36 and 46.

[22] Ibid, para 44.

distinction between the war correspondent and the human rights reporter or investigator, in terms of the importance of the information they gather or the public interest that its publication will serve. In both cases there is the danger that information will dry up if the court routinely orders them to identify their sources. *Brdanin* was a case on compellability rather than privilege, but it assumes that on the limited occasions when war correspondents are compelled to testify on core issues, they will be accorded a privilege to withhold the names of their sources.

The Appeal Court decision that the reporter was only compellable where his information was important and could not be obtained elsewhere was a compromise between the claims of news organisations and human rights NGOs—the latter were initially sceptical about journalists who refused to help war crimes prosecutors. I acted for the *Washington Post* and recall some anxious discussions with Ken Roth about whether journalists had a duty to their source or to the new war crimes tribunals. Richard Goldstone provided expert evidence about the importance of neutrality to those who have a duty objectively to report a war, and the Appeals Chamber decision, largely written by the US judge Theodore Meron, more or less satisfied both sides.

Source protection

In the important European Human Rights Convention case of *Goodwin v UK*, the Court decided that a qualified privilege to protect journalistic sources followed from the right to freedom of expression. The public right to newsworthy information entails that those who supply information to journalists, frequently in breach of the confidence of their employers or colleagues, should nonetheless be protected because otherwise these sources would 'dry up'; that is, stay silent, and much newsworthy material would not be imparted and would not in consequence be published. The European Court of Human Rights held:

> Protection of journalistic sources is one of the basic conditions for press freedom, as is reflected in the laws and professional codes of conduct in a number of contracting states and is affirmed in several international instruments on journalistic freedoms. Without such protection, sources may be deterred from assisting the press and informing the public on matters of public interest. As a result the vital public watchdog role of the press may be undermined and the ability of the press to provide accurate and reliable information may be adversely affected. Having regard to the importance of the protection of journalistic sources for press freedom in

> a democratic society and the potentially chilling effect an order of source disclosure has on the exercise of that freedom, such a measure cannot be compatible with Article 10 of the convention (the freedom of expression guarantee) unless it is justified by an overriding requirement in the public interest.[23]

Can this reasoning be applied to protect the sources of human rights reporters and fact finders, who are tasked with collecting information for public purposes—to inform the reports of the UN Secretary General or to research for reports issued to the public by NGOs like Amnesty International and Human Rights Watch? The issue arose in the UN Special Court for Sierra Leone. The prosecution called a staff member of the United Nations, who was a human rights monitor, as a witness. The UN waived its immunity rights so that he might testify freely, on condition that he be permitted to do so in closed court and that, when giving his evidence, the witness should not be compelled under cross-examination to name any human source from which he had received information. The witness' statement had been disclosed to the defence and consisted both of his direct observations of the war and of what others had told him of the 'widespread and systematic' commission of war crimes in some areas. This was relevant but secondary evidence: it was directed to establish an element of the crime charged (namely the widespread and systematic nature of the attacks) but did not directly connect any defendants with an offence. Nonetheless, one trial chamber decided that the witness could be compelled to name his sources, and this was the major issue for decision by the Appeal Chamber. We decided it in favour of the witness, primarily on the wording of the Special Court Rules of Procedure. My concurring judgment considered the broader issue of whether 'human rights reporters' are entitled, in the course of their testimony, to decline to answer questions directed to identifying the source of the information.

The Court had *amici* briefs submitted by the UN's Human Rights Commissioner, as well as from Amnesty International and Human Rights Watch, which urged that the public interest requires human rights reporters to possess such a testamentary privilege, either in absolute terms or at least on a qualified basis. But the defence lawyers argued that any such entitlement to resist source disclosure would

---

23 *Goodwin v UK* (1996) ECHR 16, para 39.

improperly undermine a defendant's right to challenge the evidence given against him. The competence and compellability of human rights reporters was not in issue; the UN official was perfectly willing to testify and the UN was agreeable so long as he did so without being subjected to cross-examination, in which questions might be asked the honest answer to which would identify a source who had been promised anonymity and who might well be in danger of harsh or even lethal reprisals if publicly named. It was my view that the principle set out in *Goodwin* was equally applicable to human rights monitors giving evidence in war crimes courts:

> There is in my judgment, little meaningful difference in this respect between an investigative journalist tracking a story in a war torn country, a war correspondent reporting on the ebb and flow of the conflict, and a researcher for a human rights organisation filing information for an "in-depth" report or for filtered use in an annual report, or for a UN monitor gathering information for the Secretary General to report to the Security Council. All are exercising a right to freedom of expression (and, more importantly, assisting their source's right of free speech) by extracting information for publication from people who would not give it without an assurance that their names will remain anonymous. The reprisal they often face in such circumstances, unlike the risk run by Mr Goodwin's source of being sacked or sued for breach of confidence, is of being killed as an "informer"—a traitor to the organisation or community on whom they are silently squealing. To identify them in court would betray a promise and open them to such reprisals: more importantly if courts routinely ordered witnesses to name their sources, then information about human rights abuses would diminish because reporters could not in good conscience elicit it by promises to protect their sources. For these reasons, I consider that "human rights monitors," like journalists, have a privilege to refuse to name those sources to whom they have promised anonymity and who are in danger of reprisal if that promise is broken. In practical terms, that means that they must not be compelled to do so by threats to invoke the court's power to hold them in contempt and to fine or imprison them. It does not mean, of course, that the evidence that they give, based on information from sources they decline to name, will be accorded normal weight. Their entitlement to protect their source has this downside for the party that calls them: it may lose some and perhaps all of the weight that might otherwise have been placed on the evidence that is given based on the anonymous source material.[24]

[24] See *Prosecutor v Brima and others* Case number SCSL-2004-16-AR73, Appeals Chamber judgment, 26 May 2006, separate and concurring opinion of Justice Geoffrey Robertson QC, para 28.

There is an overriding international public interest in UN human rights reporters being able to give an assurance of confidentiality to those who put their necks on the line to inform on the murderous activities of powerful supporters or figures within their community—two witnesses who gave evidence to Phillip Alston in Kenya suffered lethal reprisals. The public interest in protecting UN sources applies with the same force to fact finders engaged by Amnesty and Human Rights Watch who collect and expertly analyse information about human rights abuses, later published in annual or special reports which serve to inform governments and international institutions, as well as the interested public, about such abuses and are used as a basis for campaigns to end them. The public interest in the free flow of information to such publications is at least as great as to other news media. Moreover, the consequences of exposure of sources of this kind can be calamitous. It is apt to recall that the protective rule in *Goodwin* was fashioned in the context of the genteel environment of the city of London, where a business journalist was fined for refusing to name an 'insider' source of information about a company's finances—a source who would face only disciplinary action if exposed. In repressive countries, sources for fact-finding missions who tell of torture, death squads and arbitrary imprisonment, may, if exposed, face these very consequences. Not only may they be brutally treated as punishment for embarrassing the government or other power brokers, but their family and friends may also face reprisals. This fact underlines the need for the protective rule, usually identified as a 'privilege' belonging to the witness, although that 'privilege' is a reflection of the rather more weighty 'right' of the source. The privilege is qualified, not absolute, because it must yield in cases where the identification of the source is necessary either to prove guilt or to establish a reasonable doubt about guilt.

There is a problem in the proliferation of 'human rights NGOs', several thousand at last count, with 'monitors' or 'fact-finders' of varying calibre and experience. Some have been accused of sensationalising reports in order to gain support for campaigns or membership subscriptions, whilst others might have a bias derived from political connections or state funding. Certain NGOs with 'human rights' in their title have been credibly accused of undermining human rights causes.[25] Are all these monitors to be accorded a qualified privilege to

[25] See *The Economist*, 4 December 2004, 'Yanukovich's Friends – A Human Rights Group that Defends Dictators'.

withhold the names of sources? I do not see how a meaningful distinction can be made, any more than the *Goodwin* privilege can be denied to journalists who have a propaganda agenda or report on wars where they support one side or the other. The reporter's privilege is, after all, the obverse of the right possessed by the source, who may speak low, in fear and trembling, to the first fact finder who appears in his burnt out village completely unaware of any bias and concerned only that their identity be protected if they tell what they know. The prospect that what they say will be 'spun' or exaggerated by partisan journalists or monitors does not lose the source his or her right to be protected from exposure: but what it does mean is that the court must give the party which cross-examines the reporting witness every opportunity to explore any bias or hidden agenda or other motive for distortion or exaggeration. This is after all, a set of human rights which belong to defendants and must be upheld to ensure fairness of trial.

Courts must always guard against allowing prosecutors to present evidence which amounts to no more than hearsay demonisation of defendants by human rights groups or by the media. The right of sources to protection is not a charter for lazy prosecutors to make a case based on second hand reports or investigations. Unchecked hearsay has an inevitable place in the factual matrix upon which expert opinion is based. For example, in *Prosecutor v Bizimungu*, the late Dr. Alison Des Forges was called as an expert: she based her opinion upon two accounts of a meeting with the ex-president given by confidential sources. Her right to withhold their names was upheld, although the court pointed out that this would be an important factor to consider in evaluating her evidence.[26] Defendants must never be convicted solely on evidence from anonymous accusers; the Court effectuates that principle by excluding or else de-valuing hearsay accusations, rather than by compelling a witness who reports them to divulge the identity of the confidential source who made them.

Summary

Fact-finding missions to repressive or post-conflict societies must respect the undertakings they give to sources and must refuse to

[26] *Prosecutor v Bizimungu,* Case number ICTR-99-50-T, decision on defence motion for exclusion of portions of testimony of expert witness Dr. Alison Des Forges, 2 September 2005.

answer questions that might expose informants when summoned to testify in a war crimes court. Courts should respect that refusal, and decline to make any finding of contempt against a fact finder, unless the source is crucial to establishing the defendant's guilt or innocence. This approach should be applied pragmatically, by judges who recognise the danger that sources embroiled in armed conflict may be partisan and in some cases malicious, even to the extent of inventing or fabricating the information they give to fact finders. Fabrication may, without identification or cross-examination of its source, fool even the most experienced human rights monitor (it was, after all, an experienced ex-Amnesty researcher who passed on the notoriously false story about the Kuwaiti babies being thrown out of hospital incubators by Iraqi troops during the first Gulf War). On the other hand, there must be an equal recognition that score-settling will continue for long after the conflict and that sources may be assaulted, killed or driven out of their communities as the result of exposure. But testimony based on information from anonymous sources should never be the sole basis for findings of guilt.

Reprisals against fact-finders

It is a sad fact of life that those involved in law enforcement in unstable societies will sometimes be the victim of lethal reprisals. A number of prosecutors and journalists have been assassinated for finding out too much, whilst others have been taken hostage and held to ransom. An organization which sends fact finders on a mission to a dangerous country will always bear responsibility for their safety and well-being. International law offers no special protection to a member of a fact-finding mission over and above that which the member is entitled by virtue of his or her status as a civilian. Attempts have been made by journalist organisations to encourage the addition to Article 8 of the Rome Treaty (which contains an exhaustive definition of war crimes) a new international crime of killing journalists, to which might be added the intentional killing of human rights monitors and fact-finders. The Red Cross has opposed any extension, on the basis that they are already protected as 'civilians', but obviously armies locked in a civil war do not perceive journalists as civilians, which is why they kill them. The forces of the state (and sometimes insurgents), will threaten human rights investigators precisely because they do not perceive them as civilians, but as persons who are likely to expose their misdeeds to the world.

It is, of course, a war crime to direct attacks against 'personnel using the distinctive emblems of the Geneva Convention in conformity with international law'[27], (so Red Cross personnel are safe) and to attack persons 'involved in a humanitarian assistance or peace keeping mission in accordance with the charter of the UN'[28]—which would cover UN rapporteurs on fact-finding missions, but would not protect members of human rights missions dispatched by NGOs. There is a powerful case to be made for giving them specific protection.

War correspondents have the inconsequential assistance of Article 79 of the First Protocol to the Geneva Conventions 1977, which provides that

> journalists engaged in dangerous professional missions in areas of armed conflict shall be considered as civilians… [and] shall be protected as such under the Conventions in this Protocol, provided they take no action adversely affecting their status as civilians…[29]

This gives journalists, like all civilians, immunity from military discipline and they must not be made specific targets for attack or become the victims of reprisals by any party to the conflict, although their entitlement to civilian status will be jeopardised if they take any action which indicates support for a belligerent—for example, carrying a gun or rendering special assistance to one side or the other. This vague civilian status is unsatisfactory and there needs to be a specific crime to deter attacks on journalists and human rights monitors or fact-finders, for the simple reason that in conflict zones they are not perceived as innocent civilians but as enemies, real or potential, of those whose criminal acts they may expose.

Publication of the report

The fact-finding mission that finds its facts and writes its report may find that its problems are not over. They may be just beginning. English common law regards any slighting criticism liable to lower a person's reputation in the minds of right thinking people as a defamation which can require recompense of up to £200,000 and—much

---

27 Rome Statute of the International Criminal Court Article 8(2)(b)(xxiv).

28 Ibid, Article 8(2)(b)(iii).

29 Protocol Additional to the Geneva Conventions 1949 and relating to the protection of victims of international conflict, 1977.

more crippling—millions of pounds in legal costs. The burden of proving the truth of serious allegations rests on the defendant publisher, and this is virtually impossible when sources must be protected or else refuse to come forward. London is the libel capital of the world because its law is so plaintiff-friendly, and its courts are the favoured forum for the wealthy of the world to harry their critics. An NGO will not escape by the device of publishing a fact-finding mission's report in America: First Amendment protection does not cover internet downloadings in the UK. Every human rights report will be accessible in England, either via the internet or obtainable from Amazon, and English courts welcome forum shoppers.[30] Newspapers are sued in London all the time by foreign claimants—most notably Russian oligarchs, and Arab billionaires accused of supporting terrorism. Human rights reporting has so far benefited from the practical consideration that its targets—political and military leaders accused of genocide and torture—are usually reluctant to travel to the UK for fear of a Pinochet-style arrest, certainly if their libel action fails. This fear has been reduced by the House of Lords in a recent libel action brought by Roman Polanski; he was permitted to testify by video-link, safe in a Paris hotel room from the arrest and extradition warrant awaiting him from US law enforcers in London.[31] Some violators are prepared to come to London: the Head of the Ghanaian Secret Police sued *The Independent* when it informed its readers that he had been accused by a judicial inquiry some years before of masterminding the murder of three of that country's judges. This is the kind of allegation which is important for the public to know about but is virtually impossible to prove, without the massive expense of gathering the evidence of the long disbanded inquiry in a far-off country.[32]

In recent years the House of Lords has developed a public interest defence for the media against libel actions, which should cover the publication of most human rights reports. It applies whenever the subject matter is of high public interest and the allegation is made by reputable professionals who honestly and reasonably believe in its truth

---

[30] See *Berezovsky v Forbes* (2000) 1 WLR 1004.

[31] See *Polanski v Conde Nast Publications*, (2005) UKHL 10. The film director had jumped bail in California years before, when on trial for child molestation.

[32] See *Tsikata v Newspaper Publishing Plc*, 1997 1 All ER 655. The newspaper succeeded in showing that it had qualified privilege to report the inquiry finding, even though it had not led to a prosecution.

and who publish it with professional responsibility. This case—*Jameel v Wall Street Journal*—allowed the newspaper to report what it could not prove, but reasonably and responsibly believed, about Saudi co-operation with the CIA in monitoring a prominent businessman.[33] The *Jameel* case provides a valuable defence, but will not relieve an NGO from having to spend a considerable amount of money before its defence is upheld, and to cover such costs it may be wise to take out libel insurance, especially where the report criticises powerful officials or wealthy leaders.

Breach of confidence is another legal snare that NGOs must avoid in publishing investigations that have managed to obtain secret documents. Global Witness struck an important blow for human rights reporting recently when it successfully fought off an injunction from the son of the President of the Republic of Congo. His credit card statements had been obtained and placed on the Global Witness website to show that the President's son had secretly been stealing the profits of the state owned oil company. The Court held that the seriousness of the offence justified the breach of confidentiality, as there could be no confidence in iniquity: 'the profits of oil sales should go to the people of the Congo, not to those who rule it or their families'.

But the anxiety and risk attendant on any such legal action should not be underestimated. Global Witness would have been forced to pay tens of thousands of pounds in legal costs had it lost, and it was fortunate to have *pro bono* representation. The sad fact is that the United Kingdom does not have free speech, it has expensive speech.

Conclusion

The final rule for a human rights report is to make it readable. It will often be written by lawyers, who must remember that it will not be read only by lawyers: to achieve its objective, it must be comprehensible to a wide range of people involved in civil society programmes, to journalists and politicians and diplomats, to victims and even to perpetrators. Some readers will not have English as a first language, and will not have the benefit of translation. The art is to be simple without becoming simplistic: let the facts speak for themselves, and confine legislation or technical details to appendices.

---

[33] *Jameel v Wall Street Journal* (No 3) 2006 UKHL 44.

Few reports become bestsellers (one exception is 'Nunca Mas'—Ernesto Sabato's report that alerted the world to the work of death squads in South American dictatorships). Remember that good human rights reporting must stand the test of time and, increasingly in war crimes courts, the test of cross-examination.

Geoffrey Robertson QC is founder and Head of Doughty Street Chambers. He has appeared as counsel in many leading cases in constitutional, criminal and international law, and served as first President of the UN War Crimes Court in Sierra Leone, where he authored landmark decisions on the limits of amnesties, the illegality of recruiting child soldiers and other critical issues in the development of international criminal law. He has conducted many observer missions for Amnesty International and other NGOs into the trials under apartheid South Africa and under communist regimes in Eastern Europe and Vietnam.

He sits as a Recorder and is Master of Middle Temple and a visiting professor in human rights law at Queen Mary College, London. In 2008 he was appointed by the Secretary General as one of three distinguished jurist members of the UN Justice Council. His books include Crimes Against Humanity: The Struggle for Global Justice; The Justice Game (memoir) and The Tyrrannicide Brief, an award-winning study of the trial of Charles I. He has been assisted in preparing this opinion by Kate Annand, a barrister at Doughty Street chambers with a practice in international and European human rights law. He has recently released reports into the Armenian Genocide and the 1988 prison massacres in Iran.

BIBLIOGRAPHY

Ahmed, Shamima and David Potter, NGOs in International Politics 11 (2006).

Ajibade, Idowu Mopelola, University of McGill, *A Synopsis: Rights, Responsibilities and Roles of Human Rights NGOs under International Law* 18 (2008), available at http://papers.ssrn.com/sol3/ papers.cfm?abstract_id=1300103.

Amnesty International, *Amnesty International response to Andrés Ballesteros, Jorge A. Restrepo, Michael Spagat, Juan F. Vargas,* The Work of Amnesty International and Human Rights Watch: Evidence from Colombia, *CERAC, Colombia, February 2007* (2007), available at http://www.amnesty.org/en/library/asset/AMR23/006/2007/en/83aa83aa-d399-11dd-a329-2f46302a8cc6/amr230062007en.html.

Amnesty International, *Israel/Occupied Territories: The cycle of abuse must stop* (April 8, 2002), http://www.amnesty.org/en/library/asset/MDE15/044/2002/en/66894365-d85e-11dd-9df8-936c90684588/mde150442002en.html.

Amnesty International, "Mapping for Human Rights," available at http://www.amnesty.nl/documenten/spa/mapping%20for%20human%20rights.pdf (last visited Sept. 19, 2011).

Amnesty International, *Monitoring and Reporting Human Rights Violations in Africa: A Handbook for Community Activists* (2002), available at http://www.amnesty.nl/documenten/spa/handbook_community_eng.pdf.

Amnesty International, *Statute of Amnesty International*, available at http://www.amnesty.org/en/who-we-are/accountability/statute-of-amnesty-international (last visited Jan. 9, 2011).

Amnesty International and CODESRIA, *UKWELI: Monitoring and Documenting Human Rights Violations in Africa* 41 (2000), available at http://www.amnesty.nl/documenten/ukw_eng.pdf.

Amnesty International Nederland, *Programme on Africa*, available at http://www.amnesty.nl/special-programme-africa (last visited Sept. 19, 2011).

Amnesty International Nederland, *Special Programme on Africa – Publications*, available at http://www.amnesty.nl/special-programme-africa-publication (last visited Sept. 19, 2011).

Anderson, Kenneth, *Questions re: Human Rights Watch's Credibility in Lebanon Reporting*, Kenneth Anderson Laws of War Blog, Aug. 23, 2006, available at http://kennethandersonlawofwar.blogspot.com/2006/08/questions-re-human-rights-watchs.html.

Anheier, Helmut K. and Amber Hawkes, "Accountability in a Globalising World: International Non-Governmental Organisations and Foundations," in Leadership in Sozialen Organisationen (J. Eurich and A. Brink, eds., 2009).

Arkin, William M., "Divining Victory - Airpower in the 2006 Israel-Hezbollah War," Air University Press (2007), available at http://www.4shared.com/document/NRfziHeq/Divining_Victory_-_Airpower_in.html.

Asian Human Rights Commission (ARDC), *Human Rights Monitoring and Fact-Finding* (2000), available at http://www.hrschool.org/modules/6.pdf.

Baker, Alan, *Just what did Goldstone expect?* Jerusalem Post, Oct. 18, 2009, available at http://www.jpost.com/Opinion/Article.aspx?id=157889.

Ballesteros, Andres, Jorge A. Restrepo, Michael Spagat, and Juan F. Vargas, Conflict Analysis Resource Center and the University of London, *The Work of Amnesty International and Human Rights Watch: Evidence from Colombia* 2–3 (2007), available at http://www.ngo-monitor.org/data/images/File/evidencefromcolumbia_feb2007.pdf.

Barry, Ellen, *E.U. Report to Place Blame on Both Sides in Georgia War*, N.Y. Times, Sept. 29, 2009, available at http://www.nytimes.com/2009/09/29/world/europe/29georgia.html?pagewanted=allhttp://www.nytimes.com/2009/09/29/world/europe/29Georgia.html.

Barry, Ellen, *Georgia Challenges Report That Says It Fired First Shot*, N.Y. Times, Sept. 30, 2008, available at http://www.nytimes.com/2009/10/01/world/europe/01russia.html.

Baylis, Elena, *Tribunal-Hopping with the Post-Conflict Justice Junkies*, 10 Oregon Rev. Int'l L. 361, 386 (2008).

Bell, Abraham, *Human Rights Watch has some explaining to do*, Opinio Juris, September 1, 2006.

Bell, Abraham and Gerald M. Steinberg, *Methodologies for NGO Human Rights Fact-Finding in Modern Warfare: The 2006 Lebanon War as a Case Study*, Report to the Israel Science Center, October 2011.

Ben-Ari, Har'el, *The Normative Position of International Non-Governmental Organizations (INGOs) Under International Law* (2010)(unpublished Ph.D. dissertation, Bar-Ilan University)(on file with the author).

Bennet, James, *Death on the Campus: Jenin; U.N. Report Rejects Claims Of a Massacre Of Refugees*, N.Y. Times, Aug. 2, 2002, available at http://query.nytimes.com/gst/fullpage.html?res=9D04E6DD1E3BF931A3575BC0A9649C8B63&scp=2&sq=jenin&st=cse.

Bernstein, David, *Human Rights Watch (and Amnesty International) on Goldstone Retraction*, The Volokh Conspiracy, Apr. 6, 2011, available at http://volokh.com/2011/04/06/human-rights-watch-lies-re-goldstone-retraction/.

Bernstein, Robert L., *Rights Watchdog, Lost in the Mideast*, N.Y. Times, Oct. 19, 2009, available at http://www.nytimes.com/2009/10/20/opinion/20bernstein.html.

Betts, Wendy S. and Gregory Gisvold, *Conflict Mapping: Innovation in International Responses in Post-Conflict Societies*, 10 No. 3 Hum. Rts. Brief 24 (2003).

Blitt, Robert Charles, *Who will watch the watchdogs? Human rights Nongovernmental Organizations and the case for regulation*, 10 Buff. Hum. Rts. L. Rev. 261, 348 (2004), available at http://www.ngo-monitor.org/data/images/File/SSRN-id753487.pdf.

Blom-Cooper, Louis, Guns to Antigua (1990).

Bothe, Michael, *Fact-Finding as a means of ensuring respect for international humanitarian law*, in International Humanitarian Law Facing New Challenges 249, 265 (Volker Epping and Wolff Heintschel von Heinegg, eds., 2007).

Brett, Peggy, and Murzenberg, Patrick, Centre for Civil and Political Rights, *UN Human Rights Committee, Participation in the Reporting Process: Guidelines for Non-Governmental Organisations (NGOs)* (2nd ed. 2010), available at http://www.ccprcentre.org/doc/CCPR/Handbook/CCPR_Guidelines%20for%20NGOs_en.pdf.

Bukovská, Barbora, *Perpetrating Good: Unintended Consequences of International Human Rights Advocacy*, 9 Sur Int'l J. on Hum. Rts. 6, 11 (2008).

Chandler, David, Constructing Civil Society: Morality and Power in International Relations (2004).

Clark, Ann Marie, Diplomacy of Conscience: Amnesty International and Changing Human Rights Norms (2001).

Clark, Roger, Amnesty International Canada Section (English Speaking), *The Evolution of the Mandate* (Oct. 28, 1996), available at http://www.amnesty.org/aboutai/eom.htm.

CNN Transcripts, *CNN Reliable Sources: Coverage of the Mideast Conflict* (July 23, 2006), available at http://edition.cnn.com/TRANSCRIPTS/0607/23/rs.01.html.

Combes, Nancy Armoury, Fact-Finding Without Facts: The Uncertain Evidentiary Foundations of International Criminal Convictions (2010).

Conflict Research Consortium, University of Colorado, *International Online Training Program On Intractable Conflict* (1998), available at http://www.colorado.edu/conflict/peace/problem/factfinding.htm.

Conflict Research Consortium, University of Colorado, *International Online Training Program On Intractable Conflict* (1998), available at http://www.colorado.edu/conflict/peace/problem/cinterest.htm.

Cook, Robin, *Statement at the Launch of the Torture Reporting Handbook* (2000), available at http://www.essex.ac.uk/torturehandbook/news.htm.

Cooper, Anderson, Hezbollah Remains Secretive Organization, *Anderson Cooper 360 on CNN*, Aug. 9, 2006.

Council of the European Union, *Mandate of the Independent International Fact-Finding Mission on the Conflict in Georgia* (2008), available at http://eur-lex.europa.eu/Notice.do?mode=dbl&lang=en&ihmlang= en&lng1=en,fr&lng2=bg,cs,da,de,el,en,es,et,fi,fr,hu,it,lt,lv,mt,nl,pl,pt,ro,sk,sl,sv,&val=484042:cs&page.

Dershowitz, Alan, *First Word: What is 'Human Rights Watch' watching?*, Jerusalem Post, Aug. 26, 2006, available at http://www.jpost.com/Opinion/Columnists/Article.aspx?id=32731.

Development Assistance Committee, Organization for Economic Co-operation and Development, *Guidance on Evaluating Conflict Prevention and Peacebuilding Activities: Working draft for application period* 33 (2008), available at http://www.oecd.org/secure/pdfDocument/0,2834,en_21571361_34047972_39774574_1_1_1_1,00.pdf.

Differences Relating to Immunity from Legal Process of a Special Rapporteur of the Commission on Human Rights, Advisor y Opinion, ICJ Reports 1999.

Dueck, Judith, "HURIDOCS Standard Formats as a Tool In the Documentation of Human Rights," in Human Rights and Statistics: Getting the Record Straight 127, 127–28 (Richard P. Claude and Thomas B. Jabine, eds., 1992).

El-Sarraj, Dr. Eyad, *Don't Take Part in War Crimes: Boycott Israel Now*, available at http://www.gcmhp.net/File_files/PressApr222k2.html.

Ermacora, F., *The Competence and Functions of Fact-Finding Bodies*, in International Law and Fact-Finding in the Field of Human Rights 90 (1982).

Fisher, William F., *Doing Good? The Politics and Antipolitics of NGO practices*, 26 Ann. Rev. of Anthropology 444 (1997), available at http://www.jstor.org/stable/2952530.

Fitzpatrick, Joan, *Human rights fact-finding*, in The UN Human Rights Treaty System in the 21st Century (Anne F. Bayefsky ed., 2000).

Franck, Thomas M., ed., *The Belgrade Minimum Rules of Procedure for International Fact-Finding Missions*, 75 AM. J. INT'L L. 163 (1981).

Franck, Thomas M. and H. Scott Fairley, *Procedural Due Process in Human Rights Fact-Finding by International Tribunals*, 74 Am. J. Int'l L. 308 (1980).

Gaer, F., Reality Check, in NGOs, The UN, and Global Governance 56 (T.G. Weiss & L. Gordenker, eds., 1996).

Georgia 'started unjustified war,' BBC News, Sept. 30, 2009, available at http://news.bbc.co.uk/2/hi/8281990.stm; *Uncomfortable conclusions for Georgia*, BBC News, Sept. 30, 2009, available at http://news.bbc.co.uk/2/hi/europe/8284046.stm; *EU: Russia, Georgia share responsibility for 2008 conflict*, CNN World, Sept. 30, 2009, available at http://articles.cnn.com/2009-09-30/world/russia.georgia.eu_1_south-ossetia-russia-and-georgia-georgian-territory?_s=PM:WORLD.

Giffard, Camille, Human Rights Centre, University of Essex, *Torture Reporting Handbook* 4 (2000), available at http://www.essex.ac.uk/torturehandbook/handbook(english).pdf.

Giffard, Camille and Kate Thompson, Human Rights Centre, University of Essex, *Reporting Killings as Human Rights Violations Handbook* (2002), available at www.essex.ac.uk/reportingkillingshandbook/.

Goldstone, Richard, *Reconsidering the Goldstone Report on Israel and war crimes*, Wash. Post, Apr. 1, 2011, available at http://www.washingtonpost.com/opinions/reconsidering-the-goldstone-report-on-israel-and-war-crimes/2011/04/01/AFg111JC_story.html.

Great Lakes Policy Forum, "Congo: The UN Mapping Report and the Responsibility to Justice," December 2, 2010, available at http://www.sfcg.org/programmes/forums/pdf/GLPF%2012-02-10%20Summary.pdf.

Griffiths, Hugh, Crimes of War Magazine: The Tribunals, *Evidence Gathering: The Role of NGOs* (2001), available at http://www.crimesofwar.org/tribun-mag/relate_ngo_print.html.

Groome, Dermot. The Handbook of Human Rights Investigation: A Comprehensive Guide to the Investigation and Documentation of Violent Human Rights Abuses (2000).

Guzman, Manuel and Bert Verstappen. HURIDOCS, *What is Documentation* (2003), available at http://www.huridocs.org/wp-content/uploads/2010/08/whatisdocumentation-eng.pdf.

Hafner-Burton, Emilie M., *Sticks and Stones: Naming and Shaming the Human Rights Enforcement Problem*, 62 Int'l Org. 689, 693 (2008), available at http://ilar.ucsd.edu/assets/001/11945.pdf.

Hannum, Hurst, *Implementing Human Rights: An Overview of NGO Strategies and Available Procedures*, in Guide to International Human Rights Practice (4th ed. 2004).

Heins, Volker, Nongovernmental Organizations in International Society 58 (2008).

Human Rights First, *The Role of Human Rights NGOs in Relation to ICC Investigations* (2004), available at http://www.amicc.org/docs/Human%20Rights%20First%20NGO_Role_Discussion_Paper.pdf.

Human Rights Watch, *Fatal Strikes: Israel's Indiscriminate Attacks Against Civilians in Lebanon* 9 (2006), available at http://www.hrw.org/en/reports/2006/08/02/fatal-strikes.

Human Rights Watch, *Israel/Lebanon: Israel Responsible for Qana Attack* (July 29, 2006), available at http://www.hrw.org/en/news/2006/07/29/israellebanon-israel-responsible-qana-attack.

Human Rights Watch, *Israel: Investigate Attack on Civilians in Lebanon* (July 16, 2006), available at http://www.hrw.org/en/news/2006/07/16/israel-investigate-attack-civilians-lebanon.

Human Rights Watch, *Our History*, available at http://www.hrw.org/en/node/75134 (last visited Apr. 11, 2011).

Human Rights Watch, *Rockets from Gaza: Harm to Civilians from Palestinian Armed Groups' Rocket Attacks* (Aug. 6, 2009), available at http://www.hrw.org/en/reports/2009/08/06/rockets-gaza-0.

Human Rights Watch, *Sri Lanka: Urgently Evacuate Civilians* (Mar. 4, 2009), *available at* http://www.hrw.org/en/news/2009/03/04/sri-lanka-urgently-evacuate-civilians.

Human Rights Watch, *Why They Died: Civilian Casualties in Lebanon during the 2006 War* (2007), available at http://www.hrw.org/en/reports/2007/09/05/why-they-died.

Ibhawoh, Bonny, *Human Rights INGOs and the North-South Gap: The Challenge of Normative and Empirical Learning*, in Daniel A. Bell and Jean-Marc Coicaud, Ethics in Action: The Ethical Challenges of International Human Rights Nongovernmental Organizations (2007).

Ileka Atoki, *Justice for the Victims in Congo*, Huffington Post, October 1, 2010, available at http://www.huffingtonpost.com/amb-ileka-atoki/post_976_b_746003.html.

Independent International Fact-Finding Mission on the Conflict in Georgia (2009), available at http://www.ceiig.ch/Index.html.

Intelligence and Terrorism Information Center at the Center for Special Studies, *Hezbollah's use of Lebanese civilians as human shields: the extensive military infrastructure positioned and hidden by Hezbollah in populated areas. From within the Lebanese towns and villages deliberate rocket attacks were directed against civilian targets in Israel* (Dec. 5, 2006), available at http://www.terrorism-info.org.il/malam_multimedia/English/eng_n/html/human_shields.htm.

International Advocacy Non-Governmental Organizations (IANGO) Workshop, *International Non Governmental Organization Accountability Charter* (2005), available at http://www.ingoaccountabilitycharter.org.

International Counsel on Human Rights Policy, *Crime, Public Order, and Human Rights* 118 (2003), available at http://www.ichrp.org/files/reports/8/114_report_en.pdf.

International Crisis Group, *Reality Demands: Documenting Violations of International Humanitarian Law in Kosovo 1999* 1 (2000), available at http://www.crisisgroup.org/~/media/Files/europe/Kosovo%2021.ashx.

International Humanitarian Fact-Finding Commission, *About Us*, available at http://www.ihffc.org/index.asp?Language=EN&page=aboutus_general/ (last visited Sept. 19, 2011).

International Humanitarian Fact-Finding Commission, *Rules of the International Humanitarian Fact-Finding Commission* (1992), available at http://www.ihffc.org/.

International Rehabilitation Council for Torture Victims, *The Istanbul Protocol*, available at http://www.irct.org/investigation—documentation/the-istanbul-protocol.aspx.

Kalb, Marvin, and Carol Saivetz, Harvard University Kennedy School of Government, *The Israeli-Hezbollah War of 2006: The Media as a Weapon in Asymmetrical Conflict* (2006).

Kaldor, Mary, Global Civil Society: An Answer to War (2003).

Keck, Margaret E. and Kathryn Sikkink, Activists beyond Borders, Advocacy Networks in International Politics (1998).

Landman, Todd, Studying Human Rights (2006).

Letter from Angolan Minister of External Relations to UN Secretary General, Ban Ki-Moon, July 30, 2010, available at http://www.ohchr.org/Documents/Countries/ZR/DRC_Report_Comments_Angola.pdf.

Letter from the Burundi Ministry of External Affairs and International Cooperation to Ban Ki-Moon, September 21, 2010, available at http://www.ohchr.org/Documents/Countries/ZR/DRC_Report_Commetnts_Burundi.pdf.

Logister, Louis, *Global Governance and Civil Society: Some Reflections on NGO Legitimacy*, 3 J. Global Ethics 165 (2007).

Lynch, Colum, *UN waters down genocide charges against Rwandan forces in Congo*, Foreign Policy, October 1, 2010, available at http://turtlebay.foreignpolicy.com/posts/2010/10/01/un_waters_down_genocide_charges_against_rwandan_forces_in_congo.

Mallinder, Louis, Law, *Politics and Fact-Finding: Assessing the Impact of Human Rights Reports*, 2 J. Hum. Rts. Prac. 166, 168 (2010).

Mandel, Sarah, NGO Monitor, *Experts or Ideologues? A Systematic Analysis of Human Rights Watch's Focus on Israel* (2009).

Martins, Kerstin, *Examining the (Non-) Status of NGOs in International Law*, 10 Ind. J. Global Legal Stud. 2–3 (2003), available at http://www.sfb597.uni-bremen.de/homepages/martens/download/MARTENS_GLS2003.pdf.

Meldrum, Eric, *Time for a Change?: The Traditional Human Right NGO Fact Finding Methodology in relation to National and International Prosecutions of Gross Human Right Violations* 49 (2009), available at http://www.brookes.ac.uk/schools/be/oisd/architecture/cendep/dissertations/EricMeldrum.pdf.

Mertus, Julie, *Considerations for Human Rights Fact Finding by NGO's*, available at http://academic3.american.edu/~mertus/HR%20fact-finding.htm (last visited Mar. 3, 2011).

Mugambe, Lydia, *Lund Workshop on fact finding held from 30 November 2004–2 December 2004*.

Murphy, Kim, *Officials Say 28 Died in Qana, Not 54*, L.A. Times, Aug. 4, 2006, available at http://articles.latimes.com/2006/aug/04/world/fg-qana4.

Musselman, Tyler B., *Skirmishing for Information: The Flaws of the International Legal System as Evidenced by the Russian-Georgian Conflict of 2008*, 19 Transnat'l L. & Contemp. Probs. 317, 348 (2010), available at http://fog.its.uiowa.edu/~tlcp/TLCP%20Articles/19-1/musselman.finalfinal.mlb.022710.pdf.

Mutangi, Tarisai, Human Rights and Peace Centre, Makere University, Uganda, *Fact-Finding Missions or Omissions: A Critical Analysis of the African Commission on Human and Peoples' Rights and Lessons to be Learnt from the Inter-American Commission on Human Rights* (2005).

Myre, Greg, *Offering Video, Israel Answers Critics on War*, N.Y. Times, Dec. 5, 2006, available at http://www.nytimes.com/2006/12/05/world/middleeast/05mideast.html?_r=1&hp&ex=1165294800&en=8118d4b5432dffa0&ei=5094&partner=homepage&oref=slogin.

Neier, Aryeh, *The Attack on Human Rights Watch*, N.Y. Review of Books, Nov. 2, 2006.

Nye, Joseph S., Jr., Soft Power: The Means to Success in World Politics (2004).

Observations of the Congolese government on the DRC mapping project August 2010, available at http://www.ohchr.org/Documents/Countries/ZR/DRC_Report_Comments_DRC.pdf.

Office of the United Nations High Commissioner for Refugees, *Refworld: The Leader in Refugee Decision Support*, available at http://www.unhcr.org/cgi-bin/texis/vtx/refworld/rwmain (last visited September 13, 2011).

Official Government of Rwanda Comments on the Draft UN Mapping Report on the DRC, September 30, 2011, available at http://www.gov.rw/IMG/pdf/DRC_Report_Comments_Rwanda.pdf.

Orenstein, Mitchell A. and Hans Peter Schmitz, *Review: The New Transnationalism and Comparative Politics*, 38 Comp. Pol. 470–500 (2006).

Orentlicher, Diane F., *Bearing Witness: The Art and Science of Human Rights Fact Finding*, 3 Harv. Hum. Rts. J. 83, 105–06 (1990).

Powell, William W., *Neither Market nor Hierarchy: Network Forms of Organization*, 12 Research in Org. Behav. 295–96, 303–04 (1990).

Ramanathan, Usha, "Human Rights in India: A Mapping," Environmental Law Research Center, available at http://www.ielrc.org/content/w0103.pdf.

Raoul Wallenberg Institute of Human Rights and Humanitarian Law, *Guidelines on International Human Rights Fact-Finding Visits and Reports (The Lund-London Guidelines)* (2009), available at http://www.factfindingguidelines.org/guidelines.html.

Raoul Wallenberg Institute of Human Rights and Humanitarian Law, International Bar Association, and British Institute of International and Comparative Law, *Human Rights Fact-Finding Missions: Seminar Report* 8 (June 1–2, 2009), available at http://www.biicl.org/files/4462_fact_finding_report_updated_2.pdf.

Report of the Independent International Fact-Finding Mission on the Conflict in Georgia (2009), available at http://www.ceiig.ch/index.html.

Risse, T. & K. Sikkink, *The Socialization of International Human Rights Norms into Domestic Practices, in* The Power of Human Rights: International Norms and Domestic Change (Thomas Risse, Stephen C. Ropp, & Kathryn Sikkink, eds., 1999).

Roberts, Adam, *Lives and Statistics: Are 90% of War Victims Civilians?*, 52 Survival 115 (2010), available at http://www.iiss.org/publications/survival/survival-2010/year-2010-issue-3/lives-and-statistics-are-90-of-war-victims-civilians/.

Robertson, Geoffrey, *Human Rights Fact Finding: Some Legal and Ethical Dilemmas*, Hum. Rts. Inst., Int'l Bar Ass'n, Thematic Papers 4 (May 2010).

Roth, Kenneth, *Gaza: the stain remains on Israel's war record*, GUARDIAN (UK), Apr. 5, 2011, at A28, available at http://www.guardian.co.uk/commentisfree/2011/apr/05/gaza-stain-remains-israel-war-record.

Schmitt, Michael N., *Investigating Violations of International Law in Armed Conflict*, 2 HARV. NAT'L SEC. J. 31, 84 (2011).

Sida, Division for Peace and Security Through Development Cooperation, *Manual for Conflict Analysis* 5 (2006), available at http://www.conflictsensitivity.org/sites/default/files/.

Simmons, P.J., *Learning to live with NGOs*, 112 FOREIGN POL'Y 82, 83 (1998).

Slaughter, Anne-Marie, A NEW WORLD ORDER (2004).

Slim, Hugo, "Claiming a Humanitarian Imperative: NGOs and the Cultivation of Humanitarian Duty," in *Human Rights and Conflict: Exploring the Links between Rights, Law, and Peacebuilding* 159, 161 (Julie Mertus and Jeffrey W. Helsing, eds., 2006).

Slim, Hugo, International Council on Human Rights Policy, BY WHAT AUTHORITY? THE LEGITIMACY AND ACCOUNTABILITY OF NON-GOVERNMENTAL ORGANISATIONS (2002).

Stearns, Jason, DANCING IN THE GLORY OF MONSTERS (2011).

Steinberg, Gerald M., *Ken Roth's blood libel*, JERUSALEM POST, August 26, 2006, available at http://fr.jpost.com/servlet/Satellite?cid=1154525949034&pagename=JPArticle%2FShowFull.

Steiner, Henry J., DIVERSE PARTNERS: NON-GOVERNMENTAL ORGANIZATIONS IN THE HUMAN RIGHTS MOVEMENT – THE REPORT OF A RETREAT OF HUMAN RIGHTS ACTIVISTS 34 (1991).

Steiner, Henry J., Philip Alston and Ryan Goodman, INTERNATIONAL HUMAN RIGHTS IN CONTEXT: LAW POLITICS AND MORALS 748 (3d ed. 2008).

Sthlm Policy Group, *Evaluation of the Diakonia IHL program: Occupied Palestinian territory (oPt) and Israel* 39 (2009), available at http://www.diakonia.se/Documents/public/RESULTS_AND_HIGHLIGHTS/Evaluation_IHL_Programme_2009.pdf.

Terms of Reference, *U.N. Office of the High Commissioner for Human Rights, "Report of the Mapping Exercise documenting the most serious violations of human rights, and international humanitarian law committed within the territory of the Democratic Republic of the Congo between March 1993 and June 2003,"* August 2010, at Annex 3.

The Interim Winograd Report (April 2007), available at http://www.vaadatwino.org.il/pdf/???%20????.pdf.

Thoolen, Hans and Berth Verstappen, HUMAN RIGHTS MISSIONS: A STUDY OF THE FACT-FINDING PRACTICE OF NON-GOVERNMENTAL ORGANIZATIONS 135–36 (1986).

Uganda's Position on the Draft DRC Mapping Exercise Report, September 30, 2010, available at http://www.ohchr.org/Documents/Countries/ZR/DRC_Report_Comments_Uganda.pdf.

UN Commission on Human Rights, *Study of reported violations of human rights in Chile, with particular reference to torture and other cruel, inhuman or degrading treatment or punishment* E/CN.4/RES/12 (1978), available at http://www.unhcr.org/refworld/ publisher,UNCHR,,CHL,3b00f0b22c,0.html.

United Nations, *Code of Conduct for Special Procedures Mandate-Holders of the Human Rights Council* (2007), available at http://www1.umn.edu/humanrts/codeofconduct.html.

United Nations, *Declaration on Fact-finding by the United Nations in the Field of the Maintenance of International Peace and Security* A/RES/46/59 (1991).

United Nations, *Final Act of the International Conference on Human Rights: Tehran, 22 April to 13 May 1968* A/CONF. 32/41 (1968).

United Nations, *Guidelines for the Conduct of United Nations Inquiries into Allegations of Massacres* (1995), available at http://www.icrc.org/themissi.nsf/

b5a5eed1a93ca649c12569dd00505aca/ee82c7e78d0175d3c1256b02002984df!Open Document.

United Nations, *Manual for the Prevention of Extra-Legal, Arbitrary and Summary Executions* (1991), available at http://www1.umn.edu/humanrts/instree/executioninvestigation-91.html.

United Nations, *Report of the Secretary-General prepared pursuant to General Assembly resolution* ES-10/10 (June 7, 2002), available at http://www.un.org/peace/jenin/.

United Nations Human Right Council, *Methods of Work of the Special Rapporteur on torture*, available at http://www2.ohchr.org/english/issues/torture/rapporteur/docs/methodswork.doc.

United Nations Human Rights Council, *Report of the Special Rapporteur on extrajudicial, summary or arbitrary executions* (2010), available at http://daccess-dds-ny.un.org/doc/UNDOC/GEN/G10/135/03/PDF/G1013503.pdf?OpenElement.

United Nations Human Rights Council, *United Nations Fact-Finding Mission on the Gaza Conflict* ¶170 (Sept. 25, 2009), available at http://www2.ohchr.org/english/bodies/hrcouncil/specialsession/9/factfindingmission.htm.

United Nations Interregional Crime and Justice Research Institute and the International Criminal Tribunal for the former Yugoslavia, *ICTY Manual on Developed Practices* (2008).

United Nations Office of the High Commissioner for Human Rights, *Istanbul Protocol: Manual on the Effective Investigation and Documentation of Torture and Other Cruel, Inhuman or Degrading Treatment or Punishment* (2004), available at http://www.ohchr.org/Documents/Publications/training8Rev1en.pdf.

United Nations Office of the High Commissioner for Human Rights, *Manual on Human Rights Reporting* (1997), available at http://www.ohchr.org/Documents/Publications/manualhrren.pdf.

United Nations Office of the High Commissioner for Human Rights, *Training Manual on Human Rights Monitoring* 100 (2001), available at http://www.ohchr.org/EN/PublicationsResources/Pages/TrainingEducation.aspx.

United Nations Office of the High Commissioner for Human Rights, *Training Manual on Human Rights Monitoring* 113 (2001), available at http://www.ohchr.org/EN/PublicationsResources/Pages/TrainingEducation.aspx.

Viljoen, Frans, *Fact-Finding by UN Human Rights Complaints Bodies – Analysis and Suggested Reforms*, MAX PLANCK YEARBOOK OF UNITED NATIONS L. 49 (2005), available at http://www.mpil.de/shared/data/pdf/pdfmpunyb/viljoen_8.pdf.

Vivanco, Jose Miguel, *HRW Response to CERAC Charges about our Colombia Work* (2007), available at http://www.hrw.org/en/news/2007/03/15/hrw-response-cerac-charges-about-our-colombia-work.

Weissbrodt, David and James McCarthy, *Fact-Finding by International Nongovernmental Human Rights Organizations*, 22 VA. J. INT'L L. 1. (1981).

Willetts, Louis, *Introduction*, *in* THE CONSCIENCE OF THE WORLD': THE INFLUENCE OF NON-GOVERNMENTAL ORGANISATIONS IN THE UN SYSTEM (Peter Willets, ed., 1996).

Willetts, Louis, *The Impact of Promotional Pressure Groups in Global Politics*, *in* PRESSURE GROUPS IN THE GLOBAL SYSTEM: THE TRANSNATIONAL RELATIONS OF ISSUE-ORIENTED NON-GOVERNMENTAL ORGANIZATIONS (Peter Willets, ed., 1982).

Wilson, Woodrow, *Transcript of President Woodrow Wilson's 14 Points* (1918), available at http://www.ourdocuments.gov/doc.php?doc=62&page=transcript.

Wouters, Jan and Ingrid Rossi, Institute for International Law, University of Leuven, HUMAN RIGHTS NGOS: ROLE, STRUCTURE AND LEGAL STATUS 5 (2001).

INDEX

www.ingramcontent.com/pod-product-compliance
Lightning Source LLC
Chambersburg PA
CBHW031324230926
51848CB00001B/73